THE NAVAJO INDIANS
AND
FEDERAL INDIAN POLICY

THE NAVAJO INDIANS
AND
FEDERAL INDIAN POLICY
1900-1935

Lawrence C. Kelly

THE UNIVERSITY OF ARIZONA PRESS
Tucson, Arizona

About the author . . .

LAWRENCE C. KELLY developed his interest in Navajo history at the University of New Mexico while pursuing the graduate studies that earned him the Ph.D. degree from that institution. He is the author also of *The Navajo Roundup,* and a contributor to various historical journals. A Fellow of the National Endowment for the Humanities during 1970-71, Dr. Kelly has taught at Lewis College and at Indiana University/Fort Wayne Campus. Since 1968 he has been a member of the history faculty at North Texas State University.

First printing 1968
Second printing 1970

THE UNIVERSITY OF ARIZONA PRESS

I.S.B.N. -0-8165-0065-7
L.C. No. 66-27381

For My Parents
Esther and Charles Kelly

Preface

IN THIS BOOK I originally intended to examine the Indian policy of the New Deal as it affected the largest tribe in the nation, the Navajos. As I worked my way through the documents preserved in the National Archives, however, it became apparent that New Deal Indian policy was not so much a new response to an old problem as it was the liberation of forces and ideas which had been building up since the end of World War I. It also became clear that the pivotal period in modern Navajo history lay between the years 1913 and 1935. As a result my research took me back beyond the 1930's rather than forward into the 1940's.

While accepting full responsibility for all errors and the sundry other failings reviewers are always quick to note, it is my pleasure to gratefully acknowledge the assistance of the many persons who have made the task of writing this book both a pleasure and a rewarding personal experience.

To Professor Frank D. Reeve, Emeritus, University of New Mexico, my greatest debt is due. When I was incapable of distinguishing a Navajo from a Pueblo he introduced me to the fascinating history of the Southwestern Indians and suggested I couple my interest in the New Deal with their story, thereby exploring a field which recent historiography had not seen fit to treat.

Professor E. E. Dale, Research Professor Emeritus, University of Oklahoma, a member of the original Meriam Survey task force, shared with me his experiences on that historic mission. He also read the original manuscript, offering helpful advice and encouragement. Dr. Phillips Thygeson, Director, Francis I. Proctor Institute of Ophthalmology, University of California, generously aided me in composing a layman's description of the tarsectomy operation employed during the Southwest Trachoma campaign. Mr. Robert W. Young, Tribal Operations Officer, Navajo Agency, shared with me his intimate knowledge of recent Navajo history and procured the maps reproduced here. The late Mrs. Charles Dietrich and her secretary, Mrs. Sylvia Loomis, kindly permitted me to use the Herbert J. Hagerman papers in their possession.

I am heavily indebted to the excellent staff of the Indian Records Division, National Archives: Jane F. Smith, Evans Walker, and Robert Kvasnicka. My special thanks go to Mrs. Carmelita Ryan who guided me through the maze of records under her care and who repeatedly uncovered materials which I would otherwise have overlooked.

The initial research for this book was made possible by a grant from the Sandia Fund of the University of New Mexico. The Graduate School of Indiana University provided assistance in preparing the final typescript.

Lastly, I wish to acknowledge the assistance and encouragement of my wife, Pecky, whose patience, good humor, and overall sense of proportion were qualities which sustained me on not a few occasions.

LAWRENCE C. KELLY

Fort Wayne, Indiana

Contents

1. THE PEOPLE TO 1913   1
   Navajo History   1
   Navajo Society   7

2. RESERVATION EXPANSION BEFORE 1922   16
   The Dawes Act   16
   Executive-Order Indian Reservations   17
   The Checkerboard   20
   Executive Orders of 1900 and 1901   21
   New Mexico   23
   The Sub-Agencies   27
   Opposition   27
   Compromise   30
   A New Plan   31
   Stalemate   34

3. MINERAL LAW   37
   Conservationists versus Exploiters   37
   The Metalliferous Minerals Act   39
   The General Leasing Act   43

4. OIL   48
   Discovery   48
   Albert B. Fall and John Collier   55
   Herbert J. Hagerman   61
   A Change of Policy   64
   Jurisdictional Rivalry   65
   First Navajo Tribal Council   69
   Santa Fe Auction   70
   Indian Bureau Conflict   72
   The Stone Decision   74

5. LEGISLATION   76
   Initial Attempts   76
   Congressional Proposals   78
   Lee's Ferry Bridge   81
   Solution   88
   Role of Commissioner Burke   93
   Significance of the Solution   99
   Decline of Oil   101

6. RANGE MANAGEMENT   104
   The Problem   104
   Scabies Eradication   106
   Horse Reduction   108
   Scientific Sheep Breeding   111
   An Overgrazed Range   112

7. RESERVATION EXPANSION   115
    The Hagerman Plan   115
    Ineffectual Legislation   117
    Navajo Initiative   119
    Ashurst Proposes Bill   121
    Renewed Allotment   122
    Unopposed Additions   124
    Success and Failure   127
    Conclusion   130

8. TRANSITION   132
    The "New Policy"   132
    Under Fire   135
    Meriam Commission   138
    Bureau of the Budget   142
    Senate Investigation   145
    The Hoover Years   148

9. NEW DEAL FOR THE NAVAJOS   154
    New Philosophy   155
    Sheep Reduction   158
    Wheeler-Howard Bill   163
    Navajo Rejection   167

10. EDUCATION, HEALTH AND POLITICS   171
    Education   171
    Health   181
    Voting   187

11. NAVAJO TRIBAL COUNCIL   190
    The Myth   190
    A Correction   192

EPILOGUE   195

BIBLIOGRAPHY   200

INDEX   210

TABLES

I.   Extent of Overgrazing on the Navajo
     Reservation   114
II. Comparison of Recommendations, Appropriations
     and Expenditures of Indian Bureau Funds,
     Fiscal 1922-1930   144
III. Navajo Vote on the Wheeler-Howard
     Bill by Jurisdictions   169

ILLUSTRATIONS

1. Navajo Reservation Additions   18
2. Jurisdictional Boundaries of the
   Navajo Reservation Prior to 1928   26

CHAPTER 1

The People To 1913

NAVAJO HISTORY

Navajos call themselves Diné: The People. They are members of the Athabascan language group which migrated from Asia to the northwest Pacific coast of North America some thirteen to sixteen hundred years ago. Anthropologists tell us that perhaps as early as A.D. 700 groups of these Athabascans began a gradual migration to the southwestern United States. The route or routes they took, the frequency of their migrations, the number of people involved, are all unknown. Probably they arrived in the Southwest by A.D. 1000, but the first definite signs of their presence date from the years 1450-1550. The pueblo dwellers at Zuñi called them *Apachu,* a word which probably meant "enemy" or "stranger" but which may have been derived directly from the word *Apadje,* "people," by which some of the invaders referred to themselves. The Spanish translated this word as "Apache" and thus it has remained to our day.[1]

In 1626 the Spanish friar Gerónimo Zárate Salmerón reported the existence of a separate group of these Apaches whom he called *Apaches de Navahu.* In 1630 his fellow missionary Alonso Benavides also referred to these people and explained that the term *Navahu* came from the Pueblo Indian (Tewa) word meaning "large cultivated fields." Scholars who follow Benavides in accepting the Tewa origin of the name nevertheless are divided over its meaning. Some say it

---

[1]The best account of the Athabascan migration and Navajo prehistory is Evon Z. Vogt, "Navaho," in *Perspectives in American Indian Culture Change,* ed. Edward H. Spicer (Chicago: University of Chicago Press, 1961). See also Clyde Kluckhohn and Dorothea Leighton, *The Navaho* (2d ed. rev.; Garden City, N.Y.: Doubleday, 1962); Clyde Kluckhohn and Evon Z. Vogt, *Navaho Means People* (Cambridge: Harvard University Press, 1951); Ruth Underhill, *The Navajos* (Norman: University of Oklahoma Press, 1956); and Frank D. Reeve, "Seventeenth Century Navaho-Spanish Relations," *New Mexico Historical Review,* XXXII (January, 1957), pp. 36-52. (Future citations to the New Mexico Historical Review abbreviated as *NMHR.*)

is a place name designating an area where the Navajos, having abandoned their earlier migratory way of living, were now farming. Others maintain that it comes from the Tewa words meaning to "take from the fields," thus indicating the predatory aspects of early Navajo-Pueblo contact. Still others make a case for a Spanish derivation from *navaja*, "clasp-knife," or *nava*, "fields" or "flat land." Whatever the true meaning, it is certain that by the early seventeenth century the Navajos were recognized as a people distinct from the Apaches.[2]

Navajo history in the seventeenth century is sketchy at best. Spanish accounts do indicate that there were two separate bands of Navajos living in a vaguely defined area west of Jemez Pueblo, which Benavides first designated as the Navajo country. One group lived west and northwest of Jemez between Nacimiento Mountain on the east and the San Juan River on the north, in what was called the Province of Navajo. A second band lived southwest of Jemez in the Cebolleta Mountains. The records also indicate the failure of Spanish missionary activity among the Navajos, and sporadic but increasingly persistent warfare between the two peoples.[3]

It was in the seventeenth century that the transition from an agricultural to a pastoral economy occurred. We do not know precisely when this momentous event took place. Most authorities date it from the time of the Pueblo Indian Revolt against the Spanish in 1680 when the Navajos supposedly collected the stray sheep and horses produced by the general confusion, but one scholar has recently suggested that the livestock holdings, particularly sheep, may have had their origin in the decade preceeding the revolt.[4]

More than sheep and horses were acquired as a result of the Pueblo Revolt. When the Spanish governor de Vargas completed his reconquest of New Mexico and the Pueblo villages in 1696, it was

---

[2]For the debate over the meaning of *Navahu* see Edgar L. Hewitt, "Origin of the Name Navaho," *American Anthropologist,* VIII (n.s., 1906), p. 193; Frank D. Reeve, "Early Navaho Geography," *NMHR,* XXXI (October, 1956), pp. 299-300; and Kluckhohn and Leighton, *The Navaho,* p. 24. Anthropologists generally have accepted the Tewa origin of the name and for this reason have seen no good reason to hold to the Spanish spelling and pronunciation, "Navajó." Instead, they prefer the Anglicized form, "Návaho." See Berard Haile, "Návaho or Navajó," *The Americas,* VI (July, 1949), p. 87.
I have chosen the Spanish form for the simple reason that the federal records upon which this study is based employ this spelling.

[3]Reeve, "Early Navaho Geography," *NMHR,* XXXI, p. 305; also Reeve, "Seventeenth Century Navaho-Spanish Relations," *NMHR,* XXXII, p. 51.

[4]Underhill, *The Navajos,* pp. 40-41; Reeve, "Seventeenth Century Navaho-Spanish Relations," *NMHR,* XXXII, p. 49.

discovered that many of the Indians had fled westward to the Pueblo villages of Acoma and Laguna near the Cebolleta Navajos. Others fled directly into the Cebolleta Mountains and still others into the Province of Navajo. Although we are not certain of the magnitude or duration of this Navajo-Pueblo intermingling, the evidence suggests that it was "crucial" for Navajo cultural change.[5] Weaving became a part of Navajo life, and wool produced changes in clothing. Pueblo religious customs were merged into the more primitive Navajo theology and the population swelled with intermarriage.

Following the Pueblo Revolt, Navajos from the Province of Navajo became increasingly bold. Beginning in 1705, Spanish punitive expeditions were sent against them but it was not until 1720 that the raids were finally curtailed. Several reasons have been advanced for the Spanish success. For one, the Navajos were apparently convinced that the guerrilla-type warfare was going against them. Secondly, increasing Ute and Comanche pressures on the Navajos made peace with the Spaniards necessary and their support desirable. Lastly, the addition of sheep and other livestock to the Navajo economy made raiding less necessary than before.[6]

In the 1740's Franciscan friars again attempted the conversion of the Navajos. In 1744 two friars entered the Province of Navajo where they were warmly received. Although only six days were spent among the Indians, the missionaries reported the conversion of 5,000 Navajos, a beginning so promising that the King of Spain two years later approved the establishment of four missions in the area. This overly optimistic decree was never implemented for a variety of reasons but, by 1749, two missions were established in the Cebolleta Mountains area, one near the present town of Cebolleta, New Mexico, where 500 Navajos were induced to settle, another nearby at Encinal. One year later the friars were driven from the missions. Subsequent investigation revealed that the Navajos had become angered by the inability of the missionaries to furnish them with gifts and that they were, moreover, frightened by the example of forced labor which they observed in the nearby Pueblo communities.[7]

Relations with the Spanish government were worsening again at

---

[5]Vogt, "Navaho," in *Perspectives in American Indian Culture Change*, p. 301.

[6]Frank D. Reeve, "Navaho-Spanish Wars, 1680-1720," *NMHR*, XXXIII (July, 1958), pp. 212-30.

[7]Frank D. Reeve, "The Navaho-Spanish Peace, 1720's-1770's," *NMHR*, XXXIV (January, 1959), pp. 25-40.

this time. Ute attacks forced the Navajos in the Province of Navajo to begin the abandonment of their homeland in the 1750's. Some migrated southward to the Cebolleta area, increasing the population there at a time when Spanish settlers from the lower Rio Grande valley were also pushing into the area. Others began the westward trek that was to take them eventually to the area they occupy today. By 1780 Navajos were to be found in the Chuska Mountains and in the Canyon de Chelly where intimate contact was again established with a Pueblo people, the Hopis.

In 1767 the first of a series of land grants was issued to Spanish settlers who asked permission to move west of the Rio Grande. Despite the fact that each grant contained a provision protecting Navajo rights, the gradual encirclement of Mt. Taylor in the heart of the Cebolleta range produced tensions which erupted in fighting in 1774. By 1780 the Navajos had driven the Spaniards out. Some Navajos flirted briefly with the Gila Apaches who were at war with the Spanish, but this alliance was broken and a truce concluded with the Spanish when the latter threatened to unleash the Comanches and Utes. The last decade of the eighteenth century witnessed a return once more to peaceful relations.[8]

As Spain's control over her American colonies weakened in the early nineteenth century, the Indians of the Southwest were quick to sense her declining authority. After 1800 the Navajos emerged as the "most impressive pastoral culture in aboriginal America and one of the dominant military powers in the Southwest." By 1820 their strength was felt from the Rio Grande valley to Hopiland. After Mexican independence they literally ran wild, and warfare and raiding became major occupations. When the Americans arrived in 1846 they experienced no difficulty with the Mexican authorities in Santa Fe, but the Navajos were not to be so easily quelled.[9]

Like the Spanish before them, the Americans had little conception of Navajo political and social organization. Believing that the Navajos were organized like a European nation or state, they attempted to make treaties with their leaders; between 1846 and

---

[8]Frank D. Reeve, "Navaho-Spanish Diplomacy, 1770-1790," *NMHR*, XXXV (July, 1960), pp. 200-35.

[9]Vogt, "Navaho," in *Perspectives in American Indian Culture Change*, p. 293. See also Edward H. Spicer, *Cycles of Conquest: The Impact of Spain, Mexico, and the United States on the Indians of the Southwest, 1533-1960* (Tucson: University of Arizona Press, 1962), p. 213.

1852 several treaties were negotiated but the raids continued. One report tells us that 800,000 sheep and cattle as well as 20,000 horses and mules passed into Navajo hands between 1846 and 1850.[10] In 1852 the federal government established Fort Defiance in the heart of the Navajo country; relatively peaceful conditions then prevailed until 1858. Perhaps as much responsible as the army for this lull in the raiding was the popular Indian agent, Henry Linn Dodge, who between 1853 and 1856 worked among the Navajos from his head-quarters at Sheep Springs, just northeast of Fort Defiance.

In 1856 Dodge was felled by an Apache arrow. Two years later trouble erupted at Fort Defiance when the military seized a large area of traditional Navajo pasture. After the post commander ordered some Navajo horses which had encroached on this preserve shot, the Navajos retaliated by shooting his Negro slave. A punitive expedition succeeded only in antagonizing further the Navajo leaders Barboncito, Herrero, and Manuelito, who organized a force of 2,000 warriors for an attack on the fort itself in April, 1860. Although the war party was repulsed, peace was not restored.[11]

The outbreak of the Civil War resulted in the withdrawal of the troops stationed at Fort Defiance. The Navajos, interpreting this as a confession of weakness on the part of the Americans, once again began to terrorize the white settlements in New Mexico. In 1863 Brigadier General James H. Carleton arrived in New Mexico from California to repel the Confederate forces. When he learned that the Confederates had fled before his arrival he began to cast about for some worthy task to keep his impatient men busy. Conferences with the Territorial Governor resulted in a decision to launch a campaign against the Indians.

Carleton's plan went far beyond a mere punitive campaign. He envisioned nothing less than the establishment of permanent peace through the wholesale removal of the Navajos and Apaches to a reservation in eastern New Mexico. Carleton stated it this way:

> . . . to gather them together, little by little, on to a reservation, away from the haunts, and hills, and hiding-places of their country, and then to be kind to them; there teach their children how

---

[10]Spicer, *Cycles of Conquest*, p. 216; Frank D. Reeve, "The Government and the Navaho, 1846-1858," *NMHR*, XIV (January, 1939), pp. 110-14.

[11]Spicer, *Cycles of Conquest*, p. 217; Underhill, *The Navajos*, pp. 106-108, gives a somewhat different account.

to read and write; teach them the arts of peace; teach them the truths of Christianity. Soon they will acquire new habits, new ideas, new modes of life; the old Indians will die off, and carry with them all latent longings for murdering and robbing; the young ones will take their places without these longings; and thus, little by little, they will become a happy and contented people, and Navajo wars will be remembered only as something that belongs entirely to the past.[12]

The mountain man, Kit Carson, then living in Taos, New Mexico, was commissioned field commander and given orders to bring the Indians in, peaceably if possible, forcibly if necessary. By midsummer, 1863, Carson had ended the menace of the Mescalero Apaches. He then turned his attention to the Navajos who were given until July 20, 1863, to surrender.

Only a few bands of Navajos complied with the command. As a result, Carson invaded the Navajo country with a small army. Wherever resistance was offered, he destroyed the crops, rounded up the sheep, and shot the Navajo men. On March 6, 1864, 2,400 Navajos began the "Long Walk" to the Bosque Redondo on the banks of the Pecos River in New Mexico. By May an additional 3,500 were on the way. Although an undetermined number successfully hid in the canyons and on the mountains, some 8,500 Navajos were eventually removed from their homeland.

The utopia Carleton planned was a failure. Aside from the reluctance of the dispirited and homesick Navajos to take up farming, drought, hail, and worms attacked the crops. There was friction with the Mescalero Apaches and trouble with neighboring Comanches. The civilian agent, Michael Steck, quarreled with Carleton over the plan itself; Steck called it inhumane and unfruitful. And always there was the problem of money. The first twenty months of the experiment cost the War Department $1,114,981.70 and the average cost of rations between 1863 and 1868 was $750,000 per year. In 1867 the Navajos refused to plant crops; during the winter several hundred deserted. In 1868 the Bosque Redondo scheme was officially abandoned[13] and a

---

[12]James H. Carleton to General Lorenzo Thomas, September 6, 1863, in U. S. Congress, Senate, Joint Special Committee, *Conditions of the Indian Tribes*, 39th Cong., 2d sess., 1866-1867, Report No. 156, p. 134.

[13]The Bosque Redondo experiment is well covered in a number of sources. See particularly, Frank D. Reeve, "Federal Indian Policy in New Mexico, 1858-1880," *NMHR*, XII (1937), pp. 249-55, and XIII (1938), pp. 22-24; Underhill, *The Navajos*, pp. 128-43.

treaty was signed permitting the Navajos to return to a new reservation in their former homeland.

The treaty of 1868 marked the beginning of a new era in Navajo history. It set aside for their exclusive use a reservation of almost four million acres, equally straddling northwestern New Mexico and northeastern Arizona. By the provisions of the treaty, during the next fourteen years a school was to be built and a teacher provided for every thirty children who could be "induced or compelled to attend." In return, the Navajos promised to forego raiding and pillaging as a way of life (15 Stat., 667).

From 1868 to 1913 the lot of the Navajos was a seemingly profitable and peaceable one. From an estimated and probably unreliable figure of 8,000 people at the time of their return from the Pecos River valley, their numbers grew to an estimated 22,000 in 1900 and to 30,000 in 1912.[14] Their animal holdings increased from 15,000 sheep and goats provided by the government in 1869 until they had at least as many as they had possessed at the time of Carson's roundup. The federal government, recognizing that the original four-million-acre grant was too small, continually enlarged the reservation until it totaled some twelve million acres by 1911.[15]

NAVAJO SOCIETY

The sketch of Navajo history just presented is a white man's account. It is not a history of the Navajo people or their civilization but rather the story of their contact with and reaction to succcessive waves of white invaders. If we would know something of the way Navajos view themselves and the world about them, we must turn to the writings of cultural anthropologists and ethnologists. Fortunately, during the past seventy years, "The People" have been closely examined by these social scientists who have bequeathed to us a large body of literature.

The place to start is with the land itself. The reservation today

---

[14]Ruth Underhill, *Here Come the Navaho!* (Lawrence, Kansas: Haskell Institute Press, 1953), p. 223; U.S. Bureau of Indian Affairs, *Annual Report of the Commissioner of Indian Affairs, 1912* (Washington: G.P.O., 1913), pp.74-80. (Hereafter cited as Commissioner of Indian Affairs, *Annual Report*.)

[15]Commissioner of Indian Affairs, *Annual Report, 1911*, pp. 95-96. For comparative purposes, this is larger than the combined areas of Connecticut, Delaware, Rhode Island, and Vermont.

comprises some 14,500,000 acres spread over the three states of New Mexico, Arizona, and Utah. It is part of the geological formation designated as the Colorado Plateau — an "intensely dissected rocky region of elevations that range from 3,500 feet above sea level to more than 10,000 feet." At least four separate kinds of topography are observable. There are flat, alluvial valleys at the 4,500-6,000 foot level; rolling plains between 5,500-7,000 feet; rocky tablelands or mesas at 6,000-8,000 feet; and the mountains above 7,500 feet. Over half this vast area a warm, arid, desert climate prevails; average annual rainfall is about eight inches and the vegetation is sparse. In the region of intermediate elevation — about two-fifths of the reservation — an average annual rainfall of sixteen to twenty inches makes possible a larger stand of native grasses and a shrub growth of piñon, juniper, and sagebrush. In the humid mountainous region, yellow pine, oak, aspen, and fir stands are found together with meadows used for summer grazing. Approximately 15 percent of the reservation is barren or rendered useless because of inaccessibility.[16]

Until recent times, despite its forbidding nature, this land was capable of supporting its people. Before the Spaniards came, agriculture was the most important economic pursuit, and even today many Navajos continue to raise some portion of their food supply. Corn, squash, beans, and melons, the Navajo staples, are cultivated near natural springs or, more frequently, in arroyos which are irrigated by the spring snow melt and the summer rainstorms. The introduction of sheep in the seventeenth century profoundly changed the Navajo economy. Until the 1930's nearly every Navajo was a stockman who grazed some sheep and goats; many of the flocks were quite large. Both agriculture and the livestock industry have played a role in Navajo social organization.

The basic unit in Navajo social and economic life is the biological family: husband, wife, and unmarried children. Polygamy has had traditional approval. The man who could afford a second wife (quite often his first wife's sister, niece, or daughter by a previous marriage) demonstrated economic success, a heightened sense of responsibility, and greater prestige through his many offspring. Though the custom is dying out in most areas, where it persists the two or more families, though housed in separate domiciles, live together and form one unit.

Although it is not uncommon to find the biological family living

---

[16]Robert W. Young, *The Navajo Yearbook, 1961* (Window Rock, Arizona, 1961), pp. 358-66; Kluckhohn and Leighton, *The Navaho*, p. 47.

by itself, the rigors of daily life and the need for social intercourse in a lonely land have tended to group most Navajos into larger aggregates. Because Navajo society is fundamentally matriarchal (lines of descent and property inheritance are traced through the mother) this larger functional unit is built around the mother. An older woman with her husband and unmarried children, together with her married daughters and their families constitute what the anthropologists designate the "extended family." These families live in adjacent homes or hogans and cooperate closely in agriculture and the care of livestock. Extended families also provide for the isolated individual — the aged father or mother, the widowed, childless sister, the unmarried niece.

For some tasks like planting, harvesting, sheep dipping, or the giving of important ceremonials, a loose association of relatives, comprising perhaps two or more extended families or one extended family and several independent biological families, is formed. Membership in this "outfit" is fluid and contact between the component parts is infrequent except in the cases just mentioned. Unlike the extended family, the outfit is spread over a wide geographical area.

The largest effective unit of social and political cooperation is the "community," which is based not on ties of blood but on geographical location. Failure to recognize the community's existence until the early twentieth century retarded effective political organization among the Navajos, but in recent years the community, for the most part, has been recognized as the basic unit for the selection of delegates to the Navajo Tribal Council.

Navajos are also identified by clans of which there are approximately sixty. Many of the clan names are place names, a fact which suggests that at some time in the past clan members congregated in a given locale. Today members of a clan may be found spread across the reservation but there is still a tendency to concentrate in certain areas. In the past the clan was an effective force in social control but the growth and dispersal of the Navajos have greatly weakened this function. Today the clans, which are matriarchal and exogamous, function primarily as a means of identifying distant relatives and preventing inbreeding.[17]

---

[17]For the structure of Navajo society see Kluckhohn and Leighton, *The Navaho*, pp. 100-14; Kluckhohn and Vogt, *Navaho Means People*, pp. 137-38; Alexander H. and Dorothea C. Leighton, *The Navaho Door, An Introduction to Navaho Life* (Cambridge: Harvard University Press, 1944), p. 22; and Vogt, "Navaho," in *Perspectives in American Indian Culture Change*, pp. 304-306.

It has sometimes been assumed that the introduction of the horse and the sheep made the Navajos a nomadic people. Like the Bedouins of North Africa, they have been pictured as rugged individualists with little or no community life.[18] The structure of Navajo society just presented should help to temper this erroneous judgment. While it is true that the Navajos move about with their flocks, it is likewise true that they travel, for the most part, within certain well-defined areas. It is common for a Navajo to have a summer and a winter home but the latter is a permanent structure in which the same family lives year after year. Furthermore, Navajo property concepts tend to confine the family or extended family to the use of a given area.

Water, timber, and patches of saltbush are considered communal property, open to all who need them. Farm or grazing land, once it has been appropriated by members of a given family, becomes their special preserve so long as they continue to use it. This is not the same as private ownership. Anthropologists call this kind of ownership "inherited-use ownership," which means simply that so long as a given plot of land is used by a particular family, it "belongs" to them and the right to use may be passed on from one generation to the next. No right-minded Navajo, for instance, would intentionally trespass on land which he knew was being used by another.

The mother and her children are the real owners of the family herd and farm, the husband serving somewhat like a trustee. The concept of joint ownership between husband and wife, so common in our own society, has not been generally recognized by Navajos. The wife has her income from the sale of rugs, sheep, and surplus crops, while the husband has his from any wages he might earn, the proceeds from silversmithing, or the sale of horses and sheep which are indisputably his. Because of the overriding consideration of family, however, it is not precisely correct to refer to any of these income-producing items as personal property. The only property which is truly personal and individual, i.e., the kind which one can dispose of as he sees fit, is "clothing, jewelry, saddles, ceremonial equipment and intangibles like songs and prayers."[19]

---

[18]G.E.E. Lindquist, *The Red Man in the United States* (New York: George H. Doran Co., 1923), p. 278.

[19]For a more detailed treatment of Navajo property concepts see Kluckhohn and Leighton, *The Navaho,* pp. 105-106; Alexander and Dorothea Leighton, *The Navaho Door,* p. 19; John L. Landgraf, *Land Use in the Ramah Area of New Mexico* (Papers of the Peabody Museum of American Archaeology and Ethnology, Vol. XLII, No. 1; Cambridge: Harvard University Press, 1954), p. 27; and

Just as Navajo property concepts differ from those of their white neighbors, so do their basic assumptions about life and thus their hierarchy of values and standards of ethical conduct. While it must be remembered that Navajos today are undergoing all the strains and turmoil of a culture in transition, a description of their traditional beliefs is a necessary prelude to understanding. The best treatment of these concepts is to be found in the writings of the late Clyde Kluckhohn, to whom the following account is heavily indebted.

The core of Navajo philosophy is contained in several basic convictions. One is that it is this life which counts. There is, for instance, no concept of an ultimate or master design in their cosmology. While the existence of life after death is not denied, it is mostly ignored. In addition, the Navajo is almost morbidly aware that life is full of dangers and his preoccupation with these dangers colors every aspect of daily life. He accepts nature as far more powerful than man and consequently he strives to conform to its dictates rather than attempting to change its course. He does not conceive of the human personality as a duality of spirit and matter, but, rather, as a single, indivisible whole. Nor is he concerned with whether man is basically good or evil. Man is simply a combination of both.[20]

Because he is so concerned with this life, the Navajo tends to be very practical, or, as Kluckhohn has put it, "utterly pragmatic." The virtues which he attempts to emulate are those which promote harmony and reduce friction. One should be pleasant to all, especially solicitous to one's relatives. The ideal Navajo possesses self-control, generosity, and cheerfully shoulders his portion of the community work.

Because life is considered so precarious and because bare subsistence has so often been a reality, it is not surprising that health and strength should rate highest on the list of Navajo values. With these and industry a Navajo can accumulate the other things which are conducive to the good life and a sense of security. Without them he may be unable to tend the sheep or cultivate the fields, and thus perish. Grinding poverty is greatly feared and is not socially accep-

---

Willard W. Hill, *The Agricultural and Hunting Methods of the Navaho Indians* (Yale University Publications in Anthropology, No. 18; New Haven: Yale University Press, 1938), pp. 22-24.

[20]Clyde Kluckhohn, "The Philosophy of the Navajo Indians," in *Ideological Differences and World Order*, ed. F.S.C. Northrop (New Haven: Yale University Press, 1949).

table. Neither is great wealth. The attainment of wealth as a chief aim in life is universally condemned and a successful man will take steps to prevent too great an accumulation of material goods for fear of being called a witch.[21]

Navajo morality is not based on an absolute code of ethics but is rather "contextual" and practical. Anthropologists point out that this is characteristic of the difference between a "shame" and a "guilt" culture, between one in which custom rather than individual conscience is the arbiter. With perhaps the single exception of incest, no act is considered either intrinsically good or evil. Stress is again placed on getting along with one's neighbors. Goodness is characterized by helpfulness, dependability, and generosity, while stinginess, laziness, and meanness are considered bad traits. The motivating factor in enforcing good behavior is the shame and ridicule which accompany public disclosure of transgressions. The Navajo, for instance, who has stolen or told a lie is not apt to worry about his action if it is not discovered, but the fear of being shamed if he is found out is usually sufficient to induce proper behavior. The main difference between Navajo morality and Christian morality, Kluckhohn has written, is not that of the presence versus the absence of moral standards, "It is rather a difference in the mechanism for enforcing those standards."[22]

Navajos have traditionally dealt differently than the white man with persons who commit major crimes. Murder, rape, assault, and other acts of violence were and are condemned and punished, but the offender, before the application of our legal system, was not ordinarily imprisoned or physically chastized. Instead, a fine was levied against the offending party or his family to compensate the wronged party or his family for any economic loss entailed.

A society which places great value on health and survival could be expected to be greatly concerned with warding off illness. This is

---

[21]For a discussion of Navajo virtues and values see Kluckhohn and Leighton, *The Navaho*, pp. 299-300; Kluckhohn, "The Philosophy of the Navaho Indians," in *Ideological Differences and World Order*, pp., 371-75; and Richard Hobson, *Navaho Acquisitive Values* (Papers of the Peabody Museum of American Archaeology and Ethnology, Vol. XLII, No. 3; Cambridge: Harvard University Press, 1954), pp. 28-29.

[22]Kluckhohn, "The Philosophy of the Navaho Indians," in *Ideological Differences and World Order*, pp. 373-76; Laura Thompson, *Personality and Government* (Mexico, D.F.: Ediciones del Instituto Indigenista Inter-Americano, 1951), p. 43. For the difficulties of an early Christian missionary to the Navajos see Robert L. Wilkin, *Anselm Weber, O.F.M., Missionary to the Navaho* (Milwaukee: Bruce Publishing Co., 1953), p. 112.

so true among the Navajos that while their religious ceremonials have the function of worship and instruction in the sacred myths, they are mainly concerned with the restoration or maintenance of health. Religion and well-being are inextricably knit in Navajo society.

The major problem which has faced white administrators and physicians in their attempts to deal with the very real problems of Navajo sickness and disease is the fact that the Navajos do not account for illness in biological or physiological terms. For a Navajo, sickness is the product of some imbalance or disorder between himself and the Holy People (the gods), nature, or another person. Disease or accidental injury can be brought about by a bewildering variety of taboo transgressions, or by contact with ghosts, or as the result of witchcraft. A further complication lies in the fact that for a Navajo, human nature is whole and indivisible. There is no precedent for treating the body or parts of the body separately. Navajo healing ceremonies are designed to cure the whole man.

Most Navajo ceremonials or "sings" are directed toward effecting a cure, although the most frequent ceremonial of all, the Blessing Way rite, is designed to promote or prolong health and well-being, and is therefore more precautionary than curative. Because of the great variety of ceremonies and the specific nature of the cure produced by each, correct diagnosis is extremely important. For this purpose a shaman known as the "handtrembler" is consulted. Depending upon the movement of his hands which begin to shake during his rite, the proper curing ceremony is indicated. There are at least fifty different sings which can be prescribed, varying in length from one to nine days. All of these ceremonies are expensive, for not only must the singer be paid but, since the ceremonies are also occasions for social gatherings, provision must be made for the guests.[23]

Modern medical science has demonstrated the great value of these ceremonies in cases of psychosomatic illness. The medicinal herbs employed have also proved to have beneficial effect. However, in the case of infectious diseases like tuberculosis and trachoma, both widely prevalent on the reservation within recent times, the cures are ineffective. Today the Navajos are responding in ever-larger numbers to the white man's medicine, but in the early years of the twentieth century Indian Bureau officials and physicians faced difficult

---

[23]At a Yeibichai ceremony held on the eastern reservation area in 1917, over 2,000 Navajos were in attendance. See Franc Johnson Newcomb, *Hosteen Klah, Navaho Medicine Man and Sand Painter* (Norman: University of Oklahoma Press, 1964), p. 119.

problems indeed. It was not uncommon for Navajos to delay hospital treatment until the patient had been given up by the medicine man. The resulting high death rate in government hospitals, coupled with the traditional Navajo fear of the dead, did not encourage the use of these facilities.[24]

The problem of Navajo tribal organization has baffled white men from the time of the Spanish. Accustomed to the idea of a single leader, chief, or king, they repeatedly made the mistake of attempting to deal with all Navajos through one, or at best, several spokesmen. As we saw earlier, the fundamental political entity among the Navajos is the community, not the tribe or the nation. As a result, there were always as many Navajo spokesmen as there were communities, a situation which resulted in almost continuous confusion and frustration for both sides.

Today we know that within each community there were at least two leaders or *natani,* one for peace and one for war, and sometimes there were more than one of each. Although there may have been a tendency in this direction, these positions were not hereditary, but were determined by personal ability and some mastery of religious ritual. The *natani* possessed no power of coercion over his followers; instead, he relied upon his powers of persuasion. Outside his own community he possessed no authority at all. During the period of exile at the Bosque Redondo, the army did divide the tribe into twelve bands and appoint a chief over each. Subsequent to the signing of the peace treaty in 1868, this arrangement was simplified by the appointment of Barboncito as head chief with two subordinates, Ganado Mucho in the West, and Manuelito in the East. There is no evidence that these artificial creations wrought any change in Navajo political organization. As the Navajos entered the twentieth century they were still a politically fragmented people whose cohesion lay primarily in "their common linguistic and cultural heritage, the occupation of a definite territory, a common designation for themselves, Diné."[25]

A final word must be said about the Navajo attitude toward white

---

[24]For Navajo health concepts and their relation to religious ceremonies see Kluckhohn and Leighton, *The Navaho,* pp. 192-93; Alexander and Dorothea Leighton, *The Navaho Door,* pp. 38-40; and Kluckhohn and Vogt, *Navaho Means People,* pp. 139-41.

[25]Willard W. Hill, "Some Aspects of Navaho Political Structure," *Plateau,* Vol. 13, No. 2 (October, 1940), pp. 23-25; Underhill, *The Navajos,* pp. 133, 161-62.

civilization. Unlike some of their Pueblo neighbors who have attempted to shut themselves off from the encroachments of white society, the Navajos, consistently pragmatic, have demonstrated a remarkable degree of receptivity to white technology. What is important to note here is that they have been able to do so largely without destroying the essential framework of their own culture and that the reasons which they have for this adaptation are often different from those of a white man. Despite their willingness to experiment with new methods and techniques, the Navajo mentality urges caution and limited acceptance at first. In her comparison of the Navajo and Hopi mentality, Laura Thompson has ably noted that the Navajo

> is not accustomed to prolonged, systematic work toward abstract, long-range goals. Indeed he does not have the organizational, abstract, mental approach such as characterizes the planning, foresighted mentality nor is he interested in complex relationships, but rather he thinks in terms of simple, concrete action toward immediate, obvious goals.[26]

The remainder of this book is devoted to an account of how the Navajos reacted to some of the complex, abstract, and long-range goals placed before them by the federal government in the first third of the twentieth century, and how, in turn, federal Indian policy was shaped by the Navajo confrontation.

---

[26]Laura Thompson, *Personality and Government,* p. 42.

CHAPTER 2

Reservation Expansion Before 1922

In 1911 the Navajos held 12,189,997 acres of land in Arizona, New Mexico, and Utah, but this was not enough.[1] Between 1912 and 1921 several attempts were made to enlarge the reservation boundaries. In all but one instance these measures were defeated.

THE DAWES ACT

The Navajos, like most of the other tribes of the Southwest, were fortunate in that those provisions of the Dawes Severalty Act (24 Stat., 388) which provided for the individual allotment of tribal lands were never applied to them. This act, passed in 1887, was an attempt to solve the "Indian problem" for all time. Its philosophy was a white man's philosophy, conceived with little understanding of Indian psychology. To make the Indian a worthwhile citizen, the Dawes Act said in effect, treat him like a white man: divorce him from the unprogressive tribal society, give him a farm to till, and he will soon be absorbed into the mainstream of American life. This at least was what the friends of the Indians said. Land-hungry cattlemen and farmers cared little about what was said so long as the Indian reservations were broken up.

The Dawes Act essentially provided for the division of Indian tribal lands into private holdings. The largest holding that an individual Indian could receive was 160 acres. The tribal land which remained after individual allotment was to be purchased by the federal government and subsequently opened to white homestead entry. Should an Indian refuse to choose an allotment, a federal agent would make the selection for him. To protect the Indian during his apprenticeship to the white man's way, the law provided that he could not alienate his allotment for twenty-five years. During this period he was to hold his land free from taxation. Finally, as a sign that he was on the road to progress, the Indian would be freed

---

[1]Commissioner of Indian Affairs, *Annual Report, 1911*, pp. 95-96.

from ward status and be granted U. S. citizenship (24 Stat., 388).

The Dawes Act was a victory for the forces of coercion.[2] After several blunders, conscientious officials became reluctant to recommend application of the law because it proved an evil rather than a good for the Indians. Conscientious officials, however, would probably not have been able to forestall the white land-hunger had it not been for other factors.

One of these, in the Navajo preserve, was the rugged terrain. Within all this vast expanse there was but one living stream, the San Juan River. The average rainfall over most of the area was but eight inches per year.[3] Seeps and springs there were at scattered intervals, but in most of the area farming was out of the question. Not until after 1900, when artesian wells began to be developed,[4] would even the cattlemen seriously begin to cast covetous eyes on the lands. A second and more important factor was the political one. The reservation lay within the Territories of New Mexico and Arizona. So long as the federal government controlled both the Territories and the Navajo Reservation, local feeling was relatively unimportant. But, after 1900, as the two Territories moved toward statehood, their influence in Congress increased and they were listened to more frequently.

EXECUTIVE-ORDER INDIAN RESERVATIONS

The original treaty-area reservation was not large enough for all the Navajos who returned from the Bosque Redondo; as a result, many of them settled outside the reservation proper. This situation was later remedied, in part, by the creation of what were called executive-order reservations — in 1878, 1880, 1882 (Hopi reservation), 1884, 1900, and 1901 (see map No. 1).

---

[2]Loring Benson Priest, *Uncle Sam's Stepchildren* (New Brunswick: Rutgers University Press, 1942), p. 247.

[3]Herbert E. Gregory, *The Navajo Country*, U.S. Geological Survey, Water Supply Paper 380 (Washington: G.P.O., 1916), p. 123.

[4]E. M. Sweet to E. B. Meritt, July 24, 1915. National Archives, Record Group 75, Pueblo Bonito Agency, unnumbered report in the 160-168 file. Since the bulk of the documentation for this study is taken from the National Archives, Record Group 75, subsequent citations to this source will be abbreviated to include only the title of the record division within Record Group 75 and the individual file number. Thus, if the letter referred to above had been numbered, the citation might read Pueblo Bonito, 14653-15-168. See the bibliography for the various divisions within Record Group 75.

For additional material on the development of artesian wells, see U.S. Senate, Committee on Indian Affairs, *Hearings, Survey of Conditions of the Indians of the United States* (1928-1943), part 18, p. 9633. (Future citations to this source will be indicated as *Senate Survey*.)

MAP 1 **BOUNDARIES OF THE NAVAJO RESERVATION**

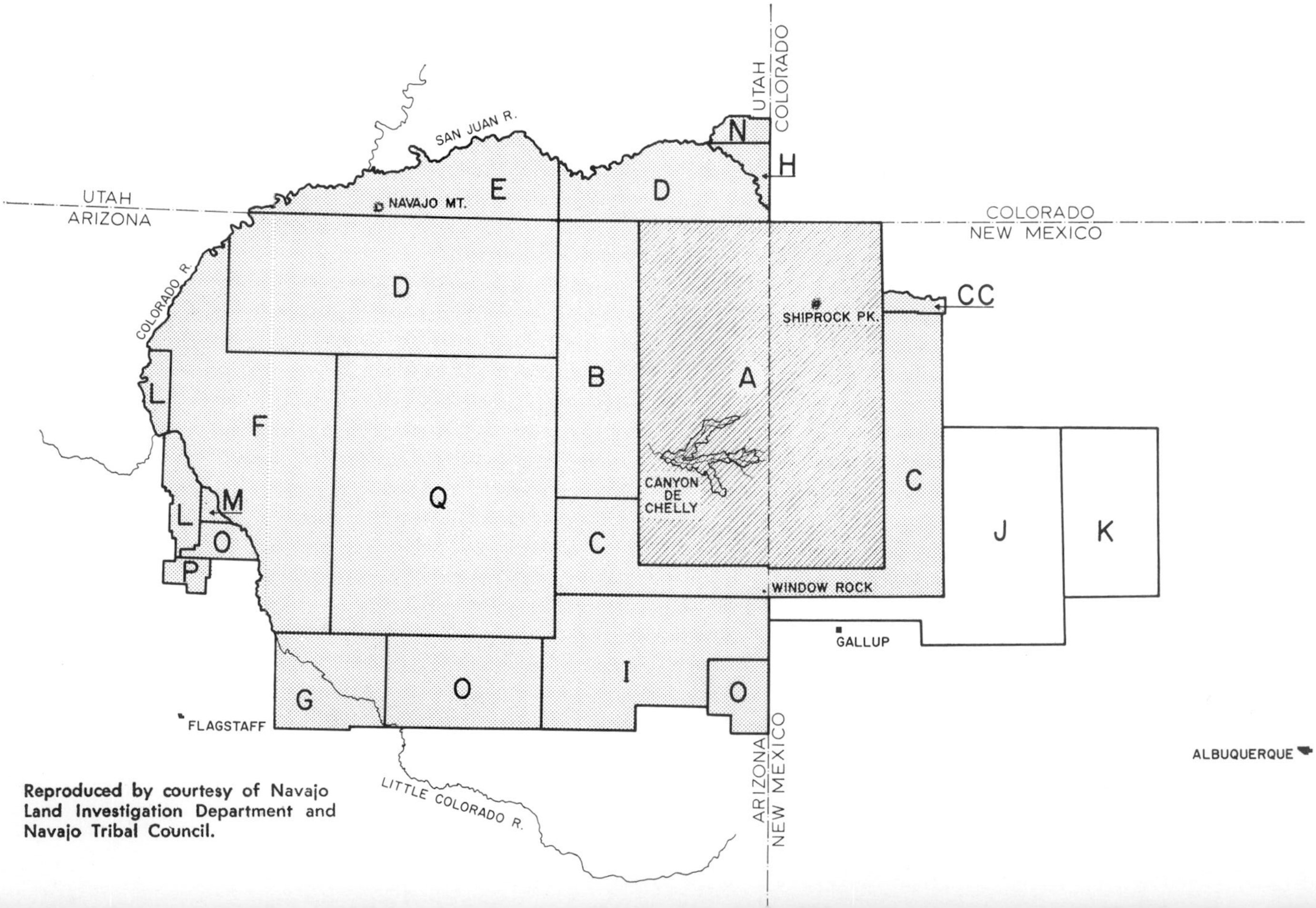

Reproduced by courtesy of Navajo
Land Investigation Department and
Navajo Tribal Council.

A Original treaty reservation. June 1, 1868.

B Executive-order addition. October 29, 1878.

C Executive-order addition. January 6, 1880.

CC Originally a part of "C"; withdrawn from the reservation by executive order, May 17, 1884; restored by executive order, April 24, 1886.

D (two parts) Executive-order addition. May 17, 1884.

E The Paiute Strip. Originally a part of "D"; in 1892 restored to the public domain; in 1908 withdrawn for the use of various Indians; restored to public domain in 1922; in 1929 again withdrawn from entry; 1933 transferred permanently to the Navajo reservation.

F Executive-order addition. January 8, 1900.

G Executive-order addition. November 14, 1901.

H Executive-order addition. March 10, 1905.

I Executive-order addition. November 9, 1907.

J Executive-order addition. November 9, 1907; restored to public domain by executive order of January 16, 1911.

K Executive-order addition. November 9, 1907; restored to public domain by executive order of December 30, 1908.

L Tusayan Forest addition. Act of May 23, 1930.

M Executive-order addition. May 7, 1917.

N Act of March 1, 1933.

O (three parts) Arizona Boundary Act of June 14, 1934.

P Tusayan Forest addition. Act of February 21, 1933.

Q Hopi reservation. Executive-order reservation created on December 16, 1882.

An executive-order reservation differed considerably from a treaty reservation. Whereas the latter was, at least in theory, the result of a bilateral agreement between Indians and the government, the executive-order reservation was a unilateral creation of the President which the Congress had neither the power to approve nor reject. Title to the treaty reservation was vested in the Indians. Title was not clearly given to the Indians by an executive order; certain lands were simply withdrawn from the public domain for their use. Although custom usually accorded them title in these cases, the legality of the title was open to serious doubt.

The executive-order reservation was a vague thing in other ways. Sometimes the documents creating these reservations reserved the land for the use of specific Indians, as did those of 1878 and 1880 in the case of the Navajos. In other cases one or more tribes might be designated, as in the case of the creation of the Hopi reservation in 1882 when it was provided that the land was to be used by the Hopis[5] "and other such Indians as the Secretary of the Interior may see fit to settle thereon." To make matters even more confusing, there were withdrawals like those of 1884, 1900, and 1901 in which no specific mention of any tribe was made. Although the 1884 order did state that the land withdrawn was to be "set apart as a reservation for Indian purposes," those of 1900 and 1901 did not even mention possible use of the land as an Indian reservation.[6] The executive-order Indian reservation was a creature of administrative expediency which fit into no well-defined public policy. Although well-intentioned, it inhabited a legal limbo and in the future its insecure status brought great anxiety to those for whom it was originally fashioned.

THE CHECKERBOARD

In addition to the problems which surrounded the legal status of the executive-order reservations, another serious and more concrete problem plagued the Navajos. In 1866 the Atlantic and Pacific Rail-

---

[5]The original document referred to these Indians as the "Moqui." It was not until 1923, when the Indian Office learned that the term "Moqui" was a Navajo epithet meaning "dead one," that the official use of the word "Hopi" came into existence. See press release of the Department of the Interior dated May 7, 1923, in the National Archives, Record Group 75, Hagerman Papers, Commissioner's File, January-June, 1923.

[6]Printed copies of the various executive orders discussed may be found in Charles J. Kappler, *Indian Affairs, Laws and Treaties* (5 vols.; Washington: G.P.O., 1904-38).

road Company was chartered by Congress to build a railroad from Springfield, Missouri, to the California state line. To finance this road a liberal land grant of forty sections per mile in the Territories (twenty above and twenty below the line) was granted to the company.[7] In 1876 all of the original grant except that portion from Albuquerque, New Mexico, to the California line was forfeited (24 Stat., 123), and the remainder passed into the control of the St. Louis and San Francisco Railroad Company. In 1880 the Atchison, Topeka, and Santa Fe Railroad bought a one-half interest in the St. Louis and San Francisco charter. In 1894 the Atlantic and Pacific Railroad Company was formally liquidated; what remained of the land grant was divided between the two owners. An affiliate, the Santa Fe Pacific Railroad Company, took control of the Santa Fe landholdings and the St. Louis and San Francisco entrusted its lands to a subsidiary known as the New Mexico and Arizona Land Company. A third concern, the Aztec Land and Cattle Company, purchased, in 1884, one million acres, mostly in Arizona, from the Frisco. Much of the land given to the Navajos by executive-order action lay within the northern limits of the original Atlantic and Pacific land grant. Thus, where this occurred, alternate sections of the executive-order reservations belonged not to the Navajos but to one or more of the three land companies. This phenomenon was known as the checkerboard.

EXECUTIVE ORDERS OF 1900 AND 1901

The withdrawal orders of 1900 and 1901 present one of the most difficult problems in Navajo land history. These lands were settled by Navajos at the time of the return from the Bosque Redondo. No supervision was extended over them because they were not on the reservation proper. In 1897 a missionary, the Reverend W. R. Johnston, set up a mission at Tolcheco, Arizona, and began to work for the legal protection of the Navajos living there who held no title to their lands.[8] As a direct result of his work, an executive-order withdrawal of November 14, 1901, set aside some 425,171 acres "until such time as the Indians residing thereon shall have been permanently settled

---

[7]Undoubtedly the best account of the railroad land-grant problem in the Navajo country is Sanford Mosk, *Land Tenure Problems in the Santa Fe Railroad Grant Area* (Berkeley: University of California Press, 1944). This is the major source for my discussion of the checkerboard problem.

[8]National Archives, Record Group 75, Leupp Agency, "Annual Narrative Report, 1931," pp. 1-2.

under the provisions of the homestead laws or the general allotment act. . . ." (See map No. 1, area G.) In time this area became known as the Leupp reservation.

The 1900 withdrawal order simply withdrew 1,575,369 acres of land "from sale and allotment until further notice,"[9] but since this tract was, the following year, placed under the jurisdiction of the newly created Western Navajo Reservation, it is reasonable to assume that it was withdrawn for Navajo usage (see map No. 1, area F). A good one-third of the 1900 withdrawal and all of the 1901 order lay within the land-grant area of the three land companies, so that only a portion of this land was available for Indian use. Friction between the Navajos and the white lessees of the railroad sections was inevitable.

In 1904 an attempt was made to solve the checkerboard problem. A rider was attached to the Indian appropriation bill providing that where private land had been included within an executive-order Indian reservation, such lands could be exchanged by the interested parties for "vacant, nonmineral, nontimbered, surveyed public lands of equal area and value and situated in the same State or Territory" (33 Stat., 211). Law in hand, the Indian Bureau set out to effect the transfer.

On December 17, 1912, a deed was executed relinquishing to the United States, in trust for the Navajo Indians, the odd sections held by the Santa Fe and Pacific Railroad Company within the two withdrawal areas. The deed was recorded in Coconino County, Arizona, on January 16, 1913, for 327,000 acres and the Santa Fe proceeded to claim its lieu lands. The surprise of the Santa Fe officials must have been great when they discovered that the Solicitor in the Department of the Interior refused to approve the transfer. He argued that the holdings of the Santa Fe were not located within an executive-order Indian reservation, but rather within an area only temporarily withdrawn from homestead entry, and that the act of 1904 was thus not applicable.[10] What could have been a test case for the

---

[9]Herbert J. Hagerman, *The Navajo Indian Reservation*, Senate Document 64 72d Cong., 1st sess., 1932, pp. 5-6. Hagerman confuses the 1900 withdrawal with that of 1901 and vice versa but his citation of the withdrawal orders is textually correct. (This document is hereafter cited as the *Hagerman Report.*)

[10]The history of this transaction and the opinion of the Solicitor is contained in a letter from J. H. Edwards, Solicitor, to the Secretary of the Interior, February 9, 1924. Navajo, 7126-22-313.

exact status of the executive-order withdrawals was postponed when the Santa Fe offered other checkerboard lands in the eastern area of the reservation as a base for its lieu selections. The title which had been vested in the United States in 1913, however, was not voided, nor was the land returned to the Santa Fe. The land problem in the Leupp and Western Navajo reservations remained unsolved.

It was not perverseness which had led the Navajos to disregard the treaty of 1868 by settling outside the treaty boundaries, but rather ignorance. For many years before their removal to the Bosque Redondo they had roamed over a much greater area than was given them in the treaty. Few of them had any idea of the reservation boundaries and when they were permitted to leave the Pecos Valley they naturally returned to their former haunts. The executive orders of 1900 and 1901 were attempts to accommodate those Navajos who had settled to the west and to the southwest of the original treaty reservation. Two other bands remained to be provided for. One of these lived due south of the Hopi reservation in Arizona. A second, and by far the largest group, had settled to the east and the southeast of the treaty reservation in New Mexico.

NEW MEXICO

When, after 1900, artesian water was discovered east of the reservation, making the land profitable for grazing, the Santa Fe began to lease increasingly large portions of its alternate holdings there. The Navajos living in the area, threatened by a white invasion of their traditional grazing area, pleaded with the Commissioner of Indian Affairs to incorporate this area by executive-order. In 1906 Commissioner Leupp visited them and, viewing their plight at first-hand, returned to Washington to recommend executive-order action.[11] But the white stockmen, through their lease of the Santa Fe lands, now had a vested interest and the best that could be arranged was a compromise. The area where most of the Navajos lived was to be withdrawn from white entry for a specified period during which the Indians within the withdrawal area were to be allotted lands from the public domain under section four of the Dawes Act. Although section four was originally designed to provide land for Indians who had never been granted a reservation, it was now interpreted to per-

---

[11]Testimony of Anselm Weber in U.S. House, Committee on Indian Affairs, *Hearings, Indians of the United States*, 66th Cong., 1-3d sess., 1920, Vol. 3, p. 707.

mit any Indian not residing on a reservation to have allotted to him and his children an amount of land from the public domain equivalent to what he would have received had he resided on a reservation that was divided in severalty.[12] When the allotment work was completed the remainder of the land would be restored to white entry. Accordingly, on November 9, 1907, a large tract of land to the south and east of the Navajo treaty reservation, in both Arizona and New Mexico, was withdrawn from entry. (Map No. 1, areas I, J, and K.) On May 13, 1908, a second, smaller tract between the withdrawal of 1901 and that of 1907, in the Castle Butte area of Arizona, was also withdrawn pending allotment to the Navajos.[13] (Map No. 1, that portion of area O between G and I.)

A clerical error in the order of 1907 extended the area of withdrawal to range number five east (New Mexico Principal Meridian) rather than the intended range five west. This greatly excited the people of New Mexico.[14] Although this error was quickly corrected, white opposition in New Mexico to the 1907 withdrawal continued. In response to this opposition a third executive order, dated December 30, 1908, restored twenty-six townships in New Mexico to the public domain (map No. 1, area K). Then in 1911, with New Mexico on the verge of statehood, sufficient pressure was put on President Taft by the New Mexico delegate to Congress, W. H. Andrews, to secure yet a fourth executive order restoring to the public domain all of the remaining portion of the 1907 withdrawal in New Mexico (map No. 1, area J). There is no evidence that the Arizona delegate in Congress protested either the 1907 or 1908 withdrawals in his Territory. As a result, these lands remained in a withdrawn status until 1934.

---

[12]The origin of this novel interpretation is explained at length in a letter from Indian Commissioner Cato Sells to agent T. K. Adreon at Leupp, dated January 12, 1915, printed in *Hagerman Report*, pp. 67-68. Noting that the contents of the letter were "of a confidential nature," Commissioner Sells stated that the purpose of this interpretation was to permit the Navajos to gain control of all the springs and water holes in the area so that they would gain "effectual and undisputed control of the entire range . . . ." He concluded by saying: "In other words, the step of allotting these Indians under the fourth section of the general allotment act was devised for the purpose of combatting the aggressive white owners of stock in the free use of the range where the Indians were located."

[13]Anselm Weber, *The Navajo Indians. A Statement of Facts* (St. Michaels, Ariz.: St. Michaels Press, 1915), p. 8. Also, *Hagerman Report*, pp. 6-7, which gives the date as March 13, 1908.

[14]U.S. House, *Hearings, Indians of the United States*, 66th Cong., 1-3d sess., Vol. 3, p. 707.

The strategy attempted by the Indian Office under the withdrawal orders of 1907 and 1908 was to allot to the Navajos only those lands containing water. In this way the Indians could control large sections of surrounding land which contained no water and thus, in practice if not in law, have the controlling rights to most of the withdrawn area.[15] The strategy, however, was imperfectly executed in two particulars.

In the first place, the 1907 and 1908 withdrawals were in the checkerboard area. Many of the waterholes were on the railroad lands and had already been sold or leased to white cattlemen. In the second place, many of the Navajos at the time of the withdrawal were squatters on railroad land. In the absence of a survey and in the rush to comply with the withdrawal order before it was revoked, many of these Indians filed applications on railroad land. No attempt was made to exchange these lands under the act of 1904 before the withdrawal in New Mexico was voided in 1911. After that date the act of 1904 became inoperative because the area was no longer within an executive-order Indian reservation. Thus, many of the Navajos in New Mexico were still without legal title in 1911. The plan for the Castle Butte area in Arizona was even less successful because all the important waterholes there had been previously bought from the railroad companies by whites.[16]

The situation in 1912 on the eve of statehood for New Mexico and Arizona was this: The attempt to provide for the nonreservation Navajos had been compromised by the existence of the checkerboard. The attempt to overcome this obstacle to the west and southwest of the reservation had been blocked by legal technicalities in the Department of the Interior. The attempt to provide for those Navajos to the east and southeast of the reservation had been blocked by interests in the Territory of New Mexico who secured the restoration of unallotted lands in 1911 before the allotment policy had been carried to completion, or exchanges effected under the law of 1904. In the area south of the Hopi reservation, the whites controlled most of the area through purchase of the water sites from the railroad companies. Furthermore, the two Territories had been angered by the attempt of the Bureau of Indian Affairs to beat them at their own game of controlling the public ranges.

---

[15]H. J. Hagerman to Senator A. A. Jones, November 26, 1923. Pueblo Bonito, 74907-23-308.3. Also, Mosk, *Land Tenure Problems in the Santa Fe Railroad Grant Area*, pp. 18-19.

[16]*Hagerman Report*, p. 21.

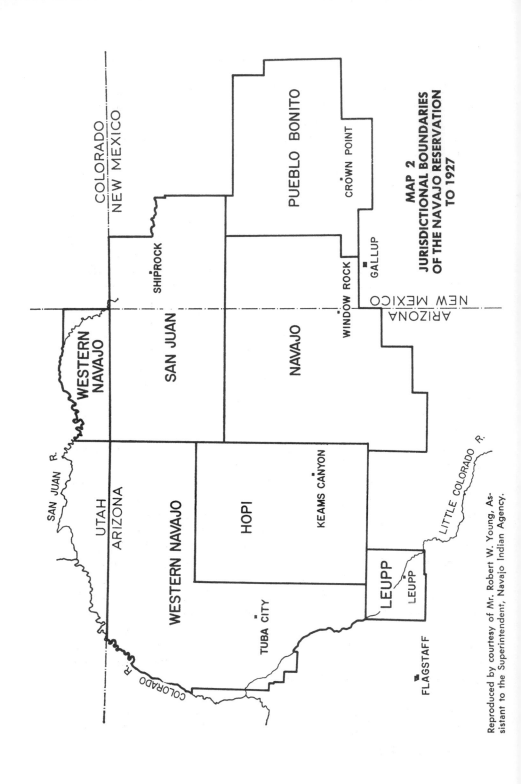

COLORADO
NEW MEXICO

PUEBLO BONITO

CROWN POINT

MAP 2
JURISDICTIONAL BOUNDARIES
OF THE NAVAJO RESERVATION
TO 1927

GALLUP

SHIPROCK

WINDOW ROCK

ARIZONA
NEW MEXICO

WESTERN
NAVAJO

SAN JUAN

NAVAJO

SAN JUAN R.

UTAH
ARIZONA

WESTERN NAVAJO

HOPI

KEAMS CANYON

LITTLE COLORADO R.

LEUPP

LEUPP

TUBA CITY

COLORADO R.

FLAGSTAFF

Reproduced by courtesy of Mr. Robert W. Young, Assistant to the Superintendent, Navajo Indian Agency.

THE SUB-AGENCIES

It should clarify things to note that by 1908 the Navajo reservation was no longer administered as a single reservation. The executive-order additions had so greatly increased the size of the Navajo country that it had become physically impossible for one man to oversee it completely. Accordingly, in 1901, a second jurisdiction was established at Tuba City, Arizona, to administer the areas added in 1884 and 1900. This was called the Western Navajo reservation. (See map No. 2 for the boundaries of this jurisdiction as well as the ones mentioned below.) In 1903 the San Juan agency at Shiprock, New Mexico, was established in the northern section of the original treaty reservation. The original Navajo agency at Fort Defiance was at this time given charge of the southern half of the treaty reservation; it continued to be called the Navajo reservation. In 1907 the Pueblo Bonito agency at Crownpoint, New Mexico, was established to care for the Navajos in the 1907 addition in New Mexico and that portion of the 1880 addition which had not been included in the San Juan jurisdiction. In 1908 the Leupp agency was created at Leupp, Arizona, with authority over the 1901 addition and the Castle Butte area. In 1902 the Hopi reservation, which contained a large number of Navajos and had been previously administered from Fort Defiance, was separated and agency headquarters were set up at Keams Canyon, Arizona.[17]

OPPOSITION

The successful return of the 1907 withdrawal area in New Mexico to the public domain in 1911 temporarily stalled the off-reservation allotment program of the Bureau of Indian Affairs. However, by 1912 the decision had been made to continue allotting Navajos under section four of the Dawes Act despite the fact that they could not now hope to control the entire range.[18] This was essentially a stop-gap measure and as such was quickly criticized by both the friends and the enemies of the Navajos. White elements in Arizona and New Mexico

---

[17]See Underhill, *Here Come the Navaho!*, p. 220-21. On July 1, 1927, the names of the San Juan, Navajo, and Pueblo Bonito reservations were changed to Northern Navajo, Southern Navajo, and Eastern Navajo, respectively. The boundaries of the five reservations were changed to some extent at this same time, but I have failed to uncover a map which gives these new reservation boundaries. In 1935 the five jurisdictions were again consolidated into one agency at Window Rock, Arizona.

[18]*Hagerman Report*, pp. 67-68.

now began to charge that this interpretation of the Dawes Act was unwarranted and illegal. Various eastern Indian associations looked upon it as unwise because it was obvious that a mere 160 acres in grazing country was not sufficient to support a family.[19]

New Mexico became a state on January 6, 1912, and Arizona on February 14, 1912. The first memorial of the first legislature of the state of New Mexico called upon the United States Congress to allot in severalty the Navajo reservation and to open the "surplus lands" of the reservation to white entry. The memorial also requested the Congress to prohibit "further withdrawal of the lands of New Mexico for any purpose whatever."[20] In October, 1912, the Bureau of Indian Affairs decided, in the face of the mounting New Mexican opposition to its off-reservation allotment policy, to discontinue the work pending a Congressional investigation of the Navajo land problem. In a letter to Senator Benjamin F. Shively (Dem., Indiana), the Commissioner of Indian Affairs wrote:

> . . . there is no authority under existing law for the disposal of the surplus lands within the Navajo Reservation. Owing to the climatic conditions, the character of the soil, etc., the Office is firmly convinced that allotments in the area specified by the General Allotment Act would be far from being sufficient for the needs of these Indians, and accordingly, . . . steps will not be taken pending further action by Congress with a view of making further allotments in severalty to the Navajo Indians within their reservation in Arizona and New Mexico. In fact it might be said that the Office would seriously question the wisdom of making allotments in severalty, in larger areas under present conditions, even should the authority therefor be granted by the Congress.[21]

In 1913 Senator Albert B. Fall (Rep., New Mexico) proposed an amendment to the fiscal 1914 Indian appropriation bill which, as amended in committee, seemed to promise the investigation that the Bureau of Indian Affairs had in mind. The original Fall amendment

---

[19]For opinion in New Mexico and Arizona see the statement of Senator Albert B. Fall in U.S. Senate, Committee on Indian Affairs, *Hearings, Indian Appropriation Bill, Fiscal 1914,* 63d Cong., 1st sess., 1913, pp. 502-503. For a statement on the eastern position see the letter of J. Weston Allen, Vice-President, Boston Indian Citizenship Committee, to the Commissioner of Indian Affairs, May 7, 1913. Navajo, 55414-14-150.

[20]For a copy of this memorial, see Navajo, 33368-12-308.1.

[21]F. H. Abbott to Benjamin F. Shively, October 9, 1912. Navajo, 98072-12-308.1.

would have prohibited the further allotment of Indians on the public domain in New Mexico and Arizona. Fall's argument was based on several "facts" which warrant attention.

One of these was his contention that the Navajos who were being allotted on the public domain had recently moved off the reservation where they had large landholdings. According to his figures,[22] if every Navajo on the reservation were allotted, each would have at least 1,100 acres. Thus, the Bureau's program of allotting Navajos on the public domain simply enabled these Indians to take up 160-acre tracts in strategic locations in order to blackmail legitimate stockmen into buying them out. The Senator claimed that:

> They may take a thousand or five thousand or ten thousand head of sheep and run them on the range within the country adjoining my ranch, take the grass away from my cattle; occupy 160 acres each under allotment; pay no taxes; support the government not at all; and tomorrow, if they choose to do so, after having eaten off the public range, return to the Navajo Reservation and have allotted to them in severalty 1100 acres.[23]

His second argument was that a government report in 1903 stated that $85,000 for water development would enable every Navajo in existence to be accommodated on the reservation proper with no necessity for anyone to move off.[24] A third thesis was that the Bureau of Indian Affairs knew no limits to its allotment policy, as when it had located 137 "renegade Navajo Indians in Socorro County, New Mexico," between April and June, 1913, despite the fact that each had 1,100 acres on the reservation and Socorro was 250 miles from the reservation.[25] The Bureau, he charged, for so long in the past had had a free hand in dealing with the Territories of New Mexico and Arizona that it was now incapable of recognizing that the two had become sovereign states.[26]

---

[22]No complete census of the Navajos was ever taken until 1928. The question of the exact number of Navajos at any given time was a constant plague. The figures usually fluctuated widely with the argument at hand.

[23]*Cong. Record*, Vol. 49, 63d Cong., 1st sess., pp. 2032-33.

[24]U.S. Senate, Hearings, *Indian Appropriation Bill, Fiscal 1914*, 63d Cong., 1st sess., pp. 502-503.

[25]Whether Fall was ignorant of the fact that this group of Navajos was a segment of the Enemy Navajo who had remained behind with the Pueblo Indians when the Navajo migration in the 1750's took place, or whether he was attempting to gain sympathy from his less well-informed colleagues is difficult to judge.

[26]*Cong. Record*, Vol. 49, 63d Cong., 1st sess., p. 2031.

The Senate Indian Affairs Committee decided that, in view of its ignorance and the conflicting evidence presented by Fall and the Bureau, it would be better to prohibit the use of funds for the allotment of Indians on the public domain within the two states for fiscal 1914. This decision was agreeable to both sides. Assistant Commissioner Abbott stated before the committee that he favored the plan "pending an investigation"; it was obvious that he felt the investigation would prove the necessity of more land for the Navajos. Fall was equally certain that his views would be borne out by the investigation.[27]

As a result of this compromise, a proviso in the 1914 appropriation bill stated "that no part of said sum shall be used for . . . allotment of any land in severalty upon the public domain to any Indian, whether of the Navajo or other tribe, within the State of New Mexico and the State of Arizona" (38 Stat., 78). The allotment of the public domain was brought to a halt on the day the law went into effect.[28]

COMPROMISE

By the time the Senate met to take action on the Fall amendment the following year, the Bureau had undergone a change of personnel. The new Assistant Commissioner, E. B. Meritt, seemed unaware when testifying on the Navajo situation that the previous Bureau policy had been based on the assumption that those Navajos living on the public domain had been there since the return from the Bosque Redondo and before. Like Fall, he told the committee that these Indians "voluntarily left the reservation to go on the public domain in order that they might make a better living for themselves."[29] No mention was made of the investigation which had been a condition of the Bureau's consent to the Fall amendment the year before. Instead, a new plea for the original Fall amendment was put forth by Senator Henry F. Ashurst (Dem., Arizona).

He had no objection to the extension of the reservation, Ashurst said, where such an extension was necessary. But it was his duty to

---

[27]U.S. Senate, *Hearings, Indian Appropriation Bill, Fiscal 1914,* 63d Cong., 1st sess., pp. 502-507.

[28]C. F. Hauke to Peter Parquette (Paquette), July 16, 1913. Navajo, 81301-13-304.

[29]U.S. Senate, Committee on Indian Affairs, *Hearings, Indian Appropriation Bill, Fiscal 1915,* 63d Cong., 2d sess., 1914, p. 297.

protest any extension "when in truth and in fact the extensions are made not for the benefit of the Indians but that the coffers of a vast corporation may be still further filled." The vast corporation to which Senator Ashurst referred was none other than the Santa Fe Railroad. According to Ashurst, the law of 1904 which had provided a solution to the checkerboard was not passed for the benefit of the Indians but for the benefit of the Santa Fe Railroad. Under cover of this law, he charged, some 370,000 acres of land assessed at from ten to twenty-five cents an acre had been swapped for other lands in Arizona worth from two to four dollars an acre. The pressure now for additional lands for the Navajos was simply more of the old Santa Fe propaganda.[30]

Senator Ashurst's introduction of this new issue was enough to postpone discussion of the Fall amendment when it first came before the Senate committee. Ten days later when the matter was recalled, Assistant Commissioner Meritt announced that the Bureau and Senator Fall had compromised on the issue by an agreement to allot on the public domain only those Navajos who had been residing there prior to June 30, 1913. Both Fall and Meritt professed satisfaction with the compromise.[31]

What happened behind the scenes, if anything, is not evident. What is clear, however, is that the compromise was in fact no compromise at all in terms of previous Bureau policy. At best it was a concession, at worst it was a betrayal of the Navajo need for land. If it had been true before 1912 that 160 acres was not sufficient for the Navajos who lived off the reservation, that fact had not changed in 1914. The original approval given by the Bureau to the Fall amendment had been based on the idea that an investigation would be made to determine the Navajo land needs. This Fall-Meritt compromise of 1914 meant simply that the nonreservation Navajos must be satisfied with less land than they needed for a livelihood and that allotment as a policy would cease with the present generation.

A NEW PLAN

Following the decision of Congress, special agents were sent into the nonreservation areas to allot as many Navajos as could qualify under the Fall rider. President Wilson signed numerous executive

---

[30]*Ibid.*, p. 294.
[31]*Ibid.*, pp. 464-65.

orders which withdrew small areas of land in regions where groups of Navajos were known to be settled, in order that these could be exchanged under the terms of the law of 1904. Congress helped by passing a second exchange act in March, 1913 (37 Stat., 1007). Unlike the act of 1904 which permitted exchanges only where an executive-order reservation was extended over railroad grant lands, this latest act permitted the companies to exchange any lands upon which the Indians had settled for other lands within the state. When the stock-raising homestead act was passed in 1916 (38 Stat., 862), authorizing homesteads on 640 acres of grazing land, the Commissioner of Indian Affairs, Cato Sells, prevailed upon the President to withdraw 94,000 acres in Arizona so that Navajos could be given time to qualify under the act.[32]

By 1916 an inspector in the field could report that in the Pueblo Bonito area 2,900 allotments had been made to the Navajos;[33] we may suppose that in other areas the work was going steadily ahead. The success of the program was, however, dubious. Allotments under section four of the Dawes Act were not finally approved and patented by the Bureau of Indian Affairs, but by the General Land Office, and this office was not as lenient toward the Navajos as was the Indian Bureau. Certain improvements and residence requirements were necessary before title was granted and Navajos often cared little about either. Despite the large number of allotments reported, the Commissioner was also informed that all of the 2,900 allotments "may be cancelled for lack of residence or lack of conformity with other requirements," and that at Leupp "the situation is no better; it may be worse . . . . The outlook is serious."[34]

Nor were the railroad land-grant companies cooperating. In one case, even after the President had withdrawn a certain area so that it could be exchanged, the Santa Fe refused the terms and the New Mexico and Arizona Land Company took no action. The lands which the government wished to exchange were scattered over a wide area and the companies felt, rightly, that the only efficient way to exchange was in large blocks of land.[35]

---

[32]Cato Sells to Franklin K. Lane, March 24, 1917. Navajo, 46090-17-307.4.

[33]S.A.M. Young to Commissioner of Indian Affairs, December 2, 1916. Pueblo Bonito, unnumbered report in 160-168 file.

[34]*Ibid.*

[35]Cato Sells to Edmund Platt, October 13, 1918. Pueblo Bonito, 59607-18-308.2.

The Bureau's allotment policy was, at this same time, again coming under fire from the whites. Because of the existence of the railroad sections in the checkerboard, the allotting agents were forced to go farther away from the reservation in search for suitable lands for the Navajos. As these allotments penetrated farther and farther into the public domain, the white settlers resented more and more the encroachment on land which they themselves hoped to get. These same people had become wary of the railroad exchange acts, because for every acre of land which the railroad companies relinquished to the Navajos, another acre somewhere else in the state was withdrawn from homestead entry and title patented to the land companies. The citizens of New Mexico and Arizona were losing on both ends.

The land situation grew steadily worse after 1914. In 1918 Superintendent Janus of Leupp stated that until the land situation in his area, particularly at Castle Butte, was solved, he was powerless to plan for the future of his Navajos — "until this is done, all is uncertainty." The Board of Indian Commissioners sent one of its members to investigate the situation in Arizona. He reported clearly the state of affairs that prevailed in most of the checkerboard and recommended that the Board "urge upon the Government the wisdom of changing the status of this land to that of an Indian Reservation."[36] With such reports coming in from the field, the Bureau of Indian Affairs prepared to encounter the wrath of the West by requesting a major executive-order withdrawal.[37]

Before the plan was completed, however, the Bureau's hands were tied by Congressional action. Word of the proposed withdrawal traveled quickly to the Senate where the representatives of the state of Arizona decided the matter had gone far enough. During debate on the Indian Appropriation bill, Senator Marcus A. Smith (Dem., Arizona) proposed an amendment from the floor which stated that "hereafter no Indian Reservation shall be created, nor shall any addition be made to one heretofore created, within the limits of the States of

---

[36]Report of Commissioner Frank Knox on the Navajo Indians, May 28, 1917. Leupp, 58075-17-150. The Board of Indian Commissioners was created by President Grant in 1869 to aid the Indian Bureau in formulating a more humane policy toward the Indians. The members of the Board were usually men of prominence and very often they were representatives of the major religious denominations. The Board was abolished by executive order in 1934 and its records deposited with the National Archives.

[37]U.S. House, *Hearings, Indians of the United States*, 66th Cong., 1-3d sess., Vol. 3, p. 707.

New Mexico or Arizona, except by act of Congress."[38] Senator Ashurst, now chairman of the Senate Indian Affairs Committee, warmly supported the amendment. It was accepted in both houses of Congress without opposition (40 Stat., 575). One year later the prohibition was extended to all the states (41 Stat., 34). A melancholy note by Superintendent Stacher of Pueblo Bonito summed up the situation:

> The plan to extend the reservation has been blocked. No one in politics seems to care a rap what becomes of the Navajo and is willing to see him crowded out from his little range in the desert where he has been content to plug along. . . . Where is the law maker that raises his voice in their behalf?[39]

STALEMATE

The executive branch of the federal government was now severely limited in its program to provide the Navajos with adequate land. Executive-order Indian reservations were illegal and so were exchanges under the act of 1904, because the Smith rider had provided that no additions could be made to reservations previously created. All exchanges which were pending under this law at the time of the passage of the appropriation bill were refused approval under a Department of the Interior ruling.[40]

Several possibilities, none very satisfactory, remained. All Navajos residing on the public domain prior to June 30, 1913, could still be allotted, but greater care would have to be taken to comply with the General Land Office regulations. The Bureau could go before Congress and request funds with which to buy lands for the Navajos. Authority could be requested for "blocking" the checkerboard, a new concept. A cursory analysis of these possible plans will demonstrate their shortcomings.

Following the act of 1918, the Bureau sent a special allotting agent, A. W. Simington, into the nonreservation area to survey the situation. His report was extremely disheartening. Despite the figures which had earlier been reported on the number of allotments, he could find only 2,410 applications; of these, only 618 had been ap-

---

[38]*Cong. Record*, Vol. 56, 65th Cong., 2d sess., p. 4194. Representative Carl Hayden, at a later date, also took credit for this act. See *Senate Survey*, part 11, p. 4762.

[39]Pueblo Bonito Agency, "Annual Narrative Report, 1918," p. 5.

[40]Memorandum, October 3, 1921. Leupp, 38599-21-150.

proved and but 100 patented. The special agent who, in the past, had made a survey and issued allotment certificates to Navajos all the way from Thoreau, New Mexico, to the Arizona line, "never filed any of the applications in the local Land Office, so that several hundred Navajos think they are allotted, but there is no official record."[41] Allotment work would have to begin again but, as a means of controlling the public domain, its usefulness was ended. The land companies, with no possibility now of extensive exchanges, began to lease more and more of their land to the whites. The land situation would grow worse. Soon whites and Navajos would be at each other's throats as each accused the other of trespassing on his land.

In 1919 Cato Sells himself went to plead with the Congress for funds to buy land around Crownpoint, New Mexico, for the Navajos. He was given $100,000 (41 Stat., 423). On August 24, 1922, $93,628.24 of this money was expended for some 12,000 acres owned by the Chaco Land and Cattle Company of Gallup, New Mexico.[42] Although the purchase gave the Navajos control of five townships, this action of Congress was but a token gesture. With some 4,000 to 6,000 Navajos living off the reservation,[43] five townships would not go far. Authorization for more funds was not forthcoming. The $100,000 had not been a gift but was rather to be reimbursed by the Navajo tribe. Since the Navajos had, at this time, very little prospect of repaying the sum, it was useless to talk of further loans.

A third possibility lay in "blocking" the checkerboard. By blocking it was envisioned that all railroad sections in a given area be given to the Navajos in return for their abandoning all their allotments in another to the land companies. In this way Navajo lands and the railroad holdings would be consolidated in several large areas and the friction produced by the checkerboard would be obviated. Blocking alone, however, was obviously no solution to the Navajo land problem, because through such an exchange they stood to lose half the land they had been using. But blocking would serve two other important purposes. As a defensive measure it would tend to lessen

---

[41]Simington to Sells, December 18, 1919. Pueblo Bonito, 65898-18-304.

[42]See the correspondence of October 31, 1922, and June 23, 1927, in Navajo, 17824-16-371, part 3.

[43]U.S. Board of Indian Commissioners, *Annual Report of the Board, 1922* (Washington: G.P.O., 1923), p. 11, hereafter cited as Board of Indian Commissioners, *Annual Report.*

the friction which was daily becoming more serious in the area.[44] As an offensive device it would provide an answer to those whites who decried the Navajo advance because his allotment could not be taxed. To have all the railroad lands consolidated into one block would greatly enhance their value over the scattered, alternate tracts previously held. As the value of these lands went up, local tax revenues would also increase. By thus making a concession to local whites, it would perhaps be possible to gain their sympathy for boundary extensions in the future. One important group, the merchants in the towns ringing the reservation, was already sympathetic to the Navajo cause. By now they had begun to see that cowboys and absentee stockmen made poor customers, and if the white stockmen should gain the upper hand in the checkerboard and succeed in driving the Navajos off, the merchants would be grievously hurt financially.[45]

With both Bureau and local white support, an act providing for consolidation of the checkerboard in New Mexico was passed on March 3, 1921 (41 Stat., 1239). The law applied to the three counties of McKinley, San Juan, and Valencia, all of which had been involved in the 1907 withdrawal order. No exchanges were effected under the law, however, until 1931, because the regulations issued by the Bureau were so complicated as to make compliance nearly impossible.[46] Such was the Navajo land situation on the eve of the discovery of oil.

---

[44]General Hugh L. Scott of the Board of Indian Commissioners reported to the Board in October, 1921, that "the feeling between the two interests has been very strong, and both sides are well-armed. . . . the situation any day may result in a serious clash because of the failure of the Department to settle the problem equitably." "They [the Navajos] charge that the white stockmen are fencing the country; that the cowboys employed by the white stockmen threatened children and older people and took cattle having Indian brands; that cowboys tore down hogans and Indian fences and that the cattlemen took possession of springs and waterholes so that the Indians could not get water for their sheep." National Archives, Record Group 75, Board of Indian Commissioners, *Special Reports*, Vol. 4, pp. 49-56.

[45]*Ibid.*, Vol. 2, pp. 146-47.

[46]Hagerman to Rhoads, August 1, 1931. Navajo, 64874-34-066

CHAPTER 3

Mineral Law

The concerted effort after 1900 to halt the enlargement of the Navajo reservation culminated in 1918 in the prohibition of new executive-order Indian reservations. At the time this battle was being waged by stock and farming interests, a second was being conducted by Western mining interests who wished to open the Indian preserves to the mining laws of the United States. This latter struggle must, for full perspective, be viewed in light of the conflict between conservationists and exploiters of the public domain.

CONSERVATIONISTS VERSUS EXPLOITERS

In 1909 oil was discovered in the West, mainly in California and Wyoming. The law under which the operators were drilling was the old Placer Act of 1870, amended in 1897 (29 Stat., 526) to make it applicable to petroleum.[1] In many ways this act was ill-adapted to the petroleum industry. Oil claims were limited to twenty acres per individual or 160 acres per association of eight or more individuals — in either case, an area much too small for efficient exploitation of oil reserves. Furthermore, title to a claim was not granted until discovery had been made. While this regulation proved no hardship

---

[1]The exact status of oil lands had been a moot question until 1897. The Placer Law of 1870 provided certain regulations for placer claims as opposed to lode claims, defining as subject to its juridiction "all form of deposit excepting veins of quartz or other rock-in-place." When oil was first discovered, an attempt was made to place it in this broad category. In 1875 the Commissioner of the General Land Office ruled that such a construction was valid. The Secretary of the Interior in 1883 ruled that while the validity of this interpretation was "an undetermined question" he would permit oil leases to go patent under the Placer Law. His successor in 1885 ruled definitely that the interpretation was valid. In 1896 Secretary of the Interior Hoke Smith reversed these earlier rulings, thereby throwing great consternation into the infant oil industry. It was Smith's ruling which united western Congressmen behind the bill that became law in 1897, giving legal status to the hitherto-disputed interpretation that oil could be mined under the Placer Law. See John Ise, *The United States' Oil Policy* (New Haven: Yale University Press, 1926), pp. 295-96.

to the gold and silver prospector, it was quite unreasonable in the case of the oil prospector who would be forced to drill an expensive well on land to which he had no title. It was always possible that on the verge of a discovery, some other prospector could obtain title on the basis of discovery of another mineral. But while the Placer Act was thus undesirable in several respects, it did possess the virtue of vesting complete title to the land in the successful prospector. In the face of conservationist demands for a leasing system on the public domain, many exploiters felt such unpleasantries could be overlooked.

The conflict between exploiters and conservationists came to a head on September 27, 1909, when President Taft, extending the conservation program of his predecessor, withdrew large areas of the public domain in California and Wyoming from mining entry. Between October 1, 1909, and June 30, 1910, some thirteen additional withdrawals were signed by the President. All of them were made upon the recommendation of the Director of the Geological Survey, George Otis Smith, who since 1908 had been urging upon Secretary of the Interior Richard A. Ballinger the need for some such action to assure a fuel supply for the Navy.[2]

The Taft withdrawals provide an amusing, if uninspiring, commentary on the workings of the Presidential Cabinet system. Immediately following the withdrawal orders the oil operators descended on Congress seeking redress of their grievances. No aid was forthcoming in the Taft administration. But after 1913 when President Wilson succeeded Taft, the companies found an ally in Secretary of the Interior Franklin K. Lane who approved their requests. Secretary of the Navy Josephus Daniels, however, refused to have anything to do with their proposals and, with the support of Attorney-General Thomas W. Gregory, was successful in blocking legislation to reopen the withdrawals to prospecting under the Placer Act. Since both Lane and Daniels had their supporters in the Congress, a stalemate resulted.[3]

Blocked in the Congress, the oil companies took the issue to the courts. In 1915 the Supreme Court upheld Taft's withdrawal order. The conservationists, heartened by the decision, now set out to obtain a leasing bill for mineral resources on the public domain. Western opposition, however, successfully blocked this legislation for five years.

---

[2]*Ibid.*, p. 313.
[3]*Ibid.*, pp. 314, 334-35.

THE METALLIFEROUS MINERALS ACT

There was, in 1915, no indication of oil on any Indian reservations other than those of the Five Civilized Tribes in Oklahoma. However, there were known deposits of valuable metalliferous minerals on Indian reservations, particularly in the Southwest. While some of these lands, notably the Papago Indian reservation, were open for prospecting under the law, the great majority were not, and Western mining interests were greatly interested in securing admission to these hitherto-closed preserves.

The only law in existence which permitted access to Indian minerals was passed in 1891. This provided that, "where lands are occupied by Indians who have bought and paid for the same," and where such lands were not needed for farming or were not desired for individual allotments, they might be leased by "the authority of the council speaking for such Indians," for a maximum of ten years for mining "in such quantites and upon such terms as the agent in charge may recommend, subject to the approval of the Secretary of the Interior" (26 Stat., 795). The Department of the Interior subsequently ruled that the phrase "bought and paid for the same" meant that treaty reservations could be exploited under the law. Since executive-order reservations had not been "bought and paid for," they were not subject to the terms of the act. Most of the Indian reservations of the Southwest were executive-order reservations so there was no law to permit mining on them.

The first attempts to get at the mineral deposits on these executive-order reservations had been so crude that they were easily defeated. In 1904 Representative John Hall Stephens of Texas introduced as an amendment to the Indian Appropriation Bill a rider which he had been unsuccessfully pushing since 1900. Stephens wanted the opening of the Indian reservations, treaty and executive-order, to the same laws that applied to mineral deposits on the public domain. It bothered him not at all that the treaty lands were not public domain and that the Indians had, through custom and usage, some claim to title even on the executive-order portions. Stephens' plan would make allotment mandatory so that the surplus lands could be sold and opened to mining. The Indian would get a good price for these lands, he assured his colleagues. This was, he stoutly maintained, "legislation demanded by the people of the West."[4] The amendment was defeated by a point of order.

---

[4]*Cong. Record,* Vol. 38, 58th Cong., 2d sess., p. 2882.

The next serious attempt to gain access to the executive-order reservations came shortly after statehood for Arizona and New Mexico. There was nothing crude in the bill introduced by the new Senator from Arizona, Henry F. Ashurst, in July, 1912. It merely provided for an extension of the act of 1891 to executive-order reservations with a certain assured portion of the net proceeds of any minerals found to be set aside for the Indians. The bill, however, encountered opposition. Senator Weldon B. Heyburn (Rep., Idaho) refused it unanimous consent under the Senate rules, and thus killed it, on the ground that Indian executive-order reservations were in certain respects similar to public-domain lands, and to admit the legitimacy of leasing them was to give strength to those forces which favored a general leasing policy for the entire public domain.[5] Thus, despite the fact that leasing was the only just way to develop the Indian lands — the alternative was Representative Stephens' plan — by the time the mining interests of Arizona and New Mexico obtained a voice in Congress, they ran headlong into the larger fight between the forces opposing or favoring leasing of the public domain as a national policy.

The fact that the Ashurst leasing bill related to this larger problem is extremely important for the study of the Navajo Indians in the 1920's. The Senators and Representatives from Arizona, deeply interested in the profits which they believed could be obtained from the exploitation of the large Indian holdings within their state, were hard-pressed to disassociate their bills for the leasing of executive-order Indian reservations from those being proposed by the advocates of the general leasing policy for the public domain. In their attempt to do so, they consistently maintained that there was no true parallel between the two because the title to the executive-order Indian reservation was vested in the Indians in much the same fashion as the title of the treaty reservation. When oil was discovered on the Navajo reservation in 1922, this argument was abandoned by these same Congressmen in favor of one which vested title to the executive-order reservation in the federal government.

Representative Carl Hayden (Dem., Arizona) next attempted to open the executive-order reservations. In 1916 he introduced a bill which had, in the previous session of Congress, secured the approval of the House, only to be lost in the Senate during the closing days

---

[5] *Ibid.*, Vol. 48, 62d Cong., 2d sess., p. 9677.

of the session. His bill was essentially a restatement of Ashurst's bill of 1912. It called for a leasing system to be applied to "unallotted lands within *any Indian Reservation* in the State of Arizona heretofore withdrawn from entry under the mining laws."[6] At the suggestion of the Secretary of the Interior, the House Committee on Indian Affairs amended the bill to apply to Indian reservations in any state, and raised the leasing royalty from 2 percent to 5 percent of the net proceeds.[7]

The bill was further amended on the floor of the House to reduce the lease period from fifty years to thirty years, and to fix the lease royalty at a minimum of 5 percent rather than the absolute royalty of 5 percent prescribed by the Committee.[8] Hayden defended the bill before the House on the ground that since the executive orders granting these lands to the Indians had not included provision for retaining the mineral rights in the United States, "the minerals have been given to the Indians, and there is no other way to proceed except to recognize their ownership."[9] In the Senate, although the bill did not come to a vote, the Indian Affairs Committee reported the bill favorably, referring to the lands affected by the bill as the "tribal property of the Indians. . . ."[10] The following year the bill was re-introduced into the Senate but again failed to pass.

By 1918 the bill had a new twist. Senators Ashurst, Albert B. Fall, and A. J. Gronna (Rep., North Dakota) now maintained that the minor minerals provided for in the bill were needed desperately for the war effort.[11] To overcome the opposition to a leasing bill, Senator Ashurst patiently explained once again that the Indian leasing act had no connection with the leasing bills for the public domain. "We are," he said, "leasing lands belonging to the Indian tribes and that do not belong to the United States."[12] He realized, he continued, the very genuine fear of the other Western Senators who felt that the passage of such an act would be the insertion of "the camel's nose

---

[6]The italics are mine.

[7]U.S. House, *Metalliferous Minerals on Indian Reservations*, 64th Cong., 1st sess., 1916, Rept. 533.

[8]*Cong. Record*, Vol. 53, 64th Cong., 1st sess., p. 13777.

[9]*Ibid.*

[10]U.S. Senate, *Metalliferous Minerals on Indian Reservations*, 64th Cong., 2d sess., 1916, Rept. 880, p. 3.

[11]*Cong. Record*, Vol. 56, 65th Cong., 2d sess., pp. 7477-7483, and p. 7523.

[12]*Ibid.*, p. 7894.

under the tent, and that the whole animal will get in completely later on," but

> this bill is not the setting of a precedent. If this bill were for leasing public domain, the Senator would be correct in his contention that we are setting a precedent to be pointed to in the future, but we are not leasing public domain.[13]

At the close of the debate, for the first time, the Senate voted to accept the metalliferous mining bill for Indian reservations, and sent it to the House.

There was little opposition to the bill in the House where it had received favorable attention earlier. Ironically enough, the war was over by the time the House got the bill. Hayden was confronted with this fact, but he fielded the token resistance neatly. The original need for the bill was still to be met, he said: executive-order Indian reservations could not, without legislation of this kind, be mined under the present laws. To a Congress already concerned with the staggering cost of World War I, he presented an almost overwhelming argument: the bill would, in some cases, make possible profits of such magnitude as to make gratuity appropriations for the tribes concerned unnecessary.[14]

As events had it, the House did not have to take a vote on the bill itself. Once the Senate resistance had broken down, it was easier to tack the substance of the Hayden-Ashurst bills onto the appropriations act for fiscal 1920. Section twenty-six contained the following provisions. Any part of any Indian reservation within the states of Arizona, California, Idaho, Montana, Nevada, New Mexico, Oregon, Washington, or Wyoming, previously withdrawn from entry under the mining laws of the United States, could now be leased by the Secretary of the Interior for the purpose of mining "deposits of gold, silver, copper and other valuable metalliferous minerals." A royalty of not less than 5 percent of the net value of the output was to be credited to the Indian benefit. All funds so received were to be subject to appropriation by Congress for the tribal benefit and for *pro rata* distribution (41 Stat., 31). Thus 30,880,000 acres of land, over 19,000,000 of it in Arizona, became open to prospectors.[15]

---

[13]*Ibid.*, p. 7525.

[14]U.S. House, *Metalliferous Minerals on Indian Reservations*, 65th Cong., 2d sess., 1918, Rept. 730. And *Cong. Record*, Vol. 57, 65th Cong., 3d sess., p. 2634.

[15]*House Report 730*, 65th Cong., 2d sess., p. 3.

THE GENERAL LEASING ACT

The act which was to cause so much grief for the Navajos in the 1920's was not the Metalliferous Minerals Leasing Act, but the General Leasing Act of 1920.[16] The Metalliferous Minerals Leasing Act was based on the theory that the mineral rights of the executive-order Indian reservations belonged to the Indians. Never at any stage was there any argument to the contrary. The Congressmen from Arizona only wanted the executive-order lands opened to development; there was no opposition to giving all the royalties received from such leases to the Indians. But, after oil was discovered on the Navajo reservation in 1922, an attempt was made to exploit this natural resource, not along lines outlined in the Metalliferous Minerals Leasing Act but along those worked out in the General Leasing Act, which was tantamount to stating that the executive-order Indian reservations did not belong to the Indians but to the federal government.

The General Leasing Act was the focal point of the conflict between the forces of conservation and those of unrestrained exploitation of natural resources. In general, the East was on the side of the former and the West on the side of the latter. The arguments in favor of conservation have become so firmly established in our minds today that there is little reason to discuss them here. Those in favor of exploitation, however, deserve some treatment lest we be guilty of underestimating the appeal of a theory now discarded.

First there was the argument that a leasing policy was counter to the whole tradition of the United States' land policy. In the past, the lands of the United States were turned over to private individuals for exploitation. Private ownership was a cornerstone of American economic life; leasing smacked of socialism. In the East, men had risen to fortune through their development of lands obtained from the federal government. Now it was proposed to withhold from the citizens of the West this same right. The East, having made its fortune, was now denying the West its birthright.

A second argument was that the leasing system entailed the reservation of land titles in the federal government. Federal land was not subject to local taxation. What were the Western states to do for tax money with these huge areas exempted from taxation? Revenue

---

[16]By far the best account of the General Leasing Act is J. Leonard Bates, *The Origins of Teapot Dome; Progressives, Parties, and Petroleum, 1909-1921* (Urbana: University of Illinois Press, 1963). Bates' research is based on the papers of the major participants in the debate and the records of the various federal agencies and departments.

from the taxation of private property had permitted the eastern states to provide the roads, schools, and other public services for which they were justly famous. If, in the West, those lands which produced wealth were to remain outside the tax power of the state, how could these states encourage immigration? How could they provide for their citizens those goods and services which the eastern states, unhampered by conservationist ideas, had come to take for granted?

Leasing was, furthermore, an abdication of congressional responsibility. In effect, such a law, covering such a vast area, could not possibly be supervised by the Congress. It meant "unlimited, unrestrained" authority and power in the hands of an appointive official, the Secretary of the Interior, who would be charged with its execution. To be successful, leasing would have to be competitive; but, to allow the exploitation of the public domain to be entrusted to the highest bidder was "unwise, undemocratic, and un-American" because it would put the land in the hands of the wealthy and deny to the little man, the pioneer, his chance to make good.[17]

To meet these seemingly valid arguments on the part of the West, the conservationists sought to placate the pride which engendered them, all the while retaining the essence of their own program. Despite the argument that the Placer Mining Act allowed the greatest opportunity for the little man to develop his abilities, the proponents of conservation charged that all too often it had had just the opposite result. The Placer Mining Act, like the Homestead Act, had been so abused that the large oil companies, through fraud and deception, had gained control of large areas of valuable lands. Once established, they exploited the resources with great waste. Extortion as a means to force the small operator out of business was not unknown. Both producers and consumers had become the victims of a great monopoly. Leasing under government supervision was the only means of keeping the remainder of the public domain from this monopoly and of insuring true competition through acreage limitations.

Nor had the Placer Act protected the little man even when the forces of monopoly were not active. In the case of oil especially, since he had no title until he discovered oil, he was constantly subject to the possibility of losing his claim to a speculator or similar low type

---

[17]These arguments and others may be found in almost any discussion on the General Leasing Act from 1914 to 1920. Those selected here are taken from the *Cong. Record*, Vol. 56, 65th Cong., 3d sess., pp. 402-405, and U.S. House, *Exploration for and Disposition of Coal, Oil, Gas, etc.*, 63d Cong., 2d sess., 1914, Rept. 668, part 2.

who could file on his land under the pretext of having found some other mineral there. The Placer Act was chaotic in practice, no matter how beneficent it was in theory.

The argument of the states that they needed tax money to grow and expand was met by the proposal to divide with the states the royalty and rental monies received under the leasing act. Although the actual percentages changed from year to year, the basic idea was to divide the proceeds derived from leasing between the reclamation fund and the states in lieu of taxes. Only enough money was to go into the federal treasury to administer the law.[18]

The struggle over the leasing bill was in part between the House (conservationists) and the Senate (exploiters). As a tentative proposal, the House, in the first bill introduced in 1914, agreed to grant the successful prospector title to one-fourth of his find. The remaining three-fourths of his maximum 2,560-acre prospecting permit would be leased at competitive bidding.[19] The Senate, however, held out for title to the entire amount and the bill was killed. Thereafter the House insisted that full title remain in the federal government.

In 1917 the Senate forces ingeniously attempted to use the war-necessity argument in their favor. An immediate, increased production and supply of "coal, oil and gasoline is absolutely essential to the successful conduct of the war," the Senate report read. "Oil must be taken wherever and whenever it can be got. It is better to let future wars take care of themselves than to lose the present one through dreams of far-off conservation."[20] The House, however, remained adamant and the Senate bill was defeated.

By 1918 the unity in the Senate was breaking down; many of the Western senators favored opening the land in their states at any price. The Senate version of the leasing bill, granting partial title to the successful prospector, was passed by a close vote of thirty-seven to thirty-two. It was completely rewritten in the House and a strong statement that "the right to lease one-fourth of the area of his permit at a fixed royalty of one-eighth is thought to be ample reward for

---

[18]Again, these arguments may be found in a variety of places. Those which I have chosen are from U.S. House, *Exploration for and Disposition of Coal, Phosphate, Oil, Oil Shales, or Gas,* 65th Cong., 2d sess., 1918, Rept. 563, p. 13. U.S. House, *Mining of Coal, Phosphate, Oil, Gas, and Sodium on the Public Domain,* 66th Cong., 2d sess., 1920, Rept, 600, p. 21. *Cong. Record,* Vol. 57, 65th Cong., 3d sess., p. 3828.

[19]*House Rept. 668,* 63d Cong., 2d sess., p. 6.

[20]U.S. Senate, *Mining of Coal, Phosphate, Oil, Gas, Potassium, and Sodium on the Public Domain,* 65th Cong., 1st sess., 1917, Rept. 116.

the prospector" was incorporated in the report. The reservation of
the remaining three-fourths of a successful permit to competitive
bidding was "in the interest of conservation, in the public interest,
and gives the government the power to grapple with the monopoly
in oil."[21] The Senate was also placed in an unfavorable light when
on January 19, 1918, Congressman Scott Ferris (Dem., Oklahoma),
Chairman of the House Committee on Public Lands, submitted both
the House and the Senate versions of the leasing bill to Attorney-
General Gregory for his analysis, with the caustic comment that,
"as you are aware, the Senate bill is being insisted upon by the oil
men and also strenuously contended for by certain of the Senators."[22]
The issue had passed from one of private versus public control to
the people versus monopoly.

As the Senate became gradually identified in the public eye
with the oil monopoly, some members of that body began to appeal
more strongly to their colleagues to compromise with reality. The
opposition to granting title was so intense and violent in the House,
they said, that the Senate's insistence on such a provision was
unreasonable. Senator Key Pittman (Dem., Nevada) voiced the
changing sentiment of the West. Something must be done to open
up the West and if that meant leasing, it was, he said, "O.K." with
him.[23] In 1919 conference committees were twice appointed to iron
out differences, but each time Senate opposition to the leasing
provision was still strong enough to kill the bill. In 1920 the Senate
opposition at last collapsed and a compromise bill was passed. The
Senate insistence on title to one-fourth of the prospecting permit
was shelved for the House plan to grant the prospectors only a
guarantee of lease to one-fourth of his find. As a concession, the
House lowered the royalty on the one-fourth from 12.5 percent to
5 percent and granted the prospector a preferential right to lease the
remainder at 12.5 percent. A compromise was also reached on the
disposition of the royalty monies. The Senate had held out for a
45-45 percent split between the state in which the minerals were
found and the reclamation fund, with 10 percent going to the federal
treasury for administrative expenses. The House had demanded a
30-60 percent division. In conference the percentages were adjusted

---

[21]*House Rept. 563*, 65th Cong., 2d sess., p. 13.
[22]*Ibid.*, p. 29.
[23]*Cong. Record*, Vol. 56, 65th Cong., 2d sess., pp. 413-14.

to 37.5 percent for the state and 52.5 percent for the reclamation fund.[24] Once oil or gas was discovered, the area over and above the prospector's one-fourth was to be leased, in areas not to exceed 640 acres, "to the highest responsible bidder" by competitive bidding on the royalty. Leases were to run for twenty years with preferential rights to successive ten-year renewals. Failure to use all reasonable precautions to prevent waste would constitute grounds for forfeiture of the permit or the lease. A maximum of 3,200 acres within the geological structure of a proven field would be leased to one individual or corporation, irrespective of the number of permits held. The 37.5 percent of the royalties which the states received was to be used for the construction and maintenance of public roads or the support of public schools (41 Stat., 437).

---

[24]*House Rept. 600,* 66th Cong., 2d sess., p. 21.

CHAPTER 4

Oil

Before the Metalliferous Minerals Leasing Act opened the executive-order portions of the Navajo Reservation, the original treaty area was subjected to geological survey by oil prospectors. The diligence of the search intensified after the discovery of gas in southern Utah in 1921. Most of this activity appears to have been concentrated in the Four Corners area of Utah, Colorado, Arizona, and New Mexico, under the jurisdiction of the San Juan agency, although there was some activity farther south around Fort Defiance, Arizona, in the Navajo jurisdiction. In these areas of the treaty reservation the law of 1891 which provided for the lease of mineral lands by "the authority of the council speaking for such Indians" initially governed the relationship between the Indians and the prospectors.

DISCOVERY

By early 1920 the reports from Superintendent Evan W. Estep at Shiprock indicated that the Navajos there had not taken kindly to the prospectors. On March 11, 1920, Estep wrote the Commissioner of Indian Affairs that neither he nor his Indians wanted the prospectors around. Estep also voiced a sense of uneasiness concerning his role in the matter of approving leases.[1] According to the terms of the 1891 law, the local agent approved any leases made between the Indians and the prospectors, and we may easily imagine the difficulties such responsibilities brought to an inexperienced Indian agent. Less than a year later Estep again protested the situation, stating, "It has been with considerable effort that we have been able to restrain the Indians from taking vigorous action against such prospectors."[2] Nevertheless, they came, and in increasing numbers.

---

[1]Estep to the Commissioner of Indian Affairs, March 11, 1920. San Juan, 106565-19-324. "I am doing the best I know how in this matter, but it is somewhat new to me, and I don't want anything to happen that will deprive these Indians of their rights."

[2]Estep to the Commissioner of Indian Affairs, January 11, 1921. San Juan, 4292-21-322.

The United States Bureau of Mines reported in 1923 that between the summer of 1921 and the fall of 1923, geologists had combed the entire Four Corners area.[3] The Geological Survey, however, reported that within the Navajo reservation, investigations "are not encouraging."[4] Apparently the geologists of the oil companies did not agree with the Geological Survey, for they requested permission to meet with the Navajo council to discuss leasing terms. On May 7, 1921, a council was duly called at Shiprock, New Mexico.

The council among the Navajos was not a permanent organization. In 1915 a new agent at Leupp had written to his superiors in Washington requesting information concerning the jurisdiction and powers of the council which he found at his new station. The correspondence on this matter shows clearly that the Bureau of Indian Affairs was itself perplexed at the existence of such a council. The Washington Office finally advised the agent that "so long as the council can be used and controlled [so as to make the Indians take an interest in what is being done for them] it should be of great benefit to the Indians. . . ."[5]

The obvious implication was that the councils were to be subordinate to the government agent. San Juan superintendent Estep advised the Bureau as early as mid-1919 that there was no tribal organization "of any kind" in existence on his reservation. In 1921, prior to the first council sanctioned by the Bureau, he had again written that "it is probable no council of these [San Juan] Indians has been called in fifteen or twenty, or possibly more years. . . ."[6] It is apparent then that those Indians who assembled at Shiprock in May, 1921, were not members of any deliberative body which had been in existence prior to that time.

The calling of a Navajo council in these early years of the twentieth century was a routine and even casual event. The initiative came not from the Indians themselves, but from the prospectors who were interested in securing leases. The prospector first applied to the Commissioner of Indian Affairs for permission to meet with a council. If the permission was granted, the prospector then presented his

---

[3]Report of Kenneth B. Nowells, June 24, 1924. Navajo, 61584-24-150.

[4]Memorandum for the Secretary of the Interior, February 17, 1921. San Juan, 4292-21-322.

[5]See correspondence in Leupp, 114319-14-054. Ruth Underhill provides additional information on this early Leupp council in *The Navajos*, p. 221.

[6]Estep to the Commissioner of Indian Affairs, June 17, 1919, and January 11, 1921. San Juan, 26637-19-324 and 4292-21-322.

credentials to the local agent who issued a call for all adult males to convene at the agency headquarters on a given date.[7] Because of this informal arrangement, once a council had been held, the Indians disbanded and did not reassemble unless another request for a council was approved. There was no continuity to any of these early San Juan councils.

Four applicants for leases were represented at the first San Juan council: the Midwest Refining Company, the Western States Oil and Land Company, the Kinney Oil and Refinery Company, and the E. T. Williams Oil Company. When the Midwest representative requested permission to present his case the Navajos refused to hear him. The minutes of this meeting state simply that after refusing to hear the assembled oil representatives, the Indians conversed in Navajo — which was not translated — for about an hour, unanimously disapproved all requests for leases, and resolved that "we are opposed to the leasing of any of our lands for oil and gas mining purposes."[8] Estep explained later that about seventy-five Navajos had taken part in the council and that, while a number of the younger men "had taken a favorable stand on approving the lease," the older men quickly "talked them out of any leasing ideas," with the result that the vote was unanimous in disapproving the lease.[9]

Of the four companies represented at this first council, by far the most important and aggressive was the Midwest Refining Company. Created in 1913 to resolve the problem of competing claims between several parties in the rich Salt Creek field of central Wyoming, the Midwest was charged with the responsibility for all physical operations of the rival claimants — drilling, refining, and marketing. In return for these services it was to receive one-half the net profit from the field.

In August, 1920, Standard Oil Company of Indiana purchased 33 percent of the outstanding shares of stock in the Midwest Refining Company and by July, 1921, it had "a clear majority control." Once

---

[7]For detailed treatment of these early councils see Navajo, 23855-08-332 and 88897-21-322, and especially San Juan, 4292-21-322, 68840-21-322, and 83819-21-322, which contain most of the information concerning these early San Juan councils.

[8]*Proceedings of a General Council of the San Juan Tribe of Indians, May 7, 1921, Shiprock, New Mexico.* San Juan, 4292-21-322.

[9]Estep to the Commissioner of Indian Affairs, May 13, 1921. San Juan, 4292-21-322.

under the control of Standard, the Midwest began to expand its exploratory activities into Colorado and New Mexico. A battle of major proportions was shaping up in the western oil fields between Standard and Harry Sinclair who had recently entered Wyoming to challenge the Salt Creek monopoly.[10]

Between May and August, 1921, conditions changed at Shiprock. Whether it was Estep, who was generally adverse to leasing the Indian land, or the Navajos themselves who changed their minds, it is impossible to tell, but we find Estep in late July requesting permission from the Bureau to call another council "in accordance with the Midwest's desire."[11] The request was approved and a second council was called for August 13.

At this council the San Juan Navajos granted to the Midwest Company a lease to 4,800 acres on what was known as the Hogback structure. Power of attorney to negotiate the lease was given to Estep.[12] According to Estep, the Indians now had the idea that it would be wise to determine if oil really existed on their reservation, and they seemed to think that the Midwest "will determine the question sooner than any other company." It was also apparent that the Midwest was willing to employ Navajos at the drilling sites and to pay them relatively high wages, something the Navajos appeared to be more interested in than the granting of the lease.[13]

The success of the Midwest Company encouraged the other companies to bring pressure upon the Commissioner of Indian Affairs to call a third council. On November 3, 1921, Commissioner Charles H. Burke directed Estep to do this. His letter also indicated that the Bureau was reconsidering its original policy of calling a council each time a lease was to be approved, for Estep was advised at the coming council to "secure from the Indians broad authority to lease their land" or, "if the Indians so desire, this authority may be delegated

[10]See particularly Bates, *The Origins of Teapot Dome,* pp. 16, 148, 215, and 240. See also Harold D. Roberts, *Salt Creek, Wyoming: The Story of a Great Oil Field* (Denver: W. H. Kistler Stationery Co., 1956), pp. 144-45, 185. Also helpful is Paul H. Giddens, *Standard Oil Company (Indiana): Oil Pioneer of the Middle West* (New York: Appleton Century Crofts, 1955), Chapter 9.

[11]Estep to the Commissioner of Indian Affairs, July 30, 1921, and answering telegram of August 1, 1921. San Juan 4292-21-322.

[12]*Proceedings of a General Council of the San Juan Navajo Tribe of Indians, Shiprock, New Mexico, August 13, 1921.* San Juan 68840-21-322.

[13]*Ibid.* See also the letter from Estep to the Commissioner of Indian Affairs, August 16, 1921, same file.

to certain representative Indians who may sign the leases."[14] Estep, however, advised that the Navajos would refuse to grant any more leases and the matter was dropped temporarily. The Indians, he informed Burke, believed that no further leases should be granted until the Midwest determined the existence or nonexistence of oil. If oil were discovered they figured the other companies would pay a lease bonus of about twenty-five to thirty dollars per acre.[15]

On March 5, 1922, the third council which Burke had recommended the previous November was finally called. Prominent among the nine companies represented were the Western States Oil and Land Company, the E. T. Williams Oil Company, and the Kinney Oil Company, all of which had been refused at the time of the Midwest lease. Interest was running high, for two gas wells had been recently brought in on the Ute Mountain reservation in northwestern New Mexico near the Shiprock area.[16] The Navajos, however, stuck to their earlier position and refused, after an hour's discussion in Navajo which once again was not translated, to grant any new leases.[17]

The rejection of new leases brought several repercussions. For one, Estep was charged by the representative of one of the companies with influencing his Navajos to oppose the granting of new leases.[18] For a second, the Commissioner of Indian Affairs, in defending Estep, now, for the first time, clearly stated his policy for further development of the Navajo resources:

I wish to say that I am in favor of the development of the oil

---

[14]Burke to Estep, November 3, 1922. San Juan, 83819-21-322. The Bureau's attempt to avoid calling a council at San Juan each time a lease was to be approved was never successful. On the Navajo reservation proper, a council called on January 26, 1922, did establish a business council to pass on future leases. The Navajos appointed were Chee Dodge, Charley Mitchell, and Dugal Chee Bekiss. The importance of this latter action was small, however, because the three leases granted within the Navajo reservation were cancelled on August 29, 1922, after drilling tests indicated the absence of oil in this area. See the *Minutes of a General Council of Navajo Indians under the Ft. Defiance Jurisdiction, January 26, 1922.* Navajo, 88897-21-322. Also the letter of Navajo Superintendent Peter Paquette to the Commissioner of Indian Affairs, September 11, 1922, same file.

[15]Estep to the Commissioner of Indian Affairs, November 22, 1921. San Juan 83819-21-322.

[16]U.S. Department of the Interior, *Annual Report of the Secretary, 1922* (Washington: G.P.O., 1923), p. 50.

[17]*Proceedings of a Council of San Juan Navajo Indians, Shiprock, New Mexico, March 25, 1922.* San Juan, 83819-21-322.

[18]George F. Bruington to Charles V. Stafford, March 27, 1922. *Ibid.*

and gas, and other mineral resources of all the Indian Reservations as rapidly as possibly consistent with safeguarding the interests of the Indians. In the development of unproven territory, such as exists on the Navajo Reservation it is my policy to favor at first only sufficient leases in any particular structure to test the value for oil and gas purposes, reserving the remaining land to be advertised for sale [lease] to the highest responsible bidder in the event oil is discovered.

In order that the above policy may be carried out on the Navajo Reservation, I believe it would be advisable for you to call a General Council . . . and present to them the question of granting general authority to lease their lands for oil and gas mining purposes, delegating authority to you to sign the leases on behalf of the tribe.[19]

Estep, however, again advised the Commissioner that no good purpose could be served by calling such a council. "I am very doubtful," he wrote, "whether the Indians would feel disposed to place that much authority in the hands of any one white man." His uneasiness in the midst of the many pressures being exerted upon him was again apparent when he begged Burke to send someone with technical knowledge to help him.[20] Burke, in reply, made no mention of Estep's anxiety but stated that he should disregard the previous order for a council.[21]

There was no respite, however, from the oil companies. On August 28, 1922, Burke forwarded to Estep a file of letters which he had accumulated from various oil companies that had requested a council. "In view of the interest being shown," he ordered Estep to again call a council and attempt to secure general authority to make future leases. Once again Estep protested, saying that the Navajos had been angered by recent Midwest actions. Drilling had been shut down on the Midwest lease and rumor had it, Estep wrote, that the company would not continue work until the companies friendly to it, the Western States Oil and Land Company, the E. T. Williams Oil Company, and the Kinney Oil Company, were granted leases on the adjoining acreage. It was not likely under the circum-

---

[19]Burke to Estep, April 14, 1922. *Ibid.*
[20]Estep to Burke, April 21, 1922. *Ibid.*
[21]Burke to Estep, June 22, 1922. *Ibid.*

stances, he thought, that the Navajos would act favorably on any applications for a lease. This time the answer came back to issue a formal call.[22] The date was set for September 23, 1922.

This fourth San Juan council saw the largest assembly of individuals and corporations yet, nineteen in all. As Estep had foretold, the major companies that had attempted since the second council to gain leases were again refused. A lease was granted, however, by a vote of sixty to one, to W. E. Lockhart and J. J. Hall on behalf of the Producers and Refiners Corporation, a new competitor.[23] The lease covered a structure known as the Tocito Dome, a separate geological structure from the Hogback, about fifteen miles southwest of it.

The day following the council meeting, the Midwest struck oil on the Hogback. Its number one well came in as a producer of the highest grade oil in the mid-continent field and one of the three highest grade wells in the history of the oil business.[24] When Estep wrote his report on the council meeting to the Commissioner on September 29, the strike had not yet been confirmed, although there was a rumor to that effect making the rounds. In light of the rumor, he reiterated his plea for technical assistance, stating, "I am already taking a good deal of abuse when no one knows that a big strike has been made. Why not slip out of Washington quietly, yourself, and run out here and get a line on the game first hand."[25]

Events moved rapidly once the news of the Midwest strike was out. By October 3, 1922, both local and regional newspapers had bold black headlines proclaiming the discovery and making rather exaggerated claims for the field.[26] On October 1 Estep wrote the Commis-

---

[22]Burke to Estep, August 28, 1922; Estep's telegram to Burke, September 11, 1922; Burke's telegram to Estep, September 13, 1922. *Ibid.*

[23]*Record of the Proceedings of a General Council of the San Juan Navajo Indians held at San Juan Agency, Shiprock, New Mexico, September 23, 1922.* San Juan 82894-1922-322. The Producers and Refiners Corporation may have been working in concert with the Midwest Co. In 1922 it had concluded an agreement with the Midwest for the sale of its excess natural gas production. See Giddens, *Standard Oil Company (Indiana)*, p. 235.

[24]San Juan, "Annual Narrative Report, 1923," section 4, p. 24. The exact date of the Midwest strike is in dispute. Kenneth Nowell's report cited above gives August, 1922, while Ise says October. I prefer to accept the date given by the local superintendent.

[25]Estep to Burke, September 29, 1922. San Juan, 83819-21-322.

[26]See clippings from the *Denver Post*, October 3, 1922, and the *Farmington Times Hustler*, October 5, 1922. *Ibid.*

sioner that his Navajos were not "disposed" to entrust the lease-making power either to himself or to a committee. He also informed Burke of the reason for the Midwest's insistence, prior to the council, that leases be given to the three companies friendly to it. All four, he wrote, "are practically one and the same thing and the Midwest is just another name for the Standard Oil Company, as the latter Company owns 95% of the Midwest stock."[27]

By mid-October, 1922, the San Juan reservation was seething with activity. Conditions there had become a scandal. More whiskey, Estep reported, had been circulated through his jurisdiction in the past two weeks, "than in the previous five years, or probably in the previous fifteen years." The treaty portion of the reservation was almost completely covered with applications for leases. Most of the applicants were local speculators who had no experience in the oil business, who possessed no financial standing, and who had little intention of ever developing a lease should it be granted to them. Further to the east, the executive-order area of the reservation was also being overrun "by all kinds of classes of speculators, fly-by-nights, bootleggers, and other forms of criminals." Estep himself had been offered bribes and threatened.[28] That which Estep had long feared was happening:

> The Arabian Nights tales are modest compared to this country. New cities (on paper) are springing up all over the country and corner lots are on sale even before the town is platted. Farmington has a "publicity man" drawing $350 a month and he appears to want to earn some of it. And it would appear that he is doing fairly well in that capacity.[29]

ALBERT B. FALL AND JOHN COLLIER

Prior to the discovery of oil, several developments taking place outside the reservation influenced the course of future events there.

On March 4, 1921, the new Republican administration of Warren G. Harding took office. To the post of Secretary of the Interior President Harding appointed Senator Albert B. Fall of New Mexico.

---

[27]Estep to Burke, October 1, 1922. *Ibid.* I have been unable to determine if Estep's charge was true or not.

[28]Estep to Burke, October 19, 1922. *Ibid.*

[29]Estep to Burke, October 22, 1922. *Ibid.*

The new Commissioner of Indian Affairs was Charles H. Burke of South Dakota, former Chairman of the House Indian Affairs Committee, and author of the significant Burke Act which, in 1906, had modified the Dawes Severalty Act in several important aspects.[30]

Albert B. Fall had been a leading challenger to Navajo land expansion in the Senate. He had also taken part in opening the executive-order reservations to the Metalliferous Minerals Leasing Act. At the time of his amendment to the appropriation bill of 1914, he initially favored an end to all Indian allotments on the public domain. He had withdrawn from this position in the face of Senatorial and Bureau opposition, but when Senator Ashurst of Arizona offered an amendment to the appropriation bill for fiscal 1919, prohibiting the extension of the executive-order principle, Fall joined in the vote. Albert Fall was, moreover, a rancher and miner in his own right. As Secretary of the Interior he could be expected to reflect the views of these interests. The welfare of the American Indian was but one of his many responsibilities as Secretary of the Interior, and, in his own mind, a minor one.

---

[30]Burke was sixty years old at the time of his appointment. He had served as Congressman from South Dakota (Rep.) from March 4, 1899, to March 3, 1907, but was defeated for renomination in 1906. In 1908 he staged a successful comeback and served in the lower house from March 4, 1909, to March 3, 1915. In 1914 he received the Republican nomination for the U.S. Senate but was defeated. From 1915 to 1921 he was engaged in the real estate investment business in his home town of Pierre, South Dakota.

I have not been successful in obtaining reliable information concerning Burke's appointment. Apparently, however, he was not Secretary Fall's choice for the post. According to a series of letters from Malcolm McDowell, secretary of the Board of Indian Commissioners, to General Hugh L. Scott in March, 1921, Burke's selection came about in the following manner. In March, 1921, Secretary Fall sent to President Harding a recommendation for the appointment of J. George Wright, Superintendent of the Five Civilized Tribes agency in Oklahoma, as Commissioner of Indian Affairs. Burke at this time was consulted concerning a post in the administration and indicated an interest in the position of Assistant Secretary of the Interior in charge of Indian Affairs; he too favored Wright's appointment. Jim Harris, Republican National Committeeman from Oklahoma and another of Wright's supporters, was so certain that Wright would be confirmed that he publicly announced the nomination in Oklahoma, whereupon the followers of Harris' rival, Jake Harmon, began to bombard the President with telegrams against Wright. Much of this opposition came from oil companies who feared Wright because he was known to favor a recent decision to lease Indian lands at public auction rather than by means of sealed bids. According to McDowell, the uproar caused Harding to "get his mad up" with the result that he decided to ignore both factions in Oklahoma and appoint a Commissioner who was not from that state. His interest then centered on Burke who was persuaded to accept the nomination "much against [his] inclination." McDowell to Scott, March 8, 1921, and March 30, 1921. Scott Papers, Library of Congress, Box 49.

On January 14, 1922, the Commissioner of the General Land Office rejected the application of one E. M. Harrison for a prospecting permit covering a portion of the Navajo reservation withdrawn from the public domain by the executive order of May 17, 1884. The application was rejected for two reasons. The General Land Office ruled that it had no jurisdiction over Indian lands. Furthermore, under a Department of the Interior ruling, the act of 1891, as applied to oil and gas leases, pertained only to the treaty reservation: there was no law to permit leasing of executive-order reservations for oil and gas. Harrison's reason for applying to the General Land Office rather than to the Commissioner of Indian Affairs was that his request was based not on the law of 1891 but on section thirteen of the General Leasing Act. In other words, Harrison maintained that the executive-order Indian reservation was properly a part of the public domain and not a part of the Navajo reservation. Whether he was forcing a test case on the title of the executive-order reservations or whether he was genuinely interested in drilling for oil is not clear. In either case the effect of his application was to challenge the generally accepted but undefined status of the executive-order reservation.

Harrison did not stop with a rejection from the General Land Office. He appealed the decision to the Secretary of the Interior. Fall accepted Harrison's argument and in June, 1922, a bill approved by Fall was introduced into the House for opening the executive-order Indian reservations "within the Navajo Reservation in Arizona, New Mexico, and Utah," to oil and gas mining leases on terms similar to those contained in the General Leasing Act.[31] The sole difference from the General Leasing Act was that royalties were not to be split among the states, the reclamation fund, and the federal government, but among the states, the reclamation fund, and the Indians, with each to receive 33.3 percent.[32] On June 5, 1922, this bill received a hearing at which Secretary Fall testified, saying:

> It is my opinion that the provisions of the general leasing law of February 25, 1920, are applicable to deposits of oil and gas within

---

[31]E. B. Meritt, "The Government's Handling of Indian Affairs," *The Native American*, XXVII (January 15, 1927), in Board of Indian Commissioners, Tray #41.

[32]U.S. House, Committee on Indian Affairs, *Hearings, Leasing Unallotted Navajo Lands*, 67th Cong., 2d sess., p. 1. See also A. B. Fall to Homer P. Snyder, June 2, 1922. Navajo 44987-22-013.

Executive order Indian reservations, because of the fact that such reservations are merely public lands temporarily withdrawn by Executive order. . . .[33]

The bill was not reported out by the committee.

When the House took no action on his attempt to gain legal sanction for the Harrison plea, Fall, on June 9, 1922, issued an administrative decision that placed the executive-order Indian reservations under the General Leasing Act.[34] Essentially, his ruling was based on the fact that such lands were not owned by the Indians but by the United States, and that since such reservations had, in the past, been restored to entry by various Presidents, they were merely temporarily in the Indian custody. The effect of Fall's decision was to immediately withdraw the Indian claim to title from some 22,000,-000 acres of land. By far the greatest portion of this land, 9,000,000 acres, was formerly Navajo reservation.[35]

The second event had little to do with the Navajos immediately. By the terms of the treaty of Guadalupe Hidalgo in 1848, the Pueblo Indians of New Mexico were assured by the United States of their rights and property granted them by the King of Spain. In 1871 the United States Supreme Court ruled in the Joseph case that these Pueblo Indians, being superior to other North American Indians, were not "wards of the United States," nor were their lands to be under the guardianship of the federal government. In 1913, in the Sandoval decision, the Supreme Court reversed its earlier decision, declaring that the Pueblos had indeed been subject to federal guardianship since 1848. At the same time, the Pueblos were declared not to be competent to alienate lands, a practice they had been indulging in for years. The practical effect of this reversal was to jeopardize the landholdings of some 3,000 non-Indians, representing 12,000 persons who, in various ways, had obtained parts of the original Pueblo land grants. For years after 1913 these claimants used every means available to evade the Supreme Court decision. Following the disclosure of this problem by a Congressional investigation in 1921-22, Senator Holm O. Bursum of New Mexico, who had been appointed

---

[33] *Ibid.*, p. 2.

[34] Daniel M. Green (ed.), *Decisions of the Department of the Interior in Cases Relating to the Public Domain*, Vol. 49 (Washington: G.P.O., 1923), pp. 139-146.

[35] U.S. House, *Oil and Gas Mining Leases Upon Unallotted Lands*, 69th Cong., 2d sess., 1927, Rept. 1791, p. 11.

to fill Fall's seat, introduced a bill to disentangle the land situation.[36]

On the surface, the Bursum bill seemed to provide for an equitable settlement of the problem. Close study, however, led some friends of the Indians to decide that in reality the bill placed the non-Indian claimants in an unjustly favorable position to obtain clear title to the disputed holdings. These people charged that the "notorious Bursum bill" would place the burden of proof to title upon the Pueblos, a departure from normal procedure in similar cases which would have placed the burden of proof upon the non-Indian claimants. When Senator Bursum informed the Senate that the Pueblos had endorsed his bill, violent opposition began to the bill and Bursum.

On Sunday, November 6, 1922, one hundred Pueblo delegates, including the governors of eight pueblos, assembled at Santo Domingo Pueblo to adopt a memorial opposing the Bursum bill. They charged that the Pueblos had not been consulted by Bursum, that official explanation had been denied them, and that they had been deserted by the federal government.[37] Out of this assembly was born the Council of All the New Mexico Pueblos, a council formed without the permission of the government and indeed in opposition to it.

The Bursum bill was backed by Secretary Fall and Commissioner Charles Burke. It was opposed by a small but increasingly vocal group of persons from the eastern seaboard and the Southwest who denounced it as a brazen attempt to destroy the Pueblo Indians. The bill was eventually defeated but the opposition did not subside. Instead, the Indian Bureau came under even greater attack as the victors, led by a young social worker named John Collier, pressed their advantage and called for a thorough reorganization of the Bureau and a complete rethinking of federal Indian policy.

Collier's interest in the American Indian was relatively new. He had spent most of his career on New York City's lower east side where he worked among the immigrant masses as a staff member of the Peoples Institute. Established in 1897 by the former head of Columbia University's department of comparative literature, Charles Sprague Smith, the Institute sought "to give knowledge, leadership, and public voice to the wage earning masses." According to the urban reformer Frederick C. Howe, Smith's successor as director of the

---

[36]Herbert O. Brayer, *Pueblo Land Grants of the "Rio Abajo"* (Albuquerque: University of New Mexico Press, 1939), pp. 26-27. *New York Times,* March 16, 1924, section IX, p. 3.

[37]*New York Times,* November 7, 1922, p. 6.

Institute, it was "a kind of popular university." From 1908 to 1919 Collier served in a variety of posts at the Institute; his main interests centered upon the regulation of the burgeoning cinema industry and the training of social workers.

Like many thoughtful persons of this generation, the staff members of the People's Institute were deeply concerned with the vast social changes which urbanization and technology were effecting in American life. They deplored the materialism and the selfish individualism which they observed around them and they sought to combat these evils through programs and forums stressing community participation and cooperation. A major objective was the preservation of immigrant customs and traditions which could enrich the American cultural heritage. Traditional resistance to foreign customs and ideas, however, was heightened by the outbreak of World War I, and in the wake of the intolerance and nativism which accompanied the war, the Institute collapsed.

In 1919 Collier headed for California where he had been offered an opportunity to carry on the work of community organization under the auspices of the California State Immigration and Housing Commission. For almost a year he conducted forums throughout the state in which he emphasized the need for a communal and cooperative approach to the problems of modern society. To some state legislators this smacked too much of Bolshevism and Collier soon found himself without a job.

Now thoroughly discouraged by his failures in New York and California, Collier set out for the wilds of Mexico's Sonora Mountains. As he was traveling down the southern coast of California, he received a telegram from an old friend, Mabel Dodge Luhan, the wealthy New Yorker who had conducted a fabled salon in Greenwich Village before the war. At a time when other disillusioned Americans were emigrating to the banks of the Seine, Mrs. Luhan moved to Taos, New Mexico, married a Pueblo Indian, and discovered a new and exciting world. Determined to share her experience, she sought the support of others more articulate than herself. One telegram went to Collier, whom she had known in New York City, another went to the British novelist, D. H. Lawrence, whom she knew only through his writings. Both men answered the call. A new era in the history of the American Indian was in the making.

What Collier found in Taos that December of 1920 was the functioning communal society which he had dreamed of constructing in New York City. Repelled by the content and direction of Western

Civilization, he was thoroughly captivated by the Indian way of life. He came to believe that "only the Indians, among the peoples of this hemisphere at least, were still the possessors and users of the fundamental secret of human life — the secret of building great personality through the instrumentality of social institutions." The Bursum bill threatened the survival of these people and their way of life; their preservation became Collier's sacred crusade.[38]

HERBERT J. HAGERMAN

Meanwhile, the discovery of oil on the Midwest lease and the decision of Secretary Fall in June, 1922, to open the executive-order portions of the reservation to the provisions of the General Leasing Act, had produced doubts concerning the ability of agent Estep to handle the potential oil boom. The Commissioner of Indian Affairs was advised by Representative Carl Hayden of Arizona, shortly before the Midwest discovery, that Estep apparently lacked the experience necessary for coping with the situation, and he suggested that Burke send someone more familiar with the problems involved to aid him.[39]

On January 3, 1923, Secretary Fall requested Herbert J. Hagerman, former territorial governor of New Mexico, to accept the position of "Special Commissioner to Negotiate With Indians." The Secretary explained that there was the possibility of oil development on the Navajo reservation and that it was not feasible any longer to contract the leases through the local agents. What he wanted was one man to conduct the leasing and his choice was Hagerman. The telegram took Hagerman "by surprise, as I had not previously been in com-

---

[38]Collier has recorded the story of his career in *From Every Zenith: A Memoir* (Denver: Sage Books, 1963), but see especially his *Indians of the Americas* (New York: New American Library, 1961), pp. 9-11, for an account of the Taos experience. For the People s Institute see Frederick C. Howe, *Confessions of a Reformer* (New York: Charles Scribner's Sons, 1926), p. 240; and John Collier, "The People s Institute," *Independent*, LXXII (May, 1912), pp. 1144-48.

I make no attempt to judge the arguments of either side in the struggle over the Bursum bill which is a story in itself, and one, incidentally, which has yet to be done adequately. When Collier charged the Indian Bureau with attempting to suppress the Pueblo land titles, the Bureau countercharged that Collier was undermining its authority and seeking personal gain and publicity. Later the Bureau attempted to form its own Council of the Pueblo Indians. Collier then accused the Bureau of seeking to destroy a self-governing organ of the Indians and the Bureau defended its action by claiming that under Collier's All-Pueblo Council the Indians were being used to further Collier's own personal ambitions.

[39]Hayden to Burke, October 11, 1922. San Juan 83819-21-322.

munication with the Secretary or anyone else in regard to the matter. . . ." However, he accepted the offer and was advised to come to Washington immediately for briefing.[40]

In Washington the ideas which had been germinating for some time with regard to the conduct of the Navajo oil leases were put down on paper. A directive dated January 27, 1923, provided for the appointment of a Commissioner to the Navajos who would have general authority over the five reservations. Oil leases henceforth were to be approved by a council of all the Navajos, not just those of the San Juan jurisdiction. One delegate and one alternate from each jurisdiction were to be elected for a four-year term on the

---

[40]The original correspondence between Fall and Hagerman on this topic can be found in the Dietrich Collection, Fall folder, and the Albert B. Fall Papers, H. J. Hagerman folder, Huntington Library. See also Hagerman's memorandum dated January 17, 1923, in Navajo, 61584-24-150.

Herbert J. Hagerman was born in Milwaukee on December 15, 1871. His father, James J. Hagerman, was one of the nineteenth century's lesser-known empire builders. The elder Hagerman began his career in an iron mining venture in Michigan and then, after moving to Colorado in the early 1880's because of his health, earned several millions in successful railroad and gold and silver mining operations. In 1889 he became involved in a huge land development scheme in the Pecos Valley of eastern New Mexico, and in 1900 he moved to Roswell, New Mexico. His son was educated at Cornell and following graduation served as second secretary at the U.S. Embassy in St. Petersburg, Russia. The appointment was secured through his father's long-time friend, Ambassador Ethan A. Hitchcock.

In 1899 Hitchcock was appointed Secretary of the Interior by President William McKinley and he continued in office under Theodore Roosevelt until 1907. By 1905 Hitchcock had become convinced that huge land frauds had been consummated in New Mexico with the connivance of some Republican territorial officials. Roosevelt simultaneously became troubled over the bitterly factional nature of his party in New Mexico and in 1905 called for the resignation of the incumbent governor. On Hitchcock's advice, the young Herbert J. Hagerman was appointed governor on January 10, 1906. In little more than a year President Roosevelt was demanding Hagerman's resignation.

Roosevelt wanted a man who could unite the party; instead he got a young, inexperienced reformer who made its divisions even deeper. One of Hagerman's first moves was to secure the resignation of the superintendent of the state penitentiary and the chairman of the Republican Territorial Committee, Holm O. Bursum, on a charge of mishandling state funds. He then supported Hitchcock's investigators whose methods and determination alienated many powerful Republicans. By April, 1907, the opposition successfully convinced the President that Hagerman must go and accused the governor of having personally approved a fraudulent deed of 10,000 acres to the Pennsylvania Development Company. Hagerman failed to explain his conduct to Roosevelt's satisfaction and resigned.

Hagerman's role in New Mexico politics did not, however, end here. In 1912 when Bursum was nominated by the Republicans for governor in the state's first election, Hagerman revived the charges he had made in 1906, assisted in founding the Progressive Republican Party, and thereby helped to secure Bursum's defeat. Following this second foray into state politics, Hagerman confined his activities to supervising his Southspring Ranch and Cattle Company and serving as president of the nonpartisan New Mexico Taxpayers Association.

There is no evidence to indicate what Fall's motives were for appointing Hagerman. It may be that since he was opposed to Bursum's appointment as his successor and had recently lost a patronage struggle with Bursum, he saw in Hagerman's appointment an opportunity to even the score.

council within thirty days after the directive was made public. If a jurisdiction failed to elect a delegate, one would be appointed by the Secretary of the Interior. No meeting of the Tribal Council was to be held without the presence of the Commissioner. The Secretary of the Interior reserved the right to remove any member of the council upon proper cause being shown.[41] Hagerman was then directed to return to New Mexico and to begin the processes necessary for the calling of the council.

Before leaving Washington, Hagerman spent some time in acquainting himself with recent events in the Navajo country by a thorough study of the Bureau's files. Before he left he drew up a memorandum for future action based on his reading. Aside from the truly remarkable grasp of the situation which this document reveals today, it gives an important insight into an opinion formed by Hagerman at this early stage which was later to cause him much grief. Fall's decision placing the executive-order portions of the Navajo reservation under the General Leasing Act was accepted by Hagerman as the best means of opening these lands to development. It is very probable that Hagerman was not acquainted with the history of Indian mining laws or that he was, like other New Mexicans generally, blind to the Indian side of the argument. In any case, Hagerman was to hold, despite criticism, that Fall's interpretation was the only possible one.[42]

Hagerman returned to New Mexico in late January or early

---

[41]For the document see *Senate Survey*, part 11, pp. 4378-79. It may seem, as it was later charged, that the provisions of this directive severely limited the rights of the Navajos. In defense of the Bureau, however, it must be pointed out that the San Juan Navajos were opposed to allowing the other Navajo jurisdictions to have any say in the disposition of oil. There was a chance that they would boycott the new council and this was the reason given for the provision that the Secretary could appoint delegates. (Burke to Hagerman, March 2, 1923. Hagerman Papers, Commissioner's file, January-June, 1923.) The reason for forbidding the council to meet when Hagerman was not present is also explained by the furor that Collier's All-Pueblo Council had stirred up. Commissioner Burke had been greatly incensed by the creation of this council outside the Bureau's jurisdiction. He warned Hagerman to report to him promptly if Collier attempted such action in the Navajo country, stating that he would issue orders immediately to suppress such action. He did not, he contended, oppose "the closest scrutiny of our official acts" or "of conditions among the Indians," but, "this is quite a different thing than to go to holding meetings and councils and by false and misleading statements get the Indians excited and to believe that they are being abused and wronged by the government." *Ibid.* The power of the Secretary to remove any delegate for cause was removed before the regulations went into effect.

[42]Hagerman memorandum, January 17, 1923. Navajo, 61584-24-150. Also Hagerman to Burke, February 5, 1923. Hagerman Papers, Commissioner's file, January-June, 1923. And, Hagerman to A. B. Fall, February 9, 1923. Dietrich Collection, Fall folder.

February, and immediately set about to acquaint himself with the situation locally. By March he felt in a position to call a meeting of all the Navajo superintendents in Albuquerque. For two days the Commissioner and the agents discussed reservation problems and the directive which the Bureau had issued on January 27. At the close of the meeting, Hagerman wrote the Commissioner of Indian Affairs that some changes would have to be made in the original instructions. One delegate from each reservation was unsatisfactory because it did not take into consideration the division of population. Twelve delegates and twelve alternates were now recommended. Since the superintendents were not happy about the clause permitting the Secretary of the Interior to remove members of the Tribal Council, it was recommended that the clause be deleted. Hagerman, moreover, believed that there should be provision made for a quorum at the council meetings, for the appointment of interpreters, and for a means of succession in the event the offices of Chairman or Vice-Chairman were vacated between elections. Accordingly, on April 24, 1923, the regulations were amended to incorporate all of Hagerman's suggestions.[43] On April 25 Hagerman's title was changed to "Commissioner to the Navajo Indians" in keeping with the amended regulations. At this time or soon afterwards his duties were also expanded to cover "minerals, timber, and development of underground water," as well as oil.[44]

A CHANGE OF POLICY

On March 4, 1923, two years to the day from his entrance into the office of Secretary, Albert B. Fall resigned. The scandal over Teapot Dome had not yet broken and the reason generally given was that he and Harding had been unable from the first to see eye to eye on many issues.[45] To succeed Fall, the President turned to Hubert Work, a Colorado physician turned politician who, prior to his appointment, had been Postmaster-General.

Work soon found himself in an exceedingly difficult position.

---

[43]Hagerman to Burke, March 19, 1923, and E. B. Meritt to Secretary of the Interior, April 24, 1923. Hagerman Papers, Commissioner's File, January-June, 1923. See also *Senate Survey*, part 11, pp. 4390-92. The final representation was as follows: Navajo, four delegates; San Juan, three; Western Navajo, two; Leupp, Pueblo Bonito, and Hopi, one each.

[44] "Annual Report of H. J. Hagerman for the Fiscal Year Ending June 30, 1924." Navajo, 61584-24-150. Also Secretary of the Interior, *Annual Report, 1923*, p. 41.

[45]*New York Times*, February 11, 1922, p. 4; December 24, 1922, p. 2; June 3, 1923, p. 19.

Aside from the Fall designs on the naval oil reserves which began to come to light during the summer of 1923, the Indian problem alone was confusing enough for a new man. Some few days after Work took office, Commissioner Burke wrote him about the Fall decision on the executive-order Indian reservations. He was opposed to the decision, he informed Work, and he requested a ruling on the matter by the Department Solicitor.[46] He also requested that the Secretary approve the lease granted to J. J. Hall and W. E. Lockhart at the last San Juan council. With criticism of the Indian Bureau coming in from all sides, especially from the Pueblo country, Work halted all Indian business initiated by Fall until he could take stock of the situation.

His first action was to disapprove the Hall and Lockhart lease on April 28, 1923, since "in view of the recent rules and regulations [the decision to call all the Navajos into council to approve oil leases] no action on this lease is necessary."[47] Burke's request for a ruling on Fall's decision was given to the Department Solicitor on April 18, 1923. The Solicitor thereupon rendered an opinion that the Fall order did not apply. Although Work had issued three prospecting permits in accordance with his predecessor's ruling, he now forbade further permits.[48] To meet the challenge of public disapproval of the Department's Indian policy, he issued a call to one hundred distinguished citizens to meet with him in December to discuss the Indian issue.[49] He also requested Hagerman, who had submitted his resignation, to stay on after calling him to Washington for a conference.

JURISDICTIONAL RIVALRY

In the field Hagerman was busily preparing for the Navajo Council now scheduled for July 7, 1923. By May he had advised the

---

[46]Burke's testimony in U.S. House, Committee on Indian Affairs, *Hearings on H. R. 15021, Leasing of Executive Order Reservations*, 69th Cong., 2d sess., 1927, p. 14.

[47]Memorandum signed by Assistant Secretary of the Interior Goodwin, April 28, 1923. San Juan, 82894-22-322.

[48]Work to Senator Charles Curtis, February 13, 1924. National Archives, Record Group 48, 5-18, Executive order reservations — Indian Office. It is interesting to note that this letter clearly states that the only prospecting permits issued on executive-order Indian reservations under the Fall ruling were all on the Navajo reservation in southeastern Utah and northeastern Arizona.

[49]*New York Times*, May 12, 1923, p. 18. When the roll call was answered the following December, among those assembled were Stella Atwood of the American Federation of Women's Clubs; John Collier; William Jennings Bryan; Bernard Baruch; the Indian historians, Clark Wissler and G. E. E. Lindquist; and three members of the Board of Indian Commissioners: Hugh L. Scott, Flora Seymour, and George Vaux, Jr.

six agents of the dates on which they were to hold elections for Council delegates: Leupp, May 19; Western Navajo, May 22; Hopi, May 26; Navajo and San Juan, May 31; Pueblo Bonito, June 5.[50] His intention was to be present at each of the elections to explain to the Indians the purpose of the new council, and in this he was successful, except in the case of the Pueblo Bonito election.

In his travels through the reservation, Hagerman learned of the existence of a problem, serious enough at present, but one destined to grow rather than diminish over the years. There was serious conflict between the Navajos at Shiprock and those at Fort Defiance. The problem was complicated by personal ill-will between the Navajo leader at Fort Defiance, Henry Chee Dodge, and the superintendent at Shiprock, Evan Estep. Although Estep would leave shortly, the rivalry between the two jurisdictions would remain.

Chee Dodge, undoubtedly the most famous Navajo of recent times, was the chief spokesman of the Navajos at Fort Defiance and, insofar as the Navajos recognized any one man as their leader, of the entire tribe. Chee was born at Fort Defiance around 1860, the son of a Navajo mother and a Mexican father who served as an interpreter to the resident agent. Young Chee mastered English as well as his native tongue and familiarity with both the Navajo and the white man's ways marked him at an early age for leadership. In 1884, the revered but failing Manuelito, one of the signers of the treaty of 1868, was superseded by young Dodge as the spokesman of the Fort Defiance Navajos.[51]

Chee Dodge had then, in 1923, been an acknowledged leader among his people for some time. The announcement of the Navajo Tribal Council must have been a dream come true for him, for in 1918 he had written Commissioner Sells about the necessity for some such cohesive force among the Navajos:

> . . . I take a deep interest in all the Navajos; not only those of my immediate neighborhood. I would like to see them all make equal progress, but I am sure that it is only possible if we have one man at the head of the tribe, an active, strong, energetic and able man. . . . A uniform educational system, uniform treatment, uniform orders and regulations, and uniform progress would be the result. The whole tribe would advance as one unit.[52]

---

[50]Hagerman to Burke, May 15, 1923. Hagerman Papers, Commissioner's file, January-June, 1923.

[51]Francis Borgman, "Henry Chee Dodge, The Last Chief of the Navajo Indians," *NMHR*, XXIII (April, 1940), pp. 82-85.

[52]Chee Dodge to Cato Sells, August 20, 1918. Navajo, 73258-18-054.

In any boom area rumors abound. One of those making the rounds was that Chee Dodge had been bribed for his influence over the tribe, that he was in the pay of Standard Oil Company subsidiaries.[53]

Whether or not he had been bribed, the Navajos at San Juan were opposed to Dodge because of his attempts to tell them how to conduct their leasing business when he had served as interpreter at several of their council meetings. On February 26, 1923, Estep forwarded to Burke a petition he had received from a group of San Juan Indians. The petition protested

> against this new order of Mr. Secretary Fall. Whare by the old order of doing buisness of the Navijo indians has been taken from us & placed in the hands of Tche Dodge & a committee of six apointed by or through the Secritary of Interior.[54]

Burke quickly advised Hagerman of a possible clash, but Hagerman at this time seemed to think that the problem was not serious and that it was the natural result of the Bureau's decision to place the lease-making power in the hands of an All-Navajo Council.[55] The meeting with the agency superintendents in Albuquerque in mid-March, however, opened Hagerman's eyes to the seriousness of the problem. At this meeting, he wrote to Burke, Estep had "asserted with some vehemence" that he was convinced Dodge was in the pay of the Midwest. The Navajo superintendent, Peter Paquette, flatly denied the charge, and Estep replied that in any event the San Juan Indians were determined not to have Dodge as the chairman of the new council. He himself had not yet met Dodge, Hagerman advised: he was keeping an open mind.[56]

On the eve of the council meeting, Estep was summarily dismissed from his post. The charge was a technical one: someone had brought to light a telegram from Estep, then in California, to the acting superintendent at Shiprock, in which the latter was directed not to allow any of the San Juan appropriation to lapse as the fiscal year drew to its close. Although several of the large newspapers professed

---

[53]Estep to Burke, January 30, 1923. Hagerman Papers, Commissioner's file, January-June, 1923. This information came to Estep through the son-in-law of the editor of the *Denver Post*. At this time Estep discounted the rumor as "baloney," but it apparently stuck in his mind for future reference.

[54]Estep to Burke, February 26, 1923. San Juan 18213-23-059.

[55]Burke to Hagerman, March 2, 1923, and Hagerman to Burke, March 7, 1923. Hagerman Papers, Commissioner's file, January-June, 1923.

[56]Hagerman to Burke, March 19, 1923. *Ibid.*

to see in this action the influence of the oil monopoly acting to oust an honest government employee, the truth of the matter seems to be that the Bureau of the Budget, which was conducting a severe economy drive, had ferreted out the telegram and put pressure on the Bureau of Indian Affairs to get rid of Estep.[57] Hagerman, who first learned of the dismissal from Estep himself on June 23, was well aware that the newspaper charges could wreck his carefully laid plans for the coming council. He therefore immediately wired Burke requesting that no "change be made" until the council had met. To do so, he warned, "may complicate an already critical situation."[58]

Hagerman followed his telegram with a lengthy and urgent plea for Estep's reinstatement on July 1:

> . . . respectfully and urgently request that dismissal Estep be not pressed to consummation and that he be reinstated for present at least. I feel sure that you have been misinformed as to the actual situation. To put matter through will, I honestly believe, stir up a hornet's nest about as bad as the Pueblo affair . . . which will cause you and office endless grief. The charges, however groundless when I took office, have, after much work, been about stopped, will be bitterly revived. I will not be able to explain matter to Indians. It will [be] coming pretty near war. [This portion of the letter is a quotation from a telegram sent by Hagerman to Burke on June 30.]
>
> Estep has undoubtedly been gruff . . . but I am fully persuaded that he is an excellent man . . . and that his summary dismissal after long years of good service will definitely discourage good men from going into or staying in the service. . . .
>
> I am aware Chee Dodge hates him . . . I think Dodge can be and will be very useful and that after my talks with him . . . he was ready to go along and use the influence which he undoubtedly has . . . so as to bring about the results we all want without friction, recriminations or unnecessary bitterness.[59]

---

[57]E. C. Finney, First Assistant Secretary of the Interior, to Hagerman, July 6, 1923. Dietrich Collection, Fall folder. For the newspapers' account see the article from the *St. Louis Post-Dispatch* in *Senate Survey*, part 11, pp. 4779-80.

[58]Hagerman to Burke, June 26, 1923. Hagerman Papers, Commissioner's file, January-June, 1923.

[59]Hagerman to Burke, July 1, 1923. *Ibid.* I have quoted a large portion of this letter for several reasons. It shows that (1) Hagerman was definitely aware of the public criticism over Indian administration and he greatly feared that it would enter the Navajo field; (2) Estep's enmity toward Dodge was reciprocated by the latter; and (3) Hagerman was aware of Dodge's influence by this time and hoped to get him on the side of the Bureau's new policy.

But Burke remained adamant and the council was held on July 7 without change in Estep's status.[60]

FIRST NAVAJO TRIBAL COUNCIL

The first meeting of the new Navajo Tribal Council, held at Toadlena, New Mexico, came off without incident despite Hagerman's fears. The minutes of the meeting are extremely short; they no doubt omit at least as much as they include. Following a brief statement by Hagerman, explaining that the purpose of the meeting was to obtain sanction from the assembled delegates for leasing their oil and gas properties, the council elected Chee Dodge Chairman and unanimously approved a resolution, drawn up in Washington, granting the Commissioner to the Navajo Tribe the authority to sign "on behalf of the Navajo Indians" all oil and gas mining leases which might in the future be granted on the treaty portion of the reservation.[61]

One of the reasons for the Navajo acceptance of the Department's prepared resolution appears to have been the assurance that in return for the Navajo consent to the oil-leasing plan, the Indians would receive government aid in securing new lands. In his opening remarks Hagerman made this clear: in fact it appears that he was not above coercing them with the argument. The Navajos, he explained, would suffer more than anyone else if they failed to take advantage of the council to grant consent. It would be difficult under any circumstances to get the federal government to consent to add more lands to the reservation but, he said, "there is a good chance to find something for you if you will cooperate with the government."[62]

The San Juan opposition to Dodge, if it was present, does not appear in the record. Hagerman attributed this to Estep's own work. Not only did the ousted superintendent not interfere with the business

---

[60]Burke agreed with Hagerman that Estep's action was not wrong, only "thoughtless," but he found himself unable to convince the Bureau of the Budget of this distinction. Instead, he planned to comply with the Bureau's demands and then appeal directly to Harding for Estep's reinstatement when the President returned from his Alaska vacation trip. Because of Harding's death on this trip, Estep's reinstatement was delayed until August 22, 1923, when he was appointed agent at the Yakima Agency in Washington. On November 4, 1925, Burke wired Estep to inquire if he wished to accept the agent's post at the Navajo Agency, but Estep replied that people there would be too opposed to his appointment. See General Services, 45918-21-013, part III.

[61]*Proceedings of the Navajo Tribal Council, July 7, 1923.* San Juan, 91993-23-054.

[62]*Ibid.*, pp. 4-5.

of the council but, Hagerman informed Burke, he actually encouraged those Indians who came to him before the council not to let his dismissal interfere "in any way with their business interests in supporting the action of the council."[63] Jacob C. Morgan of the Shiprock delegation did introduce a resolution protesting Estep's dismissal, but it was killed when Chee Dodge spoke briefly in Navajo and five of the delegates followed with statements opposing the resolution.[64]

SANTA FE AUCTION

Having secured the necessary authority from the Navajo Council, Hagerman and the Department of the Interior began making plans for leasing the oil reserves. A major problem was the decision of whether to lease at all. By 1923 it was becoming apparent that the oil industry was in or approaching a bad state of overproduction.[65] In a letter to Secretary Work on July 9, 1923, Hagerman proposed a limited leasing arrangement.

It was possible, Hagerman argued, that a sale at this time would not bring large bonuses, but it was also true that if the government postponed the sale of leases, the bonuses might be even less. Immediate exploitation was not the goal of either the Department of the Interior or the Indians, but what both did want to know was whether oil existed in structures other than the Hogback. The Navajos especially, wanted a preliminary test.[66]

Whether in response to Hagerman's letter or for reasons of his own, Secretary Work decided in late August, 1923, to lease certain areas of the Navajo reservation. Under existing law the method was left to his discretion. He decided to grant large exploratory leases on unproven structures and several smaller leases on tracts adjacent to the Midwest site. All leases were to be made on the basis of competitive bidding for bonuses.[67] The auction would be held in Santa Fe, New Mexico, on October 15, 1923. Despite a policy adopted for other Indian reservations which permitted the lease holders to postpone

---

[63]Hagerman to Burke, July 23, 1923. Hagerman Papers, Commissioner's file, June-December, 1923.

[64]*Proceedings of the Navajo Tribal Council, July 7, 1923.* San Juan, 91993-23-054.

[65]Ise, *The Oil Policy of the United States,* p. 120.

[66]Hagerman to Work, July 9, 1923. Navajo, 58407-23-322.

[67]Burke to Senator Lawrence C. Phipps. September 7, 1923. Navajo, 41972-23-322.

drilling during the period of overproduction,[68] the Navajo lease holders were to begin drilling immediately to determine if oil existed. Although this was undoubtedly a wise requirement from the Navajo viewpoint, it tended to discourage several companies from bidding at the auction.

Prior to the October 15 sale, two events of special significance occurred. The Producers and Refiners Corporation, whose lease to the Tocito Dome through J. J. Hall and W. E. Lockhart had been refused by Work in the spring, and the Ohio Company, the "two main competitors in the Navajo field" to the Midwest interests, withdrew from the field. The reason was, Hagerman was informed, "that the drilling regulations on the exploratory areas are too severe."[69] Of more importance was the feverish drilling activity of the Midwest Company just prior to the auction. "With wonderful quickness" they brought in their number four well the day before the sale. Publicly they announced that it was a waterhole. No one seemed to know for sure if this were true, but Hagerman, reporting on the sale to Secretary Work, stated that in his opinion the announcement of a waterhole caused the Navajos a loss of from $50,000 to $75,000 in bonuses on those sites which were leased at the Santa Fe auction."[70]

The auction resulted in $87,000 in bonuses for the Navajos. Only eight of the eighteen possible 640-acre tracts adjoining the Hogback structure were bid on, for a total of $22,100. The remainder of the money came from the lease of the larger exploratory tracts on the Tocito Dome, $36,000; Table Mesa, $17,500; Rattlesnake, $1,000; and Beautiful Mountain, $1,000.[71] Although the Bureau of Mines engineer had not believed, prior to the sale, that the latter two tracts would

---

[68]Commissioner of Indian Affairs, *Annual Report*, 1923, p. 17.

[69]Hagerman to Burke, September 10, 1923. Navajo, 72304-23-322. On August 29, 1923, Secretary Work had specified that the lessees on each exploratory tract would be required to drill at least two wells; each was to be drilled to 3,000 feet unless oil or gas were found at a shallower depth in paying quantities. For the document, see *Senate Survey*, part 11, p. 4386. All of the Midwest's wells had struck oil at less than 1,000 feet. In view of the current overproduction and the necessity of bidding competitively now on the Tocito structure, the Producers and Refiners Company apparently felt the additional expense of a deep well was not warranted.

[70]Hagerman to Work, October 23, 1923. Navajo, 80406-23-322.7. The Bureau of Mines engineer, following up the rumor, reported to Hagerman that the Midwest number four was "sure enough a waterhole and the Midwest wasn't trying to slip anything over at all." K. B. Nowells to Hagerman, October 22, 1923. Navajo, 82587-23-322.7.

[71]*Senate Survey*, part 11, p. 4830.

arouse as much interest as the first two,[72] the lease of these two structures for the minimum bid of $1,000 was a distinct disappointment for Hagerman who wrote: "I thought the Rattlesnake would make a good bonus. I do not understand why it did not."[73]

INDIAN BUREAU CONFLICT

Having completed the sale of leases on the treaty portion of the reservation, the Department of the Interior now directed its attention toward freeing the executive-order Indian reservations from Secretary Fall's decision.

The brief which Commissioner Charles Burke submitted to Secretary Work shortly after the latter succeeded Fall had been supported by the Department's Solicitor who declared that Fall's ruling did not apply. At first Work reacted only negatively, freezing all prospecting permits under the Fall order. The impetus for positive action came when the Committee of One Hundred met in Washington on December 12-13, 1923.

The Committee pulled no punches in letting the Secretary know why, in answer to his own questions, those responsible to the government for official acts were at variance on many details with the nongovernment Indian societies and organizations, and why "the public mind is in a state of chaos" on the subject of the American Indians. This is not the place to note all the criticism leveled by the committee, but the resolution on the executive-order Indian reservation must be examined. The committee stated that the Secretary of the Interior should immediately suspend all proceedings on the sale or lease of oil, gas, or other minerals, on or from executive-order reservations, pending action by the next Congress which, it was hoped, would "vest the title of these reservations in the Indians occupying

---

[72]K. B. Nowells to H. H. Hill, September 28, 1923. Navajo, 79640-23-322. The Rattlesnake structure was, Nowells reported after this, not looked upon with much favor because of its "close proximity to the old plug, Shiprock," and because of the possibility that the Hogback structure "might possibly cut it off from the drainage area to the east." K. B. Nowells, *Report on the Extent of Oil and Gas Development in the Navajo Indian Reservation*, June, 1924. Navajo, 61584-24-150.

[73]Hagerman to Work, October 23, 1923. Nacajo, 80406-23-322.7. In Nowells' report above, he stated that the Rattlesnake lease was passed in the morning session of the auction, and that it almost passed again in the afternoon before S. C. Munoz of New York City made the minimum $1,000 bid.

them."[74] Assured that public opinion was once again with the Department, Work, on February 14, 1924, submitted to the Attorney-General of the United States two questions: (1) What title is acquired by the Indians to lands withdrawn for their benefit by executive order; and (2) Are such lands subject to the leasing act of February 25, 1920?[75] The beginnings of a battle royal were under way.

Meanwhile the status of the executive-order reservations was being debated within the Bureau of Indian Affairs. Hagerman, it will be recalled, at the time of his initial trip to Washington in January, 1923, had decided that the Fall ruling was the correct one. As time went on he became even more convinced that Fall was right. As early as September 23, 1923, he advised Commissioner Burke that it was impossible to obtain Congressional legislation that would take from the states what they believed to be their share of the royalties from the executive-order lands. By early 1924 he was writing that "strategically the Department would be in a better position with Congress if it would assent in principal to a division of possible royalties on non-treaty lands, on a basis of giving the Indians one-third instead of trying to get Congress to grant all to the Indians." He was sure, he added, that he could obtain the Navajo assent to such a proposition without "much trouble."[76]

Burke replied to these statements in rather strong language:
We can never stand for only giving the Indians 33.3% of any royalties that may come from oil leases on lands within the Executive order reservations, and we are compelled to stand for the proposition of all proceeds going into the Treasury to be expended for the benefit of the Indians except that . . . I would be quite willing for a small per cent to be paid to the state because of the fact that Indian reservation lands are not taxable.

If we should favor the Fall proposition . . . we would come in for some very severe criticism, and, in the face of precedents, which are uniform, we must stand against any legislation that

---

[74]U. S. Bureau of Indian Affairs, *Minutes of the Meeting of the Advisory Council on Indian Affairs* (Washington: mimeographed, 1923).

[75]U. S. Bureau of Indian Affairs, *Indian Policies, Comments by Secretary Work on the Resolutions of the Advisory Council on Indian Affairs* (Washington: mimeographed, 1924), p. 13.

[76]Hagerman to Burke, September 10, 1923. Navajo, 72472-23-322. Hagerman to Burke, February 22, 1924. Navajo, 15987-24-013.

fails to recognize the principle that the Indians should be protected in their rights to Executive order reservations, the same
as others.[77]

The difference is apparent. Burke was making his stand on principle
and precedent; Hagerman on political expediency and his intimate
understanding of New Mexican opinion. These lines were paralleled
in the Congress in the coming years.

THE STONE DECISION

On May 12, 1924, Attorney-General Harlan F. Stone rendered his
decision on the two questions given him by Secretary Work. The
General Leasing Act, he wrote, was not applicable to the executive-
order Indian reservations. His brief contained citations from many
previous legal decisions and an analysis of previous legislative action,
including the Metalliferous Minerals Leasing Act, all indicating that
Congress and the courts had consistently regarded treaty and executive-
order reservations as one. The General Leasing Act, he maintained,
would, by internal evidence, have stated its applicability to executive-
order reservations if such had been the intent of Congress. "The
important matter, however," he wrote, "is that neither the Courts nor
Congress have made any distinction as to the character or extent of
the Indian rights as between executive-order reservations and reservations established by treaty or act of Congress." Until one or the
other of them did so, the matter could not be definitely settled.
Plumbing the philosophical depths of the controversy, he stated the
alternatives:

> In respect to legislation and treaties of this character, two views
> are possible. First, that the right to occupancy and use extend
> merely to the surface and the United States, in providing that
> the Indians shall ultimately receive the value of the hidden and
> latent resources, merely gives them their own property as an act
> of grace. Second, that the Indian possession extended to all
> elements of value in or connected with the lands and the Govern-

---

[77]Burke to Hagerman, February 29, 1924, and Hagerman to Burke, March
26, 1924. Navajo, 15987-24-013. Hagerman's reply on March 26 indicates that he
would serve the Bureau's line, but that he still did not believe pragmatically, that
Burke's position would win out: "I shall, of course, do all I can to help impress
upon the public the necessity of the Indians having it all, in the hope that when a
compromise is made (as I feel sure it will have to be), as large a share as possible
of the royalties shall go to the Indians."

ment, in securing these values to the Indians, recognizes and confirms their pre-existing right. If it were necessary here to decide as between these opposing views, I should incline strongly to the latter. . . ."[78]

The real problem was at last stated and the solution outlined. Final decision of the issue lay with either the courts or Congress. A decision by either would be based on whether the Indians had a pre-existing right to the subsurface minerals, in which case the executive-order reservations would be equated with the treaty reservations, or whether their rights were a matter of grace, in which case Congress could decide how much, if any, was to go to the Indians and how much to the states.

---

[78]For a statement of the entire Stone decision, see U. S. Department of Justice, *Official Opinions of the Attorneys-General of the United States*, Vol. 34 (Washington: G.P.O., 1926), pp. 171-92.

CHAPTER 5

Legislation

The Stone decision proved prophetic in the years ahead. In both the courts and the Congress there were those who supported the view that the Indian right to the executive-order reservations was a matter of Congressional grace, and there were others who claimed that the right was pre-existent to any Congressional disposition. The arguments became tangled and snarled with other issues of the day, but in the end the Indians won a great victory.

INITIAL ATTEMPTS

Within the Department of the Interior there were several opinions as to the proper solution of the problem. Commissioner Charles Burke insisted that the General Leasing Act did not apply and that the Indians should get the full royalties to any oil or gas produced on the executive-order reservations. Herbert Hagerman, like many New Mexicans, felt that Fall's decision in the Harrison case was just, and that the Indians, because of the peculiar nature of the executive-order reservations, should be satisfied with less than 100 percent of the oil royalties. Secretary Hubert Work saw no problem in mining the executive-order reservations under the General Leasing Act so long as the Indians received the entire royalties from the oil produced.[1]

Outside the Department of the Interior, however, there was more concern over the impact of Fall's ruling on the issue of title to the executive-order reservations than there was on the division of possible oil royalties. Here the leadership was provided by John Collier and Congressman James Frear (Rep., Wisconsin) who took the position that while the Indians were indeed entitled to the entire

---

[1] I have uncovered no evidence on which to form a judgment of Work's motives. John Collier and Congressman Frear consistently charged during the Congressional debates that Work and Burke were perpetrating the Fall scheme. My judgment of Burke's motives is contained later in the narrative.

proceeds from the oil royalties, the crucial issue was to establish the legality of the Indian title to the executive-order reservations and to refute the argument that these lands were in any way public domain. Since his first appearance on the Indian scene in 1922, Collier had risen to a position of prominence in circles critical of the government's handling of Indian affairs. By 1923 he had the full support of the potentially powerful General Federation of Women's Clubs and was serving as the executive secretary of the newly formed and highly aggressive American Indian Defense Association. During the controversy over the Bursum bill he emerged as a skillful lobbyist before Congressional committees and his easy access to the pages of nationally circulated magazines won him respect if not endearment at subsequent Congressional investigations. Since the successful solution of the Pueblo problem in 1924, his attention had been directed increasingly toward Navajo affairs. Frear's position appears to have been determined mainly by his removal from the powerful House Ways and Means Committee in 1924 and his demotion to the Indian Affairs Committee. Sensing the support which Collier's cause was gaining, he apparently hoped to ride the growing interest in Indian affairs to victory in 1926. In this he was to be disappointed.

The first plan offered was one by Secretary Work. On December 6, 1923, he drafted a bill, simultaneously introduced into both the House and Senate, which provided that the proceeds arising from the leasing of executive-order Indian reservations should be deposited to the credit of the tribe for whose benefit the reservation had been created, the leases themselves to be made in accordance with the provisions of the General Leasing Act.[2] No action was taken on Work's bill in the House and, although the Senate Indian Affairs Committee reported it favorably, there was no discussion on the floor. However, a bill was approved at this session of Congress which affected future legislation on this problem.

The Indian Oil Leasing Act of May 29, 1924, amended the previous act of 1891 for the leasing of Indian treaty reservations.[3] Now the departmental procedure of leasing Indian treaty lands at public

---

[2]U.S. Senate, *To Provide for the Disposition of Bonuses, Rentals, and Royalties from Unallotted Lands in Executive Order Indian Reservations*, 68th Cong., 1st sess., 1924, Rept. 669. Also U. S. Bureau of Indian Affairs, *Indian Policies, Comments by Secretary Work on the Resolutions of the Advisory Council on Indian Affairs*. Work's bill was drafted and submitted prior to the meeting of the Council of One Hundred.

[3]Although the act did not so state, the Department of the Interior later interpreted it to apply only to treaty reservations. See statements of Senators Jones and Bratton, *Cong. Record.* Vol. 67, 69th Cong., 2d sess., p. 10914.

auction was given the force of law. The leasing period was extended from ten years to so long as oil and gas were found in paying quantities. States in which oil was discovered on treaty reservations were permitted to tax oil and gas production "in all respects" the same as production on non-Indian lands (43 Stat., 244).

Work's bill was again introduced in the following session of Congress. This time the Senate approved it. In the House it was amended to permit the states to levy a production tax on the oil extracted, in the same manner as the Indian Oil Leasing Act provided for the treaty reservations. The Senate refused this amendment and in conference the House amendment was re-amended to provide that 37.5 percent of the Indian royalties be paid to the state in which the executive-order reservation was located, "in lieu of taxes." The conference report, and thus the bill, was killed on a point of order.[4] This complicated maneuver deserves some analysis.

In the first place, both the Senate and the House accepted the basic premise of Work's bill, that the General Leasing Act was the one under which the executive-order reservations should be leased. The only argument was over the percentage of taxation to be allowed the states — the House insisting that the taxation be the same as that on the treaty reservations, the Senate that the state's percentage should be the same as it would be under the General Leasing Act. Representative Frederick W. Dallinger (Rep., Massachusetts), who pressed the point of order, did so at the urging of Commissioner Burke[5] who had insisted earlier that "the Indians shall be protected in their rights to the executive-order reservations the same as others."

CONGRESSIONAL PROPOSALS

With the defeat of Work's plan by his own Commissioner of Indian Affairs, the initiative now shifted to Congress. In February, 1926, Representative Carl Hayden of Arizona presented a second plan. It provided that leasing on executive-order reservations should be in accordance with the Indian Oil Leasing Act. In lieu of a production tax, 37.5 percent of the Indian rentals, royalties, and bonuses would be given to the state in which the reservation was located, provided

---

[4]*Cong. Record,* Vol. 66, 68th Cong., 2d sess., p. 5433.

[5]Burke's testimony, U. S. House, Committee on Indian Affairs, *Hearings on H. R. 8823, Leasing of Allotted Indian Lands,* 69th Cong., 1st sess., 1926, pp. 70-71.

that such monies be used "for the construction and maintenance of public roads within the respective reservations," or "for the support of public schools attended by Indian children," a proviso similar to that contained in the General Leasing Act.[6] The remaining 62.5 percent would go to the Indians. Hayden's bill also provided that those persons who had been granted permits for prospecting under the Fall ruling should, if they discovered oil, be dealt with according to the terms of the General Leasing Act.[7] A powerful issue, that of equities under the Fall ruling, was thus interjected into the already complicated situation.

Commissioner Burke supported the Hayden bill. In testimony before the House Committee on Indian Affairs, he explained that his primary interest was to obtain a settlement which would place the leasing of Indian lands under the jurisdiction of the Bureau of Indian Affairs. Hayden's bill would do this through the provision that leasing be conducted according to the provisions in the act of May 29, 1924. Any bill which allowed the executive-order reservations to be leased under the General Leasing Act would ultimately give the administration of such leases to the General Land Office which had cognizance of the public domain. Moreover, so long as the states were compelled to expend their cut of the Indian royalty money on projects useful to the Indians, Burke would not oppose this compromise. Although in principle he opposed Hayden's clause granting the permittees any rights whatever under the Fall ruling, he would, again in a spirit of compromise, agree to the clause in return for one placing the administration of the executive-order reservations under the Bureau of Indian Affairs.[8]

Opposition to the Hayden bill developed from several quarters. The House Committee on Indian Affairs amended it by replacing the complicated tax clause with one providing for a state tax on production. It also amended the relief clause to allow the applicants for permits, as well as the permit holders under the Fall ruling, to be rein-

---

[6]The text of the bill is in U.S. House, Committee on Indian Affairs, Hearings *on H. R. 9133, Leasing of Executive Order Reservations,* 69th Cong. 1st sess., 1926, pp. 1-2.

[7]Hayden's concession to the Fall decision in this instance was obviously based on the ruling of the U. S. District Court, Utah, which, a year before, had ruled against the Stone opinion in favor of Fall's.

[8]U. S. House, *Hearings on H. R. 9133,* 69th Cong., 1st sess. p. 23.

stated.[9] Three members of the House Committee filed a minority report opposing the amended bill in which they stated that the executive-order reservations belonged to the federal government, that the amended relief clause would validate the Fall schemes, that the Navajos, already a rich tribe, did not need the additional funds.[10] Congressman Frear filed a separate minority report.

At the hearings on Hayden's bill the only opposition came from Frear and John Collier.[11] Collier agreed with Hayden's proposal to place the leasing of the executive-order reservations under the Indian Oil Leasing Act, and with Hayden's relief clause limiting the application of the Fall ruling to the permit holders, but he suggested that the clause granting the states 37.5 percent of the Indian royalties in lieu of taxes be replaced by a flat production tax as provided in the act of 1924. Hayden explained at the time that his reason for the complicated tax clause was that during the debate on Work's bill the year before, there were friends of the Indians who opposed the flat-tax proviso because they feared that, in the absence of oil discoveries elsewhere in the state of New Mexico, the state legislature might pass a production tax law which would take advantage of the Indians.[12] However, the bill was amended in committee to incorporate Collier's suggestion.

---

[9]This was a new argument, also based on the ruling of the District Court in Utah. Backed mainly by the Senators and Representative from New Mexico, whose constituents apparently made up the bulk of the applicants, the argument stated that since the court had ruled there was no fraud involved, the applicants whose opportunity for obtaining permits had been frozen by Work's order should now be reinstated. The importance of this argument was that under the General Leasing Act, the discoverer of oil would have to pay only a 5% royalty on one-fourth of his permit, while under the Indian Oil Leasing Act the royalty was a flat 12.5%. Since there were some 425 applicants and only twenty permit holders, to equate the two would mean a large loss of revenue to the Navajos if oil were discovered.

[10]The second and third arguments of this minority report played an increasingly larger role in the final disposition of the problem. By 1926 the Fall trial was in full swing and there was a tendency on the part of many to find evil in any dealing to which the ex-Secretary had been a partner. The contention that the Navajos were a wealthy tribe, preposterous as it might seem, was made possible by a reckless juggling of Bureau records and general ignorance on the part of Eastern Congressmen. Congressman John Morrow (Dem., New Mexico) and Senator Ashurst of Arizona made the most frequent use of this argument. U. S. House, Committee on Indian Affairs, *Oil and Gas Mining Leases upon Unallotted Lands,* 69th Cong., 1st sess., 1926, Rept. 763.

[11]The evidence is that Frear had no personal knowledge of the conditions among the Indians and that the source of his information was John Collier. Burke's stinging criticism of Frear's uncritical use of Collier materials throughout the various hearings on this matter drove Frear to make a tour of twenty Indian reservations between September 12, and October 22, 1926. He returned more convinced than ever that Collier was correct. *Cong. Record,* Vol. 68, 69th Cong. 2d sess., p. 1067.

[12]U. S. House, *Hearings on H. R. 9133,* 69th Cong., 1st sess., pp. 26-27.

Frear now charged in his minority report that the amended tax provision was a legislative smokescreen designed to defeat Collier's intent. The effect of thus amending the bill was to remove the possibility of debate in the House on the merits of the production tax versus the 37.5 percent grant to the state in lieu of taxes. It was certain, Frear maintained, that when the amended Hayden bill reached the Senate, it would be again amended to put the 37.5 percent provision back in the bill. Thus, when the House, for the first time, had a chance to debate the issue, it would be under the pressure of a conference report with the "time entirely controlled by the proponents of the 37.5% tax proposal." It would be the same situation as the year before except that this time, under the House rules, a point of order could not be raised to defeat the measure. Frear also attacked the clause because it was subject to the interpretation that the Indians would pay all the production taxes, while the producers would pay none.[13] Thus, by Frear's standards, the Hayden bill was objectionable no matter which tax provision was accepted. Fortunately for the narrative, Hayden's bill was more fundamentally challenged in the Senate. The final solution would be reached only after long debate on issues more substantial than those proposed by Frear.

LEE'S FERRY BRIDGE

Meanwhile, on April 27, 1925, almost a year before the time just under discussion, the United States District Court, Utah, had decided in a case brought by the Department of Justice against E. H. Harrison that the ruling of Secretary Fall in Harrison's favor was valid. The decision of Judge Tillman D. Johnson stated:

The equities are all in favor of the defendant. The claim of the

---

[13]During the hearing on H. R. 9133, Hayden had stated that under his bill the state would receive 37.5% of the 12.5% Indian royalty in lieu of all taxes including those on the producers. When Frear asked why he did not tax the producers, Hayden replied that if the producers knew that all the taxes would be paid in this manner, they would bid higher for their leases. It appears to me, as it did to Collier, Frear, and most of the members of the House Committee at that time, that such an argument is entirely specious and that it could have only been intended to give the oil companies an unwarranted advantage.

I disagree, however, with Collier and Frear in their charge that in supporting the Hayden bill Commissioner Burke was being derelict in the performance of his duty to protect the Indians. I am more willing to give Burke credit for what he time and time again insisted was a compromise between himself and Secretary Work, the General Land Office, and the representatives of the West. This is not to say that he could not have been more outspoken in defense of his own views, but merely to indicate that he was probably not entirely a free agent in the matter. This argument will be more fully treated in the narrative at a later page.

government is . . . highly technical in that no substantial rights with respect to the government or anyone else are alleged or claimed. There is no question of fraud here [a reference to the charge that, like Teapot Dome, Fall had ulterior motives in framing his decision], no claim that these lands have been occupied by Indians or can possibly be occupied by Indians in any practical way. It is a desert unfit for occupancy for any human being.

The right of the government to insist upon and to enforce what is in effect a forfeiture is too doubtful in my mind for the court to adopt that view and deprive the defendants of possible benefits to be derived from the large expenditures which they have made upon the ground in good faith.[14]

The Department of Justice immediately appealed the District Court's decision to the Eighth Circuit Court of Appeals.

Some time after the introduction of the Hayden bill, word was received that the Eighth Circuit Court had refused to pass on the validity of the District Court's decision, and had instead certified to the Supreme Court two questions: (1) was there authority in the Secretary of the Interior to issue under the provisions of the leasing act of February 25, 1920, the permit which the United States, through the Attorney-General, was now seeking to have cancelled; and, (2) if the answer to the above question was "no," could the United States in equity maintain its suit to cancel the permit? There was, moreover, a rumor that two of the Circuit Court judges leaned toward Judge Johnson's opinion, while the third sided with Attorney-General Stone.[15] Whatever the truth of the rumor, a curious state of affairs now existed. Opponents of the Stone ruling pointed to the action of the federal courts in their effort to gain passage of an act placing the reservations under the General Leasing Act. Supporters of the Stone ruling counter-balanced the argument with the reply that since Stone had now been elevated to the Supreme Court, there was no doubt that his position would win out.[16]

More important than the guessing game over the probable action of the Supreme Court was the issue of the Lee's Ferry bridge and the

---

[14]Text in U.S. Senate, Committee on Indian Affairs, Hearings on *S. 1722 and S. 3159, Development of Oil and Gas Mining Leases on Indian Reservations,* 69th Cong., 1st sess., 1926.

[15]U. S. Senate, *To Authorize Oil and Gas Mining Leases Upon Unallotted Lands Within Executive Order Indian Reservations,* 69th Cong., 2d sess., 1927, Rept. 1240.

[16]See John Collier's statement in U.S. House, *Hearings on H.R. 9133,* 69th Cong., 1st sess., p. 42. Stone was elevated to the Supreme Court on March 2, 1925.

entire problem of Indian reimbursable debts. In 1914 Congress authorized the construction of Indian irrigation projects from federal funds
with the understanding that such projects should be reimbursed from
tribal funds (38 Stat., 582). The purpose of the act was to bypass the
considerable opposition of some Congressmen to gratuitous appropriations for this purpose. In time the concept of reimbursable appropriations was stretched to cover projects other than irrigation and to include those tribes which had no tribal funds, on the pretext that someday they might come into an income.[17] Nearly everyone who was
familiar with this practice was quick to admit that it had definite pork-
barrel overtones which were usually harmful to the Indians.[18] By
means of this fiction, Congressional support could often be obtained
for measures of an otherwise doubtful nature. The customary method
of justifying such measures was to obtain a statement from the Department of the Interior that such-and-such a project, usually a bridge or a
highway, would be advantageous to a certain group of Indians. All too
often, the Indians were charged with half the expense of a project
which was of far greater importance to local non-Indian groups than
to the Indians themselves. Little opposition developed to the practice
until 1920 when Congress, by law, directed that the Secretary of the
Interior begin the collection of some of these debts.[19]

On February 26, 1925, the Indian Appropriation Bill for fiscal
1926 was signed into law (45 Stat., 694). One item, accepted at the
time without opposition, was an authorization of $100,000, reimburs-
able "from any funds now or hereafter placed in the treasury of the
Navajo Reservation Indians," for the construction of a bridge across
the Colorado River six miles below Lee's Ferry, Arizona. No expenditures were authorized until the legislature of Arizona also appropri-

---

[17]In 1920 E. B. Meritt, the Assistant Commissioner of Indian Affairs, testified
before a House Committee that this idea orginated with Charles Burke when he
was Chairman of the House Committee on Indian Affairs, and had been continued since that time. Carl Hayden in 1926 maintained that Representative James
R. Mann in 1911 had formulated the idea. See U. S. House, *Hearings, Indians of
the United States*, 66th Cong., 1-3d sess., Vol. 3, p. 213, and *Cong. Record*, Vol.
67, 69th Cong., 2d sess., p. 3326.

[18]See the following for statements to this effect: U.S. Senate, Committee on
Indian Affairs, *Hearings on H.R. 8893 and H.R. 10884, Authorizing the Secretary
of the Interior to Adjust or Eliminate Reimbursable Debts of Indians*, 72d Cong.,
1st sess., 1932, p. 12; Hubert Work to Dr. Byron Cummings, March 9, 1926. National Archives, Record Group 48, Western Navajo-Bridges, part 1; *Senate Survey*,
part 6, p. 2230.

[19]The appropriation act passed in 1920 directed that only reimbursable debts
on irrigation projects be collected, but it was obvious that other projects were also
doomed to give an accounting.

ated $100,000. A less expensive bridge across the San Juan River at Bloomfield, New Mexico, was also given approval. The Lee's Ferry bridge became in 1926, during the height of the legislative battle over the status of the executive-order reservations, the symbol of all that was onerous in federal Indian policy and the rallying point of the numerous critics of the Bureau of Indian Affairs. It was a particularly vulnerable target because critics easily revealed that the Navajo reservation in the vicinity of the bridge was sparsely populated, and that there were absolutely no Navajos living within a ten-mile radius of the bridge. It was further demonstrated that the bridge was somehow located at the best possible site for a proposed arterial highway to the northern rim of the Grand Canyon National Park.[20] There probably would have been no opposition to the measure if the Navajos were as poor as they had been ten years before but, now that oil had brought money to the tribe, it was said that this was an attempt to loot their treasury.

The Bureau's position on this issue was peculiar at best. Hagerman, who had been unaware of the reimbursable policy at the time of his appointment in 1923, encountered it at his first meeting with the Navajo superintendents in March, 1923. One of the reasons for this meeting had been to determine in what manner the oil royalty monies should be spent. The superintendents agreed that if the reimbursable debts against the Navajos did not have to be repaid, the monies should be spent on improving the Navajo stock industry, educational facilities, agriculture, and transportation.[21]

Hagerman frankly informed the agents at the time that he did not know what the outcome on the reimbursable debts would be, but that he would write Commissioner Burke for instructions, which he did. No answer, however, was forthcoming until the spring of 1925 when Hagerman, after frequent questioning by the Indians as to the disposition of their oil monies,[22] began to bombard the Bureau with requests

---

[20]*Cong., Record,* Vol. 67, 69th Cong., 2d sess., p. 4554.

[21]Hagerman to Burke, March 19, 1923. Hagerman Papers, Commissioner's file, January-June, 1923.

[22]In early 1924 the Rattlesnake lease which had been sold at the Santa Fe auction for $1,000 brought in its first well. A field larger than that of the Midwest's Hogback had been discovered and additional wells followed rapidly. There were eight producing wells on the two structures by the close of 1924; fourteen in 1925; nineteen in 1926; and twenty-nine in 1927. Although the Navajo royalties were thus growing considerably, few of the Indians themselves knew how much royalty had been accumulated or how it was being spent. See correspondence in Navajo, 40549-23-054.

for a decision on the matter. He recommended in these letters that the oil monies be placed in a special fund separate from both the gratuitous and the reimbursable funds, and that they be spent for purposes desired by the Navajos. In one letter he commented, "I cannot hold myself responsible for the future unless this is done."[23]

Impressed by the urgency of Hagerman's correspondence, Burke replied shortly before the third annual Navajo Council. It had been decided, he informed Hagerman, that subject to Congressional authorization, the policy of the Bureau would be to expend the funds in the following manner: (1) to develop the water supply in those locations where such action would make available large areas of grazing land now incapable of being used because of a lack of water; (2) to breed up Navajo sheep through the purchase of good breeding stock; and (3) to purchase agricultural implements. "It is believed," he went on, "that it will only be good business to expend a portion of the oil money for improving roads and bridges."[24] In general, the superintendents and the Commissioner had now agreed on the method of expenditure. The Navajo Tribal Council had not yet spoken.

The Navajo delegates to the third annual council in 1925 showed the results of two years' experience. No longer were they content to merely approve the government's proposals. This time they had ideas of their own which they expressed clearly and forcefully. When, for instance, Hagerman informed them that there was a good possibility of their having to accept a division on the oil royalties from the executive-order reservations, some of them challenged him, stating that they believed all the proceeds were rightfully theirs.[25] After being informed of the Commissioner's decision on the expenditure of their oil royalties, they went beyond his plan and adopted a resolution providing for a division of the royalties along lines proportionate to the council membership, Hopis excluded; the money so divided to be spent in a manner agreed upon by the agent and the council members of the particular jurisdiction. Formal objection was made to the use of tribal funds for "such purposes as the bridge at the ferry across the Colorado [Lee's

---

[23]Hagerman to Burke, April 10, 1925. *Ibid.*

[24]Burke to Hagerman, July 1, 1925. *Ibid.*

[25]Hagerman here was apparently guilty once again of introducing his own bias on this issue despite his promise to Burke to defend the Bureau position for, when the Navajos challenged his interpretation, he told them that Commissioner Burke was on their side. See *Minutes of Navajo Tribal Council Meeting, Fort Wingate, New Mexico, July 7-8, 1925.* General Services, 37534-25-054.

Ferry] and the San Juan at Bloomfield." Jacob C. Morgan of Shiprock called upon Washington to consult the council whenever future appropriations were made; no action, however, was taken on this resolution. Thus had the Navajos spoken out on several of the issues before Congress in the spring of 1926.[26]

The appropriation act of 1925 merely authorized the Lee's Ferry bridge. In 1926, when it came time to actually appropriate the funds, a furious battle broke out in Congress. Senator Ashurst and Representative Hayden, both of Arizona, led the successful fight for the bridge. They were opposed by Senator Ralph H. Cameron (Rep., Arizona), Senator Sam G. Bratton (Dem., New Mexico), Representative Frear, and John Collier.

For Senator Cameron opposition to the bridge was an about-face. It was he who had submitted the report on the bridge in 1925 when the appropriation was authorized. He had done so because he believed that a letter from Secretary Work approving the bridge had been written after the Navajo Council had given consent. Now informed that the council had never been formally consulted on the matter, and indeed, on its own initiative, had opposed the measure at its last meeting, he reversed his position.[27] Aside from the unjust nature of the bill, he said it was fruitless to require the Navajos to build half the bridge when the state of Arizona had, at its last legislative session, defeated an appropriation for the other half. The only interests who wished to have the bridge built, he charged, were the National Park Service and Fred Harvey, who controlled the concessions at the Grand Canyon Park.[28] With Bratton's support he initially succeeded in striking the funds for the bridge from the appropriation bill.[29]

---

[26]*Ibid.*

[27]*Cong. Record,* Vol. 67, 69th Cong., 2d sess., pp. 4822-30.

[28]*Ibid.,* p. 4557. Senators Cameron and Ashurst of Arizona investigated the situation at the Grand Canyon Park in the summer of 1925 as members of the Senate Committee on Public Lands. Their report contained the charge that Fred Harvey had a monopoly on the park concessions. Although I do not mean to impeach Cameron's motives, it should be noted that he had a personal dislike for the Department of the Interior which stemmed from several suits which he had had with the Department over some placer mining claims. See *New York Times,* August 10, 1925, p. 3. There is also an indication that his stand on the Lee's Ferry bridge was partially dictated by political reasons. Cameron was running for his Senate seat at the time against Carl Hayden who, Hagerman claimed, had insisted on funds for the bridge for election purposes. Hagerman to Kneale, March 1, 1926. Hagerman Papers, San Juan file.

[29]*Cong. Record,* Vol. 67, 69th Cong., 2d sess., pp. 4150-52. Bratton consistently opposed the bridge on the ground that it was primarily for the benefit of whites.

Support for Cameron's position came indirectly from Hagerman. This incident sheds some light on the peculiar role of Commissioner Burke in the controversy.

In a letter to Superintendent Kneale at Shiprock, dated February 16, 1926, Hagerman stated that because of a trip to California for his health, he had learned of the controversy over the Lee's Ferry bridge only recently. In his opinion, the bridge was unnecessary and he certainly did not believe that the Navajos, with their small tribal fund, should be charged half the cost. The minutes of the 1925 council meeting clearly demonstrated the Navajo position, he declared, but they had probably been "pigeon-holed" in Washington.[30] Later, Hagerman confided his views on the bridge to his friend, Senator George H. Williams (Rep., Missouri).

Presumably to Hagerman's surprise and later chagrin, Williams discussed the letter on the floor of the Senate, and Hagerman's views became public.[31] The day following William's statement, Burke sent a mild reprimand to Hagerman. Undoubtedly Hagerman was actuated by conscientious motives in trying to defeat the bridge appropriation, Burke wrote, but there was a presidential mandate which prohibited those in the government service from communicating directly with legislators on appropriation items contrary to the report of the Bureau of the Budget. Since the Lee's Ferry bridge had been recommended by the Bureau of the Budget, Hagerman should have kept his opinions to himself.[32]

In the last analysis, neither Hagerman, nor Bratton, nor Cameron, nor Frear, nor Collier proved able to stop the measure. On March 2, 1926, the appropriation bill, with the Lee's Ferry proviso reinstated by conference committee, passed the Senate and went to the President for signature.[33] On March 4, 1926, Congressman Frear, making his most devastating attack on the Bureau yet, introduced into the House a resolution calling for the appointment of a ten-man committee from both houses "to investigate any charges of neglect, dissipation of funds,

[30]Hagerman to Kneale, February 16, 1926. Hagerman Papers, San Juan file.

[31]*Cong. Record*, Vol. 67, 69th Cong., 2d sess., p. 4827. On this same day Bratton read into the record an interview given by Hagerman to the *Santa Fe New Mexican* on February 25, 1926, in which Hagerman criticized the bridge. *Ibid.*, pp. 4822-23.

[32]Burke to Hagerman, March 3, 1926. Hagerman Papers, Commissioner's file, January-December, 1926. The influence of the Bureau of the Budget on Commissioner Burke's actions is a topic I will deal with at greater length later.

[33]*Cong. Record*, Vol. 67, 69th Cong., 2d sess., p. 4830.

improper treatment, or mismanagement of the American Indians." He specifically charged that

>the Indian Bureau under the direction of Commissioner Burke and Assistant Commissioner Meritt has approved and supported bills that have looted the treasury of the Navajo Indians . . . and that the only justification of this looting is found in a plea that a reimbursable charge eventually to be paid by the Indians will not be paid immediately.[34]

Although this resolution was not adopted, the Lee's Ferry bridge incident had the effect of uniting various forces in the Congress behind the opposition to the Hayden Oil Leasing bill which, it was claimed, envisioned more of the same kind of looting. Thus, although the opposition to the Lee's Ferry bridge was defeated, this defeat made possible, in part, the greater victory for the Navajos in the matter of the executive-order reservations.

SOLUTION

At the same time that the Lee's Ferry bridge was being approved, the Hayden bill was coming under sharp attack in the Senate. Senators Bratton and Andrieus A. Jones (Dem., New Mexico) each introduced bills modifying the Hayden proposal, making it even more onerous to Indian supporters. Congressman Frear shifted his attack on the Hayden bill from the difficult-to-prove reasons he had given in his minority report to the more fundamental charge that the bill tended to separate the Indians from their legitimate title to the executive-order reservations.[35]

The Jones bill differed radically from Hayden's. Under its terms, the General Leasing Act would be recognized as applying to executive-order Indian reservations. The Indians would obtain only the 52.5 percent that under this act would have gone to the reclamation fund. His 37.5 percent grant to the states made no mention of the use of this

---

[34]*Ibid.*, pp. 5035, 6965. Although Frear's charge intimated that it was Burke and Meritt who offered the justification that the bill for the bridge would not be paid immediately (there was a reimbursable debt against the Navajos for $771,281.07 which had to be paid even before the Lee's Ferry bridge), this charge could more accurately have been leveled at Senator Ashurst and Representative Hayden. On separate occasions these two offered identical arguments for the bridge in these terms: "Mr. President, competent geologists have stated that the region possesses the most promising indications for oil in all the Southwest. I confidently expect the Navajos to be the richest Indians in America, and when a large fund is accumulated to their credit in the Treasury, they can and will cheerfully pay for one-half of the cost of the bridge." *Ibid.*, pp. 3326, 4152.

[35]*Ibid.*, pp. 5037, 6116.

money for the Indian benefit. Applicants as well as permittees under the Fall ruling were to be restored. Little serious discussion was devoted to this reactionary proposal.

Bratton's bill was in the nature of a compromise between Hayden's and Jones'. Like Hayden he would place the leasing of the executive-order reservations under the Indian Oil Leasing Act of 1924 and give the Indians 62.5 percent of the royalties. Like Jones he would remove the strings from the 37.5 percent grant to the states, except that his bill provided that a portion of such monies, as determined by the individual state legislatures, should be used for schools and roads within the Indian reservation. Not all the applicants but only those who could prove that they had expended money for a geological survey, built roads, and drilled or contributed to the drilling of a well, would be recognized as having equities under the Fall ruling.[36]

Commissioner Burke was called upon to testify on the new measures. He repeated his stand on the Hayden bill. He had not changed his mind "one bit" on the right of the Indians to the executive-order reservations, but he had acquiesced in the compromise which the Hayden bill contained in order to placate some of the other members of the Department of the Interior, including Secretary Work, and the opposition in the Congress. He was opposed to the clause in both Jones' and Bratton's bills which reinstated some or all of the applicants; he claimed that since they had not received permission from the Department to prospect, they had not lost anything and were, therefore, not entitled to compensation.[37]

John Collier put the matter of title to the executive-order Indian reservations squarely before the committee. It would be very difficult, "perhaps impossible," he said, to pass any law authorizing the development of the areas without adopting a theory on the nature of the title.[38] He was opposed to all the bills thus far presented because they

---

[36]U. S. Senate, *Hearings on S. 1722 and S. 3159*, 69th Cong., 1st sess., pp. 1-3. The conditions which Bratton laid down for the applicants were obviously selected to allow certain applicants to qualify who would otherwise have been shut out. Jones' bill is the more logical from the Western viewpoint.

[37]*Ibid.*, pp. 53-61.

[38]Although some Senators would remain confused to the last about the effect of a Supreme Court decision in the Harrison case (see Senator Bayard's statement in the *Cong. Record*, Vol. 67, p. 10914), it was true, as both Collier and Burke pointed out, that the Supreme Court would not decide the basic issue. If the Court held with Fall, the Indians would get nothing under the General Leasing Act. If it held that the Fall ruling did not apply, the Congress would still have to enact legislation providing for the disposition of the oil reserves on

implied that the title was in the federal government. With title vested in the federal government, the executive-order reservations could be reduced at the will of the executive as they had been in the past, thus placing in the hands of the Indian Bureau "a power that is almost inestimable, one that can be used in the control of commercial opinion, public opinion in politics, a power to give or withdraw."[39] A bill which provided for a state tax on Indian land, like any other, would imply that the title was vested in the Indians, and that was what he wanted. The question of title, however, was precisely what Bratton wanted to avoid and the fight was on.

Hagerman, too, was called upon to testify. He told the committee what he had earlier told Burke, that the Navajos would accept 62.5 percent of the royalties; in fact, he stated, they would even take 50 percent. Upon close questioning by Senator Robert M. LaFollette, Jr. (Progressive, Wisconsin), he admitted that the Tribal Council had not agreed to such a division, that there were only a few Navajos who favored such a split, and that most of them wanted to wait the issue out. He did not, however, think that "there would be any trouble . . . to get from the council a formal declaration" to the effect that the Navajos would accept 50 percent.[40]

Sentiment in the Congress was, however, shifting to the Collier-Frear position. Senators Burton K. Wheeler (Dem., Montana) and La-Follette had come out in favor of granting the Indians 100 percent of the royalties, subject to a state tax. In early May, Senator Cameron proposed a fourth bill which embraced this theory and added that when the Indian oil monies were being appropriated by Congress

---

executive-order reservations, since there was no law for their development. Collier was willing to let the Court decide, but, if legislation were written before a Court decision, he insisted that the title be vested in the Indians. Burke was fearful that the Court, in light of the lower courts' decisions, would uphold the Fall ruling, and partly to forestall this possibility he backed the Hayden bill as a realistic compromise with the opposition.

[39] U. S. Senate, *Hearings on S. 1722 and S. 3159*, 69th Cong., 1st sess., pp. 71, 75, 90. It is interesting to note that a bill granting the Indians title had now become as important to Collier and Frear for freeing the Indians from Bureau control as it had for establishing the principle that their rights to the land were pre-existent to Congressional determination.

[40] *Ibid.*, p. 108. Hagerman's testimony here, while technically correct, was probably misleading. Since it appears to have had little bearing on the outcome of the status of the executive-order reservations, I shall postpone an analysis of his position until a later chapter.

the tribal councils should be consulted.[41] Three of the seven members of the Senate Indian Affairs Committee were thus opposed to the Bratton and Jones bills, three were apparently neutral. Bratton, the seventh member, was now fighting alone.

As Cameron's bill received increasing support, Bratton resolved to amend it as much as he could. His attempt to win sympathy for the position that the states should received 37.5 percent of the Indian royalties on the ground that the federal government owned so much nontaxable land in the western states was snubbed by LaFollette who lectured him on the duty of the states to deal with the adequacy of their tax structures. "Let them," he said, "increase the production tax."[42]

Bratton then attempted an amendment which provided that until the states should levy a tax upon the Indian oil monies, they would be paid a sum equivalent to the tax on oil produced upon unrestricted lands. When the other members of the committee questioned this curious arrangement, Bratton's answers were evasive. To aid the Senators, John Collier quietly explained that under the New Mexico constitution Indians could not vote if they were not taxed; if the state was forced to levy a production tax on the oil royalties, the effect might be to enfranchise the Indians.[43] Despite this revelation, the committee adopted Bratton's amendment, with the warning that if New Mexico did not enact a tax law within a reasonable period, the matter would be reconsidered by the committee.[44]

Apparently emboldened by his success, Bratton next offered an amendment which would reinstate all applicants under the Fall ruling who had filed prior to the decision of Attorney-General Stone. He was defeated by a committee vote of six to one. He then attempted a fourth amendment which would have declared that nothing in the Cameron bill should be construed to affect the title of the lands in question, or to declare a permanent policy of Congress respecting such titles. Again he was defeated with only Senator J. W. Harreld (Rep., Oklahoma)

---

[41]An obvious reference to the Lee's Ferry bridge and Cameron's stand on that issue. U. S. Senate, Committee on Indian Affairs, *Hearings on S. 3159 and S. 4152, Development of Oil and Gas Mining Leases on Indian Reservations*, 69th Cong., 2d sess., 1926, pp. 43-44.

[42]*Ibid.*, p. 24.

[43]Although there is no evidence to support such a view, I suspect that similar reasoning was behind Hayden's complicated provision giving the states 37.5% of the Indian royalties, yet requiring them to spend it for the Indian benefit.

[44]U. S. Senate, *Hearings on S. 3159 and S. 4152*, 69th Cong., 2d sess., p. 65.

siding with him.[45] The committee then voted to submit the Cameron bill to the Senate in lieu of both Jones' and Bratton's bills. There Jones and Bratton fought the passage of the bill but again were defeated and the bill was sent to the House.[46]

The House dredged up all the arguments it had used before in opposing the Hayden bill: the Navajos were wealthy and did not need the money; the land belonged to the federal government; the bill was favored by the oil monopoly; the applicants under the Fall ruling had acted in good faith and should not now be deprived of the relief provisions. In the end, the Hayden bill was amended to the specifications of the Cameron bill with the exception that the House threw out the Senate clause permitting the state of New Mexico to accept a sum equivalent to the tax on unrestricted lands until a law taxing such resources was passed.[47] The Senate then accepted the amendment and the bill went to the President. Collier and Frear had been successful in everything they had fought for with the sole exception of a positive statement that the title of the executive-order reservations resided in the Indians.

On July 2, 1926, President Coolidge vetoed the bill. He did so for two reasons. First, the bill unfairly discriminated between the permittees and the applicants. Second, the bill was of "doubtful propriety" in that it attempted to legislate the solution to a problem pending in the courts.[48] The battle would have to be fought again.

Only token Congressional resistance was offered to an amended Cameron bill the following year. The new bill, in accordance with Coolidge's veto message, placed the permittees and those applicants who had filed prior to the Stone decision on an equal basis. No opposition was received from Collier, and while Commissioner Burke and Secretary Work remained opposed in principle to the admission of

---

[45]*Ibid.*, pp. 75, 84.

[46]For the debate on the floor of the Senate see *Cong. Record,* Vol. 67, 69th Cong., 2d sess., pp. 10919-25.

[47]For the House debate, see *ibid.*, pp. 11381-97.

[48]U. S. Senate, *Message from the President of the United States Returning Without Approval the Bill (S. 4152) to Authorize Oil and Gas Mining Leases Upon Unallotted Land Within Executive Order Indian Reservations, and for Other Purposes,* Doc. 156, 69th Cong., 1st sess., 1926, pp. 1-2. According to Coolidge's veto message, Cameron's bill discriminated between permittees and applicants in the following manner. The permittees were required to prove that they had done only one of the following: expended money for a geological survey, built a road, drilled or contributed to the drilling of a well. But those applicants who had, prior to May 27, 1924, filed an application for a permit, had to prove that prior to January 1, 1926, they had performed *all* of the above requirements.

more than the twenty permittees, they agreed that if such was the will of the Congress, no substantial injustice would be done to the Indians.[49] Chee Dodge and Deshna Clah Chischillige were on hand for both the House and Senate hearings, and they expressed the Navajo satisfaction with the bill.[50] On March 3, 1927, President Coolidge signed the bill into law (44 Stat., 1347).

ROLE OF COMMISSIONER BURKE

Commissioner Burke's stand on the Lee's Ferry bridge and the Hayden bill brought sharp criticism from the Frear-Collier opposition which charged that his position was indicative of his lack of interest in the Indian cause. On the surface this contention seems vindicated. The issue is, however, somewhat more complex than it appears and Burke's role more hedged by contingencies than his critics were inclined to admit.

The Commissioner in early 1924 had no intention of admitting the application of the General Leasing Act to the Indian executive-order reservations. The Indians, he insisted in the letter to Hagerman quoted earlier, must have all the proceeds from the oil royalties, and they must be protected in their rights to these reservations the same as to the treaty reservations. Since this was well before his position was challenged, it would seem to be a fair statement of Burke's initial position and to contain no guile.

Furthermore, it was the Commissioner himself who was responsible for the defeat of Secretary Work's bill in 1925, an action which also took place before the Frear-Collier opposition to his position. The Work bill would have placed the leasing of the executive-order reservations under the General Leasing Act, and there was complete acceptance of this plan in both Houses of the Congress until Burke succeeded in having the bill killed on a point of order. At a later date the Commissioner stated the reasons for this action. He was, first of all, intent on having the same law apply to the leasing of treaty and executive-order reservations. Secondly, he insisted that all royalties from oil go to the credit of the tribe which occupied the reservation. Thirdly, he was opposed to the amendment which allowed

---

[49]U. S. House, *Hearings on H. R. 15021*, 69th Cong., 2d sess., p. 41. Evidence was produced in the hearings to show that the great majority of applicants had applied subsequently to Stone's ruling and therefore only a few applicants would be recognized under the new bill.

[50]*Ibid.*, p. 91. See also U. S. Senate, Committee on Indian Affairs, *Hearings on S. 4893, Development of Oil and Gas Mining Leases on Indian Reservations*, 69th Cong., 2d sess., 1927, p. 19.

the permittees to be recognized under the Fall ruling.[51] Why was it then, that in the following session of Congress, the Commissioner was willing to give 37.5 percent of the Indian royalties to the states, and to recognize the permittees?

The argument which Burke presented for his approval of the Hayden bill was consistent at each of his appearances before the Congressional committees. He was, essentially, making a compromise with reality which he believed still protected the Indians in their rights. Each time he testified, Burke added more details about the nature of this compromise and the persons involved in it.

The most difficult compromise appears to have been the one which Burke was forced to make with the members of his own Department. According to Burke, after Fall's resignation, he and Secretary Work had arrived at an understanding that until the Congress met in December, 1923, to discuss the Fall ruling, nothing further would be done within the Department of the Interior to implement that decision. On November 15, 1923, however, Burke received a letter from Work stating that he now saw no reason to disturb the Fall ruling. Accompanying the Secretary's letter was a copy of one signed by First Assistant Secretary Finney to the Commissioner of the General Land Office, stating that Finney and Secretary Work had come to an understanding on the Fall order, and that the General Land Office should begin again to consider applications for permits under that ruling. Burke immediately went to Work expressing his surprise at the letters in view of the conversation he had with the Secretary earlier. The Secretary then assured him that the "matter had gotten by him through a misunderstanding," and he promised to recommend legislation at the coming Congress that would give all the proceeds from oil royalties on executive-order reservations to the Indians.[52]

True to his promise, Work in December, 1923, introduced a bill which gave the proceeds to the Indians but, at the same time, gave the control of the leasing operation to the General Land Office by placing the administration of the leases under the General Leasing Act. Burke apparently had not been successful in wooing the Secre-

---

[51]U. S. House, *Hearings on H. R. 8823*, 69th Cong., 1st sess., p. 71.

[52]See Burke's testimony, *ibid.*, p. 70, and also his statement in U.S. Senate, *Hearings on S. 1722 and S. 3159*, 69th Cong., 1st sess., pp. 53-55. In this latter statement Burke maintained that Finney "had something to do with the opinion of Secretary Fall in holding that the General Leasing Act of 1920 applied to the Executive order Indian reservations." In the former hearing he stated that in opposition to Finney, Assistant Secretary Edwards had agreed with his position.

tary away from other factions in the Department. For this reason and because the Senate Committee amended the bill to give 37.5 percent of the Indian royalties to the states in lieu of taxes, the Commissioner had the bill killed in the House.

It is not apparent from the record why Secretary Work insisted upon the application of the General Leasing Act to the executive-order reservations. It may be that he simply agreed with Fall or that he believed he was under some obligation to uphold the decision of his predecessor. It is possible that Assistant Secretary Finney and the General Land Office, who had both achieved new powers under the Fall ruling, were intent upon keeping that power and prevailed upon the new and inexperienced Secretary to support their position. Since Burke's initial opposition to the Fall ruling was primarily directed at the loss of royalties which the Indians would experience, Secretary Work may have believed that he was pacifying both bureaus when he granted the General Land Office jurisdiction of the leasing operations on the executive-order reservations, but assured the Indian Bureau that all the royalty monies would go to the Indians.

A more plausible explanation, however, is the hypothesis that Work, Finney, and the General Land Office, all of whom were more susceptible to pressures from oil men than Indians, were mainly concerned with protecting the rights of the permittees recognized under the Fall ruling. This would be most easily done by applying the General Leasing Act to the executive-order reservations. This solution, however, was too simple for it implied that the executive-order reservations were part of the public domain and by 1925 Collier and Frear had made the matter of title a major issue in the debate. Thus, when Representative Hayden presented his bill in 1926, each side was offered what it most wanted. If Burke would agree to recognize the rights of the permittees under the General Leasing Act, Work and the others would agree to administer future leases according to the provisions of the Indian Oil Leasing Act of 1924, thereby assuring the Indian Bureau control of the leasing operations and implying the equality of the executive-order and treaty reservations. When Burke agreed to this arrangement he made his first compromise.

The second was his compromise with the Western representatives in Congress. According to his own testimony, the Senate amendment to Secretary Work's bill in 1925 calling for a 37.5 percent grant to the states "in lieu of taxes," convinced him that he could not obtain legislation giving all the royalty proceeds to the Indians; some concession had to be made to the Congressional forces which insisted that the General Leasing Act did apply. He thus compromised his earlier position to the extent that the states should have the 37.5 percent grant *if* the money were to be spent on the Indians.[53] He had been told, he testified, that "unless the states were given 37.5 percent there would not be any legislation."[54]

It may legitimately be asked, as indeed the House Committee did when it threw out this curious arrangement, what advantage there was in giving a state 37.5 percent of the Indian royalties, and then demanding that it spend the money on the Indians. The reasoning is that Burke, who was above all else a practical man and a politician, knew full well that once the states got the money, they would not spend it all on schools and roads for the Indian benefit. But there was, as Burke also knew well, powerful sentiment in Arizona and New Mexico for a bill which would give the states the 37.5 percent without any strings attached at all. The bills introduced by Bratton and Jones illustrate this. In all probability, Burke felt that, under the circumstances, to get anything for the Indians was to achieve success of a kind. Furthermore, in Hayden's bill he was assured that in return for this concession, the executive-order reservations would, at least in the matter of oil leases, be equated with the treaty reservations through the provision placing them under the Indian Oil Leasing Act. Within the framework of tradition and practical politics—Burke's world—this was as fair and as advantageous a solution for the Indians as he could hope to make.

As later events proved, Burke's reasoning was defective. The moral argument of Frear and Collier proved capable of transcending the realm of politics and tradition. Once LaFollette and Wheeler took up the cause, the sentiment for giving the Indians all the proceeds began to grow, and in the end this viewpoint won out. The moral argument, however, would probably never have prevailed over the more mundane interests of the Congress had it not been for the conflict over the Lee's Ferry bridge.

Burke's position on the Lee's Ferry bridge is subject to much more criticism than his stand on the Hayden bill, but there is evidence that it, too, was a consequence of the compromise he had to make to get support for the Hayden bill.

---

[53]U. S. Senate, *Hearings on S. 1722 and S. 3159*, 69 Cong., 1st sess., p. 55.
[54]U. S. House, *Hearings on H.R. 8823*, 69th Cong., 1st sess., pp. 70-71.

Ever since the passage of the Indian Oil Leasing Act of 1924, the Midwest Company had been appealing to the Indian Bureau for an extension of its lease. This lease, it will be recalled, had been negotiated under the act of 1891 which provided for only a ten-year lease; the act of 1924 had amended this provision, but not retroactively, to extend leases beyond the ten-year limit if oil or gas were still being produced in paying quantities. Burke and Hagerman were also interested in amending the Midwest lease, but for different reasons from those of the Midwest Company.

The oil discovered on the Navajo reservation had been found at a depth of between 800 and 1,200 feet. At the time of the October 15, 1923, auction, in order to test the structures for oil at greater depths, all lessees had been required to drill test wells to 3,000 feet unless oil were discovered at lesser depths in paying quantities. By 1926 the Bureau was seeking to enforce drilling to 5,000 feet. It was believed that as a concession for extending the Midwest lease, the company would agree to drill such a well.[55]

At the 1925 council, Hagerman presented this argument to the Navajo delegates. The request for authority to negotiate with the company on this basis was refused. According to Hagerman, the Navajos reasoned that since the Midwest had paid no bonus for its lease, they were under no obligation to grant the company a favor.[56] The matter rested here until February, 1926.

In February, in a letter to Hagerman, Burke once again advised the Commissioner to the Navajos of the desirability of securing from the Tribal Council an amendment to the Midwest lease. Although in sympathy with the proposal, Hagerman advised the Commissioner against such action in view of the Council's decision the previous summer. He was going to have enough trouble, he told Burke, over "what is almost sure to be the reaction of the Navajos when they are advised of the proposed appropriation of $100,000 out of their funds for the building of the Lee's Ferry bridge." The Navajos had considered Burke's letter of last July "as an assurance that no considerable amount of these funds would be used for bridges—at least without consulting the Indians." It would be very difficult for him to go before the Navajo Council now with a request even so reasonable as the

---

[55]See Hagerman's statement on the Midwest lease before the Navajo Tribal Council, Ft. Wingate, New Mexico, June 7, 1925. General Services, 37534-25-054.

[56]Hagerman to Burke, July 11, 1925. Hagerman Papers, Commissioner's file, July-December, 1925.

Midwest's and secure Navajo acquiescence in the face of the proposed bridge expenditures.[57]

Burke's reply on February 17, 1926, was a closely reasoned defense of his stand on the issue. In the first place, he informed Hagerman, the bridge had been recommended to the Secretary of the Interior by the superintendent of the Western Navajo reservation who stated that the bridge would be of great benefit to the Navajos in his jurisdiction, both in granting them increased travel opportunities and in bringing them closer to civilization. More important than this evidence of its desirability, the bridge had become tied in with the disposition of the royalties on the executive-order reservations [Hayden's bill]: "We cannot hope to get this legislation if everything for the betterment of the Indian estate is to be paid by gratuity appropriations." If the bridge were not beneficial to the Navajos then it ought not to be paid for by them; but if it were, and if the Navajos had the money, there was no reason why they should not pay their share of the cost. Frear's charge that Burke was intent on siphoning off the Navajo tribal funds was untrue:

> I want to emphasize that there has been no thought or intention of taking a penny of the money now in the Treasury to the credit of the Navajo Indians to pay for this bridge. It is the intention to use the proceeds only as stated in the letter to you which you read to the Indians at your last Council.

With reference to a similar situation among the Pueblo villages, Burke stated that if the debt should prove embarrassing to the Indians, "a repeal of the law could probably be brought about."[58]

Burke's defense of his position on the Lee's Ferry bridge is presented ably in this letter, but it leaves much to be desired. With the exception of Hayden, Ashurst, and the superintendent of the Western Navajo reservation, everyone was agreed that the bridge was of little benefit to the Navajos and certainly not worth $100,000 of their oil monies. The opinions of Hagerman and the Tribal Council should have been given some weight in any determination of its desirability. Burke's argument that the bridge should not be built if it were not

---

[57]Hagerman to Burke, February 6, 1926. *Ibid.*, Commissioner's file, January-December, 1926.

[58]Burke to Hagerman, February 17, 1926. Dietrich Collection, Indian Oil and Other Matters, 1926, file. This letter is also printed in *Senate Survey*, part 11, pp. 4845-46.

beneficial was based on the thesis that it was beneficial and thus was begging the question. The only argument that Burke presented which makes sense was his declaration that unless he supported the bridge appropriation, the Hayden bill might fail. Here the Commissioner, in his desire to obtain the settlement of the executive-order reservation problem, went too far in his concessions to the Western representatives, particularly Hayden. There is no doubt that he was perfectly sincere in his determination to spend the Navajo royalties in the way he had indicated to the Tribal Council earlier, and that if need be he would fight to repeal the reimbursable debts heaped upon the Navajos.[59] The fact remains, however, that only a politician with long years of experience in such dealings could hold such contradictory ideas at the same time. A principle was involved which Burke could not understand. The Commissioner had gone too far and when his bluff was called, rather than admit his mistake, he took refuge in an attack on Collier and Frear that did him and his office little credit. Burke's major problem was that his long years of service in the House of Representatives had ill-prepared him for the type of executive leadership called for by his office.

SIGNIFICANCE OF THE SOLUTION

The Indian Oil Act of 1927 was a great victory for those Indians who possessed executive-order reservations. Although the question of title was not explicitly solved, it had been aired, and the debates revealed that it was the intent of Congress to equate the treaty and the executive-order reservations as nearly as possible without making a formal declaration to that effect. As if to make this clear there was a clause in the act which provided that there were to be no further changes in the boundaries of Indian reservations except by act of Congress. In addition to this major victory, it was also stated that in the future the Indians, through their tribal councils, were to be consulted

---

[59]Throughout this controversy Collier and Frear charged that Burke's every action was predicated on a desire to obtain complete and dictatorial control over the Indians. There is no documentary evidence to support this bias. There is evidence to support Burke's view that the practical consequences of saddling the Navajos with one-half the cost of the bridge would not be very serious. In a letter to Hagerman, Burke explained that the Bureau's original recommendation on the bridge had been for it to be gratuitous. This had been amended in the House to make it reimbursable. He concluded by saying that "in other words, the policy of Congress is so firmly established that it is not believed, in my opinion, that it can be reversed at this time." Burke to Hagerman, April 6, 1926. Navajo, 96947-23-322. Burke's contention was borne out by the fact that the Navajos were never charged with the cost of the bridge except for $1,715.92 for survey costs.

with regard to the expenditures of their tribal funds. Even the Lee's Ferry bridge was avenged by this act.[60]

The Indian Oil Act of 1927 was the most important single piece of general Indian legislation in the 1920's. The period is not noted for legislation that evidenced a definite philosophy or policy, but it is obvious that here was the determination of a major principle in the field of Indian law. In view of this, it is ironic that the phenomenon that touched off the fireworks, the discovery of oil on the Navajo reservation, began to die out as an important factor in Navajo history about the time that the bill was passed. Despite the victory, no oil was discovered on the executive-order portion of the reservation in this period, and during the administration of Herbert Hoover, it became a policy in the interest of conservation to discontinue the leasing of Indian reservations.

DECLINE OF OIL

At the third Navajo Tribal Council meeting in 1925, Hagerman secured from the assembled delegates unanimous approval to a second sale of leases. In early 1926 he notified Commissioner Burke that preliminary arrangements for the sale had been made; his expectations were that from $100,000 to $150,000 would be realized from bonuses.[61] The auction was held at Santa Fe on June 23, 1926.

Four exploratory leases were sold at this second auction along with eight smaller leases adjacent to the proven Rattlesnake and Hogback structures. The proven tracts brought $36,000 and the exploratory tracts $25,700, considerably less than Hagerman's estimate.[62] The over-

---

[60]The provision for consultation with the tribal council, at least in regard to the Navajos, was largely ignored. The provision that the boundaries of the executive-order reservations were not to be changed, except by act of Congress, was an interesting application, in reverse, of the law of 1919 which forbade the executive to enlarge the boundaries.

[61]Hagerman to Burke, January 12, 1926. Hagerman Papers, Commissioner's file, January-December, 1926. Hagerman was particularly interested in the success of this sale because he believed that if enough interest were aroused, the Santa Fe Railroad might decide to build a railroad or pipeline into the area, thus opening the reservation to other forms of growth.

[62]Hagerman to A. F. Duclos, June 24, 1926. *Ibid.*, Navajo Indian Agency file. Also U. S. House, *Hearings on H. R. 15021*, 69th Cong., 2d sess., p. 75. The four exploratory tracts and the bonuses bid on each were as follows: Chimney Rock, $16,500; Biltabito, $5,100; Royal Arch, $3,100; Little Shiprock, $1,000. Only the Chimney Rock produced oil. There is a letter in the Hagerman Papers (San Juan file, January 30, 1929) which discusses a proposed third sale on the Chimney Rock structure, but I have been unable to determine if such a sale was ever held.

production which had been chronic since shortly before the first sale in 1923 was growing increasingly worse. Although there were twenty-nine producing wells on the Navajo reservation in 1927, and gross production in that year doubled from that of 1926 to 860,208 barrels,[63] the market price of oil dropped disastrously in March, 1927, and many of the companies operating on the reservation curtailed production.[64]

In June, 1927, Assistant Commissioner Meritt advised Hagerman that in view of the latter's reports "noting a decline in oil production and the poor prospect for future development," the Bureau was considering leaving the Indian deposits in their natural reservoirs until the situation improved.[65] The following month, Burke confirmed Meritt's opinion, saying that for the present no more lands would be offered for lease.[66] In November, Hagerman was advised by Burke that in view of the decision to discontinue leasing on Indian reservations, his services as Commissioner to the Navajos were no longer needed, and on December 1, 1927, Hagerman was relieved of his Navajo responsibilities and directed to devote his entire time to the Pueblo Lands Board, of which he had been a member since 1924.[67]

The wisdom of the decision to curtail leasing on the Navajo Reservation was confirmed in the years that followed. In late 1927 the lease to the Tocito Dome structure, for which the Gypsy Oil Company had paid $36,000 in 1923, was cancelled by the Department of the Interior at the company's request.[68] In October, 1928, it was reported to Assistant Commissioner Meritt that of the 154 prospecting permits issued under the relief clause of the Indian Oil Act of 1927, none had resulted in the discovery of oil.[69] Shortly after President

---

[63]Secretary of the Interior, *Annual Report, 1927*, p. 58.

[64]*Minutes of the Navajo Tribal Council Meeting, Leupp, Arizona, November 12-13, 1928*. General Services, 20204-30-054.

[65]E. B. Meritt to Hagerman, June 16, 1927. Hagerman Papers, Commissioner's file, January-December, 1927.

[66]Burke to Hagerman, July 20, 1927. *Ibid.* In August, Hagerman and Burke exchanged letters on the advisability of a sale on the Leupp reservation; the consensus was again negative. Leupp, 23637-27-322.

[67]Burke to Hagerman, November 26, 1927, and Hagerman to Burke, October 11, 1924. Hagerman Papers, Commissioner's file, January-December, 1927, and July-December, 1924.

[68]Hagerman to Gypsy Oil Company, January 3, 1928. Navajo, 86096-23-322. The Gypsy Company had drilled two wells, both of which produced excellent artesian water for the Navajos.

[69]Memorandum for E. B. Meritt, October 16, 1928. General Services, 20204-30-054.

Hoover took office in 1929, prospecting permits on the public domain and Indian lands were suspended. When subsequent analysis of the records showed that 40 percent of the remaining permittees had not complied with the laws, their permits were revoked. By 1932 there were only 20,000 acres of the Navajo reservation still open to prospectors.[70]

Part of the reason for the decline in the Navajo field was the discovery of new fields elsewhere in New Mexico. In 1928 oil was discovered in the Stony Butte field, just to the east of the Navajo boundary, and also farther south near Hobbs, New Mexico. The interest of the major companies shifted to these new fields and after 1929 there was almost complete inactivity in the Navajo country. A deep test on the Rattlesnake lease struck low-grade oil in 1929 but, because the well was not properly constructed, a great quantity of water mixed with the oil. The presence of water at this depth plus the interest in the "more prolific" Hobbs field "completely eclipsed" the importance of this Rattlesnake deep test well. There was little drilling and no discovery in the Navajo area between 1929 and 1934.[71]

By 1935 there were thirty-three producing wells on the reservation. The Depression and a partial failure on the Rattlesnake cut the annual oil revenue from $119,425 in 1930 to $52,401 in 1931.[72] In all, the royalties received from oil from the beginning through 1937 were only $1,227,705.19.[73] The importance of oil in Navajo history was declining.

The discovery of oil on the Navajo reservation was not a great economic factor in the history of the Navajos in these early years of

---

[70]Ray Lyman Wilbur and Arthur M. Hyde, *The Hoover Policies* (New York: Charles Scribner's Sons, 1937), pp. 236-37. For the cancellation of the Navajo prospecting permits, see Commissioner of Indian Affairs, *Annual Report, 1932*, p. 24, and Northern Navajo, 331 file, 1929. The 154 prospecting permits issued in accordance with the Indian Oil Act of 1927 had covered 300,000 acres. See footnote No. 66 above.

[71]This paragraph is a paraphrase of information contained in Ira Rinehart, *Reference Book on the Four Corners Area* (Dallas: Rinehart Oil News Co., 1955), pp. 37-38.

[72]Hagerman to Rhoads, June 14, 1932. National Archives, Record Group 75, Special Agents file, Hagerman, #300. Also Secretary of the Interior, *Annual Report, 1934*, p. 98. The only leases that produced oil in this period were the Rattlesnake, 1,000 barrels a day in 1931; Hogback, 500 barrels; and the Table Mesa, 200 barrels. Herbert J. Hagerman, *Indians of the Southwest* (n. p.: 1931), Hagerman Papers.

[73]William Zimmerman, Assistant Commissioner of Indian Affairs, to Senator Elmer Thomas, May 28, 1937. Navajo, 15529-37-322.

the twentieth century. The total revenues divided equally among the 42,000 Navajos registered in the 1930 census would not have exceeded $30 for each man, woman, and child. Oil was, however, extremely important in another phase of Navajo life. The oil royalties made possible the pursuit of the age-old Navajo goal of land acquisition. Unlike other Indian tribes suddenly blessed with an unearned income, the Navajos refused to divide their oil royalties on a per-capita basis. Instead, they decided to use the money to purchase land in areas heretofore denied them. Although the meager royalties would not go far, the Navajo decision to purchase land from their own funds so impressed the federal government that when the funds ran out, other means were found to enlarge the reservation.

CHAPTER 6

Range Management

The last enlargement of any size to the Navajo reservation was made in 1908. In 1911 approximately half of this grant, all of it in New Mexico, was withdrawn from Navajo ownership. However, the Navajos continued to increase. In 1900 their numbers were estimated at 22,000; in 1920 at 30,500; the first census in 1930 showed 42,000.[1] Their flocks grew also, but since the land did not, it was only a matter of time until it could support no more. By 1933 the situation, having grown steadily worse during the 1920's, was acute. There were several solutions but all were based on the immediate necessity of reducing the herds.

THE PROBLEM

Just when the Navajo reservation began to be overgrazed is difficult to establish. One prominent authority has set the date as far back as the 1880's.[2] Field reports of the Indian Bureau indicate, however, that overgrazing did not become apparent until about 1910.[3] After this date the reports increase in volume and urgency as the effects of overgrazing multiplied.[4]

---

[1]Underhill, *Here Come the Navaho!*, p. 223. William H. Zeh to Lee Muck, January 31, 1931. Western Navajo, 67654-30-301.

[2]Kluckhohn, *The Navaho*, p. 33.

[3]See Leupp Reservation, "Annual Narrative Report, 1910," and report of inspector S.A.M. Young to Commissioner of Indian Affairs, May 30, 1916. Navajo, unnumbered report in 150 series.

[4]In 1921, General H. L. Scott was sent to the Navajo reservation to make a report on the extent of overgrazing. He stated that H. F. Robinson, the supervising engineer for the Indian Service, had written him as follows: "I would submit that fifteen years ago many of the washes in the Navajo country carried only a little water at any time ... the rainfall of this country has not increased but because of over-grazing and the denuding of the land of grasses and shrubbery which retarded the run-off, the water which now falls on the land rapidly runs to the natural water courses making intense floods of short duration. The rapidly moving waters are cutting gullies and washes over large areas ...." Board of Indian Commissioners, *Special Reports*, Vol. 4, p. 60.

In 1919 the Commissioner of Indian Affairs referred to the Navajo land situation as a "peculiar problem." There were, scattered throughout the reservation, large areas of forage which were not being utilized because of their great distance from water. Congress in 1916 had made the first of continuing appropriations for the development of water in these locations. A stepped-up program by the Burke administration[5] resulted in the development of 202 springs and the successful completion of 131 deep wells equipped with pump, windmill, and storage tanks by July, 1928.[6] The following year twelve separate field parties combed the reservation and developed sixty-seven springs, constructed twenty-one reservoirs, and drilled thirty-five deep wells.[7] Despite this beneficial program, however, the Navajo herds were growing faster than the acreage reclaimed for their use. In 1929 several of the agency superintendents reported that their jurisdictions had reached the limits of sheep capacity.[8] By 1933 Secretary of the Interior Harold Ickes was warning that unless the soil erosion caused by overgrazing was soon checked, it would silt out the Hoover Dam reservoir within the next ten years.[9] To prevent overgrazing and to protect the government's huge investment in the dam, he recommended additional land for the Navajos. But a solution satisfactory to all the parties concerned would not be easily reached. The Navajos and the federal government called for more land, the local white elements and their representatives called

---

[5]By 1928 some $426,000 had been appropriated, reimbursable, for the development of water supplies on the Navajo and Hopi reservations. My source does not distinguish between funds for Navajos and those for Hopis. *Senate Survey*, part 6, pp. 2689-90. This work of the Bureau was highly praised in the Meriam Report of 1928. Lewis Meriam (ed.), *The Problems of Indian Administration* (Baltimore: Johns Hopkins University Press, 1928), p. 514. Hereafter cited as *Meriam Report*.

[6]Thanks primarily to the efforts of ex-superintendent Estep at San Juan, the oil companies agreed that if they struck water rather than oil, they would turn over the well to the Navajos for the cost of the casing. In the San Juan jurisdiction there were several excellent artesian wells acquired in this manner. Hagerman to Gypsy Oil Co., January 3, 1927. Navajo, 86096-23-322.

[7]U. S. House, Committee on Appropriations, *Hearings on Department of the Interior Appropriation Bill, Fiscal 1930*, 70th Cong., 2d sess., 1928, p. 826. Also *ibid., Fiscal 1931*, 71st Cong., 2d sess., 1929, p. 676. In 1929, under the Rhoads administration, the reimbursable features of this water development program were abandoned, and gratuitous appropriations substituted.

[8]Western Navajo Reservation, "Annual Narrative Report, 1929," section IV, p. 5; Northern Navajo Reservation, "Annual Narrative Report, 1929," p. 13.

[9]U.S. House, Committee on Indian Affairs, *Boundaries of Navajo Reservation in Arizona*, 73d Cong., 2d sess., 1934, Rept. 1602. See also the introduction by Assistant Commissioner of Indian Affairs William Zimmerman, to the book by George Isidore Sanchez, *The People* (Lawrence, Kan.: Haskell Institute Press, 1948), p. 9.

for better range management and a shift of emphasis in the Navajo economy.[10] All of these measures and more were necessary to solve the Navajo problem.

SCABIES ERADICATION

During the 1920's several methods were tried to reduce the flocks on a voluntary basis. The most prominent were the attempt to eradicate sheep scabies which, it was claimed, cost an infected animal the loss of five pounds of its wool annually; the elimination of the many thousands of Indian ponies that roamed the reservation, eating the grasses that could more profitably be used for sheep; and the program to up-breed the Navajo sheep through the use of blooded breeding animals, thus making it possible to produce more wool and meat with fewer animals.

The scabies eradication program was introduced as early as 1907, according to Ruth Underhill. It did not, however, meet with any degree of success until after 1924.[11] A white stockman who lived near the reservation told General Hugh Scott in 1921 that "all efforts to get the Indian stock dipped have proven absolutely futile." The Navajos did not trust the "medicine," so when the government agents came to treat their stock they retreated into the mountains and canyons much as they had done in the 1860's when Kit Carson was passing through.[12]

The Navajo distrust of the dipping process was humorously illustrated at the 1923 Tribal Council meeting. One of the delegates, in complete sincerity, told Commissioner Hagerman that after having observed the white inspectors at a dipping vat for some time one day, he noted that they never changed the solution. Concluding that they were improperly performing their job and, as a result were actually infecting the herds, he opened the gate to the dipping trough when the inspectors' attention was focused elsewhere, turning out all the "medicine."[13] It would be some time before the average Navajo was willing to accept the benefits of the dipping process.

In addition to Navajo distrust, factional jealousy between the

---

[10]For a discussion of the various solutions proposed, see *Senate Survey*, part 18, p. 9021 ff., and part 22, p. 12275 ff.

[11]*Hagerman Report*, p. 54.

[12]Board of Indian Commissioners, *Special Reports*, Vol. 4, p. 56.

[13]*Minutes of the Navajo Tribal Council Meeting, Toadlena, New Mexico, July 7, 1923*, pp. 20-21. San Juan, 91993-23-054.

local superintendents and the agents of the Bureau of Animal Husbandry, Department of Agriculture, also worked against the success of the scabies eradication program. It was not until Hagerman was appointed to oversee all the jurisdictions that this latter problem was resolved.[14]

Although a more intensive campaign for the eradication of scabies was inaugurated by the Bureau in 1924, it was not until 1929 that the work approached terminal proportions. In that year the Bureau went before the Congress requesting increased appropriations to wipe out the disease. The argument was presented as one to protect white stockmen as much as to help the Navajos. The Indian Bureau had a representative of the Department of Agriculture testify that 50 percent of the total scabies infection in the United States was located in New Mexico and Arizona, and of this amount, fully 80 percent was on the Indian reservations in Arizona.[15] The Indian flocks were infecting those of the white stockmen, especially in the checkerboard areas where the animals tended to mix on the common pasture and at the waterholes. Congress voted the Navajos $60,000 as the first installment on a multi-year program.[16] According to the terms of this grant, the Bureau of Indian Affairs would use the money to build the dipping vats and to pay the salaries of the supervisors from the Bureau of Animal Husbandry; the Navajos would pay a dipping fee for each sheep to cover the cost of the dipping solution.

Armed with the increased appropriations, Doctor F. L. Schneider of the Bureau of Animal Husbandry went before the Tribal Council in 1930 with a program of enticement and mild coercion. Until the present, he told the delegates, he had always been hampered in his efforts to wipe out scabies by unstable and inadequate monetary backing. There was no reason now, however, with Navajo cooperation, why he could not eradicate the disease completely within a few years. Every sheep which had scabies, he told them, possessed on the average only half the wool that a noninfected sheep did. Further, some of the surrounding states had enacted quarantine laws against scabious sheep. Some of the Navajos had already learned the hard way that under these laws the sheep had to be dipped before they

---

[14]*Hagerman Report*, p. 54.

[15]U. S. House, *Hearings on Department of the Interior Appropriation Bill, Fiscal 1931*, 71st Cong., 2d sess., 1929, pp. 260-61.

[16]*Minutes of the Navajo Tribal Council Meeting, Ft. Wingate, New Mexico, July 7-8, 1930*. General Services, 24619-30-054.

would be purchased. In one way or another the Navajos would pay for their diseased sheep; if they cooperated with his men the disease could be wiped out quickly.[17]

Eighteen months after the stepped-up scabies program was inaugurated, Hagerman reported to his superiors that inspections showed the disease had been eradicated on the Western Navajo, Leupp, Hopi, and Eastern Navajo jurisdictions. Some recurrence had been noted on the Northern and Southern Navajo reservations. Indian cooperation had been generally "highly satisfactory and effective." A year or two more, he felt, and success would be theirs. There was one complication; the Navajos, while not yet in grave need as a result of the Depression, were almost devoid of cash and would experience great difficulty in paying for the cost of dipping the following year. To rescue the scabies program, he recommended that the Indians be allowed to dip free of charge for one year. Burke's successor, Charles J. Rhoads, however, feared to set a precedent of this kind. In the end the Tribal Council and the Bureau worked out a compromise whereby the Navajos would pay in sheep for the cost of dipping; the meat thus obtained would be used to feed Indian children in the schools.[18] The wisdom of this arrangement was vindicated in 1934 when, with the exception of three bands of sheep in the Southern Navajo jurisdiction, no scabies had been reported or discovered for two years. The disease was apparently eradicated; no more funds were requested.[19] If the Department of Agriculture figures were correct, the Navajos could now reduce their flocks and still produce the same amount of wool. The problem of actual reduction, however, remained.

HORSE REDUCTION

A second proposal for obtaining more grazing land was to eliminate thousands of horses that roamed the reservation. Compared to a sheep, the horse was an expensive animal in an environment where grass was sparse and water limited. The experts estimated that the horse consumed ten gallons of water daily as compared with one gallon for a sheep, and four to five times as much grass. It was obvious from these figures that if there were, as reported, 100,000 horses on

----

[17]*Ibid.*

[18]Memorandum of Dr. F. L. Schneider, July 3, 1931, in Hagerman's report on sheep dipping. General Services, 35878-31-054.

[19]U. S. House, Committee on Appropriations, *Hearings on Department of the Interior Appropriation Bill, Fiscal 1935,* 73d Cong., 2d sess., 1933, p. 48.

the reservation, and these were to be done away with, forage for 500,000 sheep would become available on the same range.[20] From a social viewpoint, however, the horse was a status symbol among the Navajos. It would take some time to change their thinking on this topic.

Sometime around 1918, dourine, a contagious disease of horses characterized by skin depigmentation, paralysis, and death, got a start and spread rapidly over the reservation. Since the disease was transferred only by copulation, the simplest method of controlling it was to slaughter or castrate the infected stallions. This was done for several years, apparently with some zest.[21] The disease was then brought under control, although not eradicated, and the Navajos ceased to kill their own animals. During the period that the dourine campaign was underway, the Bureau of Animal Husbandry enlisted Navajo cooperation by making payment for each animal that was shot. Once the disease was brought under control and the payments curtailed, the Navajos lost interest in ridding themselves of the remaining horses. The precedent set during the dourine campaign boded ill for any future horse-reduction campaign which did not reimburse the owner for his loss.

Through Hagerman, the Navajos learned of a good reason for paring down their horse herds. In 1924 Commissioner Burke instructed Hagerman to inform the Navajos in strong terms that their chances for obtaining additional land were being greatly imperiled by the obvious existence of the worthless ponies.[22] Tell them, Burke said, that until they make an effort to remove this argument from the opposition's arsenal, "we are not in a good position to make much of a fight for more land."[23] Here was an argument that a Navajo could understand.

Hagerman's presentation of this argument had the desired effect. There was opposition, of course, but the more progressive and intelligent Navajos were beginning to realize that the pony was a "nuisance and a handicap to range development." "If a way could be found to

---

[20]*Senate Survey*, part 18, p. 9128.

[21]See testimony of Superintendent Peter Paquette in U. S. House, *Hearings, Indians of the United States*, 66th Cong., 1-3d sess., Vol. 3, p. 727, and testimony of Dr. Schneider before the Navajo Tribal Council in 1928, in General Services, 20204-30-054.

[22]Throughout the 1920's attempts were made to obtain more land for the Navajos. This is the subject of the succeeding chapter.

[23]Burke to Hagerman, January 28, 1924. Navajo, 40509-23-054.

market the animals," one superintendent stated, he was sure that all surplus ponies could be gotten rid of.[24] The change in Navajo thinking was dramatically signified in 1926 when, after a strong lecture by Hagerman on the evils of the surplus horses, the Tribal Council adopted a resolution pledging the Navajos to a program of eradication, and the council members to a conversion campaign among the older Navajos who opposed the program. The effect of the dourine campaign was evidenced, however, when the delegates insisted that the surplus animals be paid for.[25] Hagerman set out to find a market.

This proved to be a more difficult task than he had anticipated. At the 1927 council meeting he told the delegates that he had several contracts lined up in the past year with chicken-feed manufacturers in Oregon and California, only to find that freight rates were so high in each case that little in the way of profit would be left to the Navajos. To tide him over, Congress appropriated $30,000 to complete the dourine program. The following year a contract was signed with a firm in California. Great strides were made under the dourine appropriation and large inroads were made into the surplus horse population on the Western Navajo, Leupp, and Eastern Navajo reservations. In 1929 Schneider wrote that dourine "has been finally and completely eradicated on the reservation."[26] He suggested a move now on the remaining surplus horses.

At this point, the superintendents balked. In the first place they disagreed with the Bureau of Animal Husbandry on the number of worthless horses remaining. At a meeting with Hagerman in February, 1931, the superintendents claimed that as a result of sale to the milling company, outright slaughter, and deaths caused by drought, the total number of horses remaining on the reservation was only 34,000. All of them agreed that the reduction program could be carried too far; each Navajo family needed from four to five horses for travel. This was not a luxury but a necessity where people often lived

---

[24]See "Annual Narrative Report, 1926," from San Juan, p. 30; Pueblo Bonito, p. 6; Western Navajo, p. 19.

[25]*Minutes of the Navajo Tribal Council Meeting, Ft. Defiance, Arizona, July 7-8, 1926.* General Services, 34976-26-054.

[26]Schneider to Hagerman, September 9, 1929. General Services, 36351-29-054. It is worth noting that the success of the horse-reduction program was proportionate to the need for additional land. The Eastern Navajo campaign was the most effective; Leupp and Western Navajo followed closely behind. See Stacher to Hagerman, September 21, 1929. Hagerman Papers, Pueblo Bonito file, 1922-1928. Also Walker to Commissioner of Indian Affairs, August 27, 1929. Western Navajo, 40373-29-150.

at great distances from water and the trader's store.[27] Here the horse reduction program came to a halt.

SCIENTIFIC SHEEP BREEDING

Since 1900 the federal government had been experimenting with various types of breeding rams to improve the quality of the Navajo wool. An experiment with 500 Merino bucks in 1904-1905 produced a runty sheep with very greasy wool which the Navajos found completely unsatisfactory for weaving.[28] Lincolns and Rambouillets were also bred but, despite the government's good intentions, two problems always plagued the agents in charge of the breeding program.

For one, the Navajos before 1920 were opposed, in the main, to innovations in their traditional methods of raising sheep. An interesting comment on this attitude was provided in 1915:

> . . . the chief difficulty which the [government] farmers encounter is to compel them to dispose of their unprofitable stock and keep the younger and stronger stock for breeding purposes. A Navajo Indian is so constituted that he very much prefers to keep an old wether, or an old ewe, or an old steer, or old cow, if they are large and "fine looking" and sell his younger stock; and what a Navajo "much prefers" he generally does regardless of the advice of the farmer.[29]

In addition to this tendency there was little interest among the Navajos in scientific breeding. Rams and ewes were run together; lambing occurred throughout the year, and the harsh Navajo winters took a heavy annual toll of the fall lamb crop; as a result the Navajo sheep were often small and scraggly. These people who showed such wisdom toward the effects of inbreeding among themselves seemingly could not appreciate its effect on their animals.

For a second reason, between 1900 and 1920 the government advo-

---

[27]The transcript of this conference is printed in *Senate Survey*, part 18, p. 9277. There is, I believe, little doubt but that the Bureau of Animal Husbandry figures were closer to reality. Its records were based on the dourine campaign while the superintendent's figures were little better than guesses. Schneider claimed that there were approximately 80,000 horses remaining or ten for each family. The superintendent's figures would indicate that between 40,000 and 50,000 horses had been killed during the 1920's. While the sources are scanty here, it does seem that such a great slaughter would have appeared somewhere in the papers.

[28]H. F. Coggeshall to Commissioner of Indian Affairs, May 28, 1917. San Juan, 7272-17-150.

[29]Report of O. M. McPherson to Commissioner of Indian Affairs, November 15, 1915. San Juan, 125171-17-150.

cated a policy of tribal herds for breeding purposes. During the period of this experiment, blooded rams were purchased for loan to Navajos. The cost of the breeding animals was reimbursable; the method of payment was in kind. For every ram that an individual Navajo borrowed in the fall, he was expected to return it in the spring with two lambs. The usual result of this plan, good in itself, was too often that reported by the new superintendent at San Juan in 1920. In 1917 his predecessor had purchased 275 high-grade Lincoln rams at a total cost of $6,500. In 1920 the new superintendent found that $4,200 was still outstanding and the tribal herd itself in poor condition. It was, he said, "a very unfortunate purchase."[30]

By 1923 when Hagerman arrived on the scene, the attitude of the Navajos toward scientific breeding was changing. The Navajos, he reported, "are rapidly awakening to the vital necessity of this feature of the situation and are no longer in any way antagonistic . . . to what they may have regarded as an innovation."[31] Thus by 1923-1924, both dipping and scientific breeding, practices long resented by the Navajos, were beginning to take hold.

AN OVERGRAZED RANGE

At the 1928 Tribal Council the first positive means of controlling the size of Navajo flocks was pressed by the government. Excess grazing fees had become standard practice on other Indian reservations, the delegates were told. In most areas the tax was imposed on herds which contained over 500 sheep belonging to a single individual. For the Navajos it was proposed to levy a tax of fifteen cents per head on herds of over 1,000 sheep, the money thus obtained to be used to develop water sources on the reservation and to assist young Navajos returning from school to get a start.

Most of the delegates seemed to think that such a law was foolish —no Navajo owned that many sheep. Chee Dodge, one of the largest owners, conceded that the government's program was both necessary and fair. However, his people were not ready to adopt such a program on short notice. He suggested that the delegates postpone the matter until they had talked it over with the people. His counsel was not heeded; the government representative forced a vote, and the measure

---

[30]See report of S.A.M. Young to Commissioner of Indian Affairs, November 7, 1916, and letter of Evan Estep to Commissioner of Indian Affairs, September 30, 1920. San Juan, 82991-20-150.

[31]Hagerman to Burke, no day, 1923. Hagerman Papers, Commissioner's file, 1923-26.

was adopted by a close vote of seven to five.[32] The desired reduction was never effected, however, for the reason that the Navajos had given: no one owned that many sheep. Superintendent Hunter in 1930 explained it this way:

> . . . they are able to show without exception that no single individual owns more than a thousand head because they belong to the son and the daughter and the wife and the son-in-law and daughter-in-law, and sometimes to wives number two and number three, and so, when it is all sifted down, there is nothing to collect.[33]

By 1929 then, despite much talk and despite the success of plans which theoretically would make reduction possible, no reduction had taken place. Moreover, the generally low prices for range products which had set in after World War I had never been relieved. As a result, each year the number of sheep grazed increased because the Navajos were always waiting for a better year to sell.[34] Furthermore, while stock prices generally dwindled during the 1920's, the price for goats had fallen even more steadily than for sheep. The goat market was simply disappearing. The Navajos, most of whom had some goats with their sheep, saved the goats and sold the sheep when they needed cash. The goats bred more rapidly and were harder on the range than sheep. As if this were not bad enough for the already overgrazed condition of the range, it was established by 1931 that the automobile industry, which had been the largest purchaser of mohair, had definitely turned to other materials for upholstery. There was no longer a market for the goats or for their fleece.[35] And all the time their numbers increased.

By 1931 the Depression began to make itself felt in the Navajo country. The price of wool fell from twenty-five cents a pound to seventeen cents. Lambs which the year before had brought forty-four

---

[32]To my knowledge this is the first instance of a program adopted by the council with less than a unanimous vote. Hagerman, who had presided over all the earlier meetings, was not present because he had been relieved of his Navajo duties. Assistant Commissioner Meritt forced the vote. See General Services, 51135-28-054.

[33]*Minutes of the Navajo Tribal Council Meeting, Ft. Wingate, New Mexico, July 7-8, 1930.* General Services, 24619-30-054.

[34]Frank B. Lenzie, Range Supervisor, to Commissioner of Indian Affairs, August 27, 1932. Southern Navajo, 42451-32-301.

[35]See *Working Plan Report of the Grazing Activities of the Northern Navajo Indian Reservation, December 10, 1930,* in Northern Navajo, 65712-30-301.

cents a pound were going at five cents. Again many Navajos did not sell. The understatement of the year was made by the Northern Navajo superintendent: "This is a rather serious situation in view of the already over-grazed condition of the reservation."[36]

TABLE I

EXTENT OF OVERGRAZING ON THE NAVAJO RESERVATION, 1931

Reservation	Total Animal Units[1]	Surplus Animal Units
Southern Navajo	114,764	73,271
Northern Navajo	61,000	32,702
Eastern Navajo[2]	6,000	2,363
Western Navajo	41,544	2,744
Leupp	10,088	2,619

[1]An animal unit is the equivalent of one horse or one cow; five goats or five sheep equal one animal unit.

[2]The figures given here for the Eastern Navajo Reservation include only those animals on the reservation proper. This reservation, including the checkerboard outside the reservation, carried 47,280 animal units in 1931. See *Senate Survey*, part 18, pp. 9111-18. I have checked the figures of the Muck report against those given by the individual superintendents to the Senate Survey committee in 1931 and find that, with a slight difference in the case of Leupp (more units by some 3,000 than Muck indicates) and in the case of Eastern Navajo, the figures are similar.

Source: Muck, *An Economic Survey of the Range Resources and Grazing Activities on Indian Reservations, Senate Survey*, part 22, p. 12304.

An investigation by the Department of the Interior in 1931 gave an appalling picture of the Navajo plight. Each jurisdiction had more animals than it could conceivably support. The conditions ranged from only slightly overgrazed on the Western Navajo reservation to 50 percent above the carrying capacity in the Northern Navajo reservation and even worse in the Southern Navajo jurisdiction (Table I). There was no chance for "real improvement of the seriously overgrazed land" other than "a material reduction in the number of animals being accommodated."[37] The problem was that many Navajos could not live with fewer animals: the distribution was uneven and there were many poor Navajos. They and the Bureau of Indian Affairs clamored more vociferously than ever for more land to relieve the situation.

[36]Northern Navajo, "Annual Narrative Report, 1931," section 2, p. 2.

[37]Lee Muck, *An Economic Survey of the Range Resources and Grazing Activities on Indian Reservations*, July 15, 1931, printed in *Senate Survey*, part 22, p. 12300.

CHAPTER 7

Reservation Expansion

The decision to refuse the Navajos more land from the public domain in 1918 did not affect their desire or their need for more land. Until the discovery of oil, however, there was very little that could be done for them. A renewed effort to obtain more land was inaugurated with the appointment of Herbert J. Hagerman as Special Commissioner to the Navajos in 1923. For two years Hagerman labored to find a way to satisfy the Navajo needs; with the failure of his plan in 1925, he began to champion a program whereby the Navajos would be allowed to purchase lands with their oil royalties.

THE HAGERMAN PLAN

Hagerman had been Special Commissioner for less than a year when he advised Commissioner Burke that it was "a matter of great importance" that the Navajos be given more land.[1] When plans were being made in Washington for the first oil-lease sale, Hagerman talked to both Burke and Work personally about the problem. As a result he was authorized "carte blanche, to go ahead . . . and do the best I could with it."[2] As he saw it, the major need for land was to the south and east of the reservation boundary in New Mexico and north and east of the Leupp reservation in Arizona.

On October 16, 1923, the day following the oil-lease auction, Hagerman held a meeting in Santa Fe of those parties who would be involved in an expansion of the Navajo reservation in New Mexico. The meeting was held against the background of the act of 1921 which had permitted reconveyance and relinquishment of private lands in the three New Mexico counties of McKinley, San Juan, and Valencia.

---

[1] Hagerman to Burke, July 26, 1923. Hagerman Papers, Commissioner's file, June-December, 1923.

[2] Hagerman to Stacher, September 6, 1923. *Ibid.*, Pueblo Bonito file, 1922-28.

No transfers had occurred under this law, primarily because no provision had been made for payments for improvements on the land being relinquished. Superintendent Stacher of the Pueblo Bonito agency, who attended the meeting, reported later that there had been agreement among all the parties represented and that the assembled representatives had worked out a plan whereby, for $200,000 for improvements, some 900,000 acres of land between Crownpoint, New Mexico, and the Jicarilla Apache reservation to the north could be obtained.[3]

The ease with which this agreement was reached, when there had been such bitter opposition previously, was occasioned by the fact that the cattlemen in the area were having a difficult time making ends meet. They had failed to make a go of it, Hagerman reported, and "they now all admit that they have failed." Local interests, realizing that if the cattlemen were experiencing financial problems their ability to pay taxes was thereby imperiled, favored consolidation.[4] It seemed for once that what was good for the Navajos was also going to be good for the other New Mexicans.

On Hagerman's recommendation, Secretary Work on January 19, 1924, forwarded to both the Senate and the House Committees on Public Lands a bill embodying the terms of the October 16 conference. In his letter, Work explained that agreement had been previously reached between Hagerman and the interested parties. The bill called for an expansion of the reservation in New Mexico by 1,084,510.91 acres.[5]

It never got out of committee. James F. Hinkle, Governor of New Mexico, Senator Jones, and Congressman Morrow all opposed it. The major opposition seems to have come from Hinkle, the New Mexico Congressmen simply representing his case in the Congress. Hagerman was reprimanded by Burke for thus embarrassing the Department when he had been advised from the beginning that it was useless to attempt such legislation unless all the factions in New Mexico favored it.[6]

---

[3]Stacher to Burke, November 8, 1926. *Ibid.* Also U. S. Senate, *Hearings on S. 1722 and S. 3159*, 69th Cong., 1st sess., p. 102.

[4]Hagerman to Congressman John Morrow, March 29, 1924. Navajo, 15987-24-013.

[5]Work to Senator Irvin L. Lenroot and Congressman N. Sinnot, January 19, 1924. Pueblo Bonito, 74907-23-308.3. Of this proposed expansion, 161,920 acres had previously been allotted to Navajos.

[6]Burke to Hagerman, March 22, 1924. *Ibid.*

The opposition had come as a surprise to Hagerman who believed that since the cattlemen were receptive to the bill,[7] all was well. He had overlooked, however, the fact that the sheepmen of New Mexico were anxious to try their luck in the area where the cattlemen had failed. The Wool Growers Association of New Mexico made a decided stand against the bill and was a major factor in its failure to receive a hearing.[8] Hagerman had several conversations with Hinkle who was reluctant to state his position.[9] When he did, it was to the effect that the Indians had no rights in the area in the first place.

Once the bill was defeated, Hagerman learned the real reason for Hinkle's opposition. Some of the lands included in the proposed consolidation were school lands. With the recent discovery of oil on the adjacent Navajo reservation, Hinkle feared exchanges might jeopardize possible oil royalties for the state.[10] The New Mexico opposition stemming from the 1908 withdrawal was still too powerful for the Bureau of Indian Affairs. The next attempt at expansion would be in the area to the east of the Leupp reservation in Arizona.

INEFFECTUAL LEGISLATION

In 1913, the Santa Fe Pacific Railroad Company deeded to the federal government some 327,000 acres of its holdings in the checkerboard within the Leupp and Western Navajo jurisdictions. Although the Department of the Interior refused to accept these lands in exchange for others, the deed of transfer had been recorded and the Navajos continued to use the company's lands. In 1924 the Santa Fe once again began to press for a settlement of this claim.

Within the Department there was a clash of interests over the manner in which this problem should be resolved. Both Hagerman

---

[7]The New Mexico Cattle Growers' Association had adopted a formal resolution calling for the adoption of Hagerman's bill. Bertha Benson to Burke, March 28, 1924. *Ibid.*

[8]Stacher to Burke, November 8, 1924. Hagerman Papers, Pueblo Bonito file, 1922-28.

[9]Hagerman to Stacher, April 8, 1924. *Ibid.* Hagerman's statement of Hinkle's position is as follows: "I talk frequently to Hinkle about it and he is entirely on the other side. It is hard to pin him down but when I do, his point of view is that by rights the Indians all over that area should be bought out or thrown out and put back on the present reservation."

[10]Hagerman to Stacher, November 21, 1924. *Ibid.* Another argument which Hagerman mentioned as a deterrent to the proposed expansion was that the Navajos were not making full use of the range they already possessed because of their large herds of "useless ponies." H. J. Hagerman, "Annual Report, July 28, 1924." Navajo, 61584-24-150.

and Burke argued that since the Leupp reservation had now proved to be a permanent addition to the reservation,[11] the Santa Fe should be granted lieu lands as originally agreed upon. The Department Solicitor, however, warned Secretary Work that such an interpretation was no longer valid because of the clause in the 1918 appropriation bill forbidding the enlargement of Indian reservations without Congressional approval.[12]

In 1925 Secretary Work decided his course of action. Fully realizing that a precedent had been set in 1921 in favor of consolidation of the checkerboard areas, he introduced a bill for similar consolidation of the land in the Leupp-Western Navajo area. He was aware, he wrote, that such consolidation would reduce by half the area the Indians had heretofore used but, he concluded, "some action of this kind is required to prevent trouble."[13] Little opposition was encountered to the bill and on March 3, 1925, it was signed into law (43 Stat., 1115). The law applied only to the executive-order additions created on January 8, 1900, and November 14, 1901.[14]

The effect of this law was slight. The Santa Fe refused to negotiate, preferring to hold out for a settlement whereby it would be allowed to select lieu lands in other, and presumably better, areas of Arizona. Not until 1929 did the company change its position when it tentatively agreed to accept a money payment for the disputed acreage. There appear to be two reasons for this change of attitude. For one, most of the desirable public-domain lands in Arizona were gone by 1929. Secondly, Howell Jones, the company's land commissioner

---

[11]It will be recalled that the Solicitor's opinion in 1913 denying the validity of the proffered base lands relied on the concept that the executive order creating Leupp had stated that the withdrawal was for the purpose of allotting the Indians residing thereon, and that after such allotment the remainder of the land should be restored to the public domain.

[12]John H. Edwards to Secretary of the Interior, February 9, 1924. Navajo, 7126-22-313.

[13]U. S. House, Committee on Indian Affairs, *To Provide for Exchange of Government and Privately Owned Lands in Navajo Indian Reservation, Arizona,* 68th Cong., 2d sess., 1925, Rept. 1249, pp. 1-2.

[14]Hagerman writing to Howell Jones, Land Commissioner of the Santa Fe, on April 8, 1925 (Navajo, 7126-22-313), voiced his disapproval of Work's action: "I am quite certain that the Navajos are not desirous of eliminating any lands from the reservation and I do not suppose that Congress consulted them on the subject before this bill was passed . . . ." Neither Hagerman nor Burke, however, offered constructive solutions to the problem. Under existing law, legislation similar to Work's was the only possibility. It is interesting to note that there was no opposition to this bill from Collier and Frear, although it was passed at the same time as the authorization for the Lee's Ferry bridge.

who was responsible for the earlier position, had died and his successor was interested in consolidating the company's lands.[15] By 1930, 52,133 acres in the Leupp-Western Navajo area had been purchased from Navajo oil royalties and negotiations were underway for an additional 295,534 acres.[16]

NAVAJO INITIATIVE

Neither the defeat of Hagerman's bill in 1924 nor the ineffectual nature of Work's bill deterred the Indian Bureau from its plans to enlarge the Navajo reservation, although progress along these lines slowed considerably until 1928. The Hoover years witnessed a renewed interest in the problem.

At the Navajo Tribal Council on July 7-8, 1926, Hagerman presented a plan suggested by the Indian Bureau which called for setting aside a certain percentage of future oil royalties for the purchase of additional land. The argument was made along these lines. In the past year both the Navajo and the Pueblo Bonito jurisdictions had been forced to expend all the tribal funds allotted to them for the rental of private lands adjacent to their boundaries. Someday the funds from oil might not be available, or the owners might refuse to lease, in which case the other jurisdictions would experience a migration of Navajos from these areas to their jurisdictions. Would it not be wise now, when the money was available, to set aside a certain percentage of it for the purchase of land for these public-domain Indians?[17] After considerable debate, the council resolved to set aside 20 percent of the oil royalties in the coming year for this purpose. It was also unanimously agreed at this session to purchase part of the Fort Wingate military reservation in New Mexico which had been made available by the Secretary of War.[18]

Before the Tribal Council met again, Chee Dodge and other Navajo

---

[15]*Minutes of the Navajo Tribal Council, Ft. Wingate, New Mexico, September 3-4, 1929.* General Services, 36351-29-054. Also Scattergood to Hagerman, August 17, 1929. *Ibid.*

[16]Memorandum prepared by Hagerman for Rhoads, February 10, 1930. Navajo, 1359-30-059. Also published in *Senate Survey*, part 18, pp. 9041-44.

[17]*Minutes of the Navajo Tribal Council Meeting, Ft. Defiance, Arizona July 7-8, 1926.* General Services, 34976-26-054. Also Hagerman to Burke, July 13, 1926. Hagerman Papers, Commissioner's file, January-June, 1926.

[18]The purchase of this land was desirable for two reasons. For one, 9,502 acres of land in New Mexico north of the Santa Fe railroad would become available for Navajo use. For a second, the buildings at Ft. Wingate were to be remodeled for use as a Navajo boarding school.

leaders journeyed to Washington in early 1927 to appear before the Congressional committees which were working out the details of the Indian Oil Bill, vetoed the previous session by President Coolidge. While in Washington, Dodge apparently placed before Commissioner Burke a plan to expend over $1,000,000 of Navajo oil monies for the purchase of lands in New Mexico.[19] This proposal was the subject of some discussion at the 1927 council meeting.

The debate shows clearly a revival of the old enmity between the Navajo and the San Juan jurisdictions. Even more apparent is the emergence of a conflict over leadership within the Tribal Council. Three letters addressed to Commissioner Burke which stated that Dodge's plan was the work of the older Navajos and was not representative of the sentiments entertained by the younger members of the tribe were introduced into the record. These younger petitioners advised Burke that a more pressing matter than land was the conservation and development of water over the entire reservation. The spokesman for the rebellious young Navajos was Jacob C. Morgan of the San Juan delegation.[20]

Morgan's arguments before the council were more provincial than any previously presented. He was opposed to spending any money for land for Navajos living off the reservation proper. The money should be spent for the benefit of the young reservation Navajos returning from school, and for water development on the reservation proper. He made no secret of his opposition to Dodge.[21] His tactics were, more-

---

[19]See correspondence in General Services, 26881-27-054.

[20]Jacob Morgan later became the fourth chairman of the Navajo Tribal Council, serving from 1939 to 1944. His growing influence over the Navajos was indicated in early 1927 by the following exchange of letters between Hagerman and Superintendent Kneale of San Juan:
Morgan "is a bigot, unreasonable, unreliable, and an ever present and apparently ever growing menace . . . . Worse than all he is an admirer of John Collier and Representative Frear and eagerly devours every word that these gentlemen write . . . the veracity of which he places on a par with Holy Writ. Deshna [Clah Cheschillige], Jim Curley, and myself have for the past year been endeavoring to hold him down but he is a hard man to hold. . . . When the tribal council is reorganized, I believe it would be well to have Allen Neskiah substituted for him on the San Juan jurisdiction." Kneale to Hagerman, February 17, 1927. Hagerman Papers, San Juan file.
". . . I wish it could be arranged so that the change could be made for him to the Indian that you indicate before the meeting of the July council. I do not know how that could be brought about, but if it can be brought about, I should be greatly delighted." Hagerman to Kneale, March 3, 1927. *Ibid.* If any attempt was made to replace Morgan, it was unsuccessful for he was reelected from San Juan in 1928.

[21]*Minutes of the Navajo Tribal Council, Crownpoint, New Mexico, July*

over, successful. Although the council, after prolonged debate, finally resolved to set aside 25 percent of the royalties for land purchases, the figure was a far cry from the 50 percent recommended by the Dodge faction.[22]

ASHURST PROPOSES BILL

Although the Navajos had thus gone on record in both 1926 and 1927 as favoring the use of some of their oil royalties for land purchases, Congress had not yet approved this plan. In early 1928 Senator Ashurst introduced a bill for this purpose.

This bill reflected Dodge's position more than Morgan's. It provided a maximum expenditure of $1,200,000, reimbursable from the Navajo tribal fund, for the purchase of land and water rights for Navajo Indians living on the public domain. According to Hagerman, who still retained great interest in the Navajos despite his release from responsibility for their welfare, the intent of this bill was to permit the purchase of only $100,000 of land in any one year, thus prolonging the final purchases until 1940.[23] Two hundred thousand dollars would be made available in fiscal years 1928 and 1929. The total figure was an estimate of the Navajo land needs figured at 800,000 acres for an average price of $1.50 an acre.[24]

The bill was violently opposed in New Mexico by the stockmen and the politicians who represented them. It was proposed to make the act applicable only to Arizona.[25] In the end, the bill passed by incorporating it within a deficiency appropriation which was urgently needed (45 Stat., 899).[26] The legislative trick which had so often in the

---

7-8, 1927. General Services, 26881-27-054. Just prior to this council, Morgan had written Hagerman denouncing Dodge and claiming that he was attempting to put the educated Navajos off the council. His criticism of Dodge has an ironic ring in the light of his own rule later: "Chee Dodge has been trying to make himself a kaiser and trying to have absolute power over the people." Morgan to Hagerman, May 20, 1927. Hagerman Papers, San Juan file.

[22]*Ibid.*

[23]Hagerman to Rhoads, March 27, 1928. Hagerman Papers, Commissioner's file, January-December, 1928.

[24]U. S. House, *Hearings on Department of the Interior Appropriation Bill, Fiscal 1930*, 70th Cong., 2d sess., p. 759.

[25]Hagerman to Rhoads, No. 23 above.

[26]Bratton made an attempt to stop the measure in the Senate but, realizing that he could not hold up the entire deficiency bill, he vowed that he "was to be reckoned with" when the time came for making further appropriations. *Cong. Record*, Vol. 69, 70th Cong., 1st sess., p. 10053.

past been used against the Navajos was now employed in their favor.[27]

RENEWED ALLOTMENT

While the authorization to purchase land from oil royalties was being secured, the Indian Bureau launched a new and intensive allotment drive on the public domain in New Mexico. Following the Congressional prohibition against executive-order reservations in 1918, Commissioner Cato Sells had sent the Bureau's allotting agent, A. W. Simington, into New Mexico with orders to allot all the Navajos who could qualify for public domain lands under the terms of the compromise worked out with Albert Fall in 1914. Simington's work progressed slowly until the summer of 1925 when someone in the Bureau apparently decided that the allotment work was completed and had him transferred. Almost immediately complaints began arriving in Washington from Hagerman, Superintendent Stacher, and members of the Tribal Council, protesting that allotments had not been completed. Requests for Simington's return continued for a year until May, 1926, when he was dismissed from the service.[28] No replacement was ordered until March, 1928.[29]

There is no evidence to determine the precise reason for the decision to resume allotment at this time, but whatever it was, the new allotting agent, Charles E. Roblin, proceeded with his work at a businesslike pace. Within a year he had stirred up the opposition in New Mexico to fever pitch.

Writing to Commissioner Burke in early 1929, Roblin reported that the resumption of allotments, coupled with the authorization for land purchases,

> has excited the people of Arizona and New Mexico and the antagonism to the Indian on the Public Domain has become intensified. Memorials have been sent to Congress asking that no

---

[27]Not a little skullduggery was associated with the insertion of this provision in the House. Two years later, Representative Louis C. Cramton (Rep. Michigan), Chairman of the House Subcommittee on Appropriations, stated that he was responsible for the measure. To get it, he said, he had to work a deal with Morrow of New Mexico whereby he, Cramton, would give his support to a bill donating from the public domain to the state of New Mexico "several hundred thousand acres of land to pay off the old bonds of Silver City or some defunct outfit down there, and those lands to be sold by the State of New Mexico and the money used to repay these bonds." Cramton agreed and the Navajo bill was not opposed by Morrow. U.S. House, Committee on Appropriations, *Hearings on Department of Interior Appropriation Bill, Fiscal 1932*, 71st Cong., 3d Sess., 1930, p. 769.

[28]C. F. Hauke to William Spry, June 29, 1925. Pueblo Bonito, 65898-18-304.

[29]E. B. Meritt to C. E. Roblin, March 14, 1929. *Ibid.*

more land be given to the Navajos; a concerted effort to cover as much "government" land as possible in the Indian Country by white homestead entries is on. . . .[30]

Roblin estimated that working alone at his present rate, it would take him from four to five years to complete his work.

In an attempt to impress upon the Navajos the necessity of filing for their allotments, Roblin went before the Tribal Council in 1929. Three areas, he said, should be allotted soon if they were ever to be allotted:[31] Leupp, with only 200 allotments in twenty-one years; the area to the south of the reservation in New Mexico between Houck, Arizona, and Gallup, New Mexico, where some 3,500 Navajos lived, most of them not allotted; and the Crownpoint area in New Mexico. He further reported that in his seventeen months on the job he had filed applications for some 65,000 acres.[32]

Despite Hagerman's assurance in the fall of 1929 that there would be "no serious objections" to a continuation of the allotment-purchase policy "if the matter is conducted rather quietly and without too much publicity,"[33] the Bureau was besieged by angry letters from New Mexicans and their Congressmen. In answer to one letter from Senator Bratton, Commissioner Rhoads reminded him that the Navajos, as citizens, had equal rights under the law "to acquire land for a home site or other purposes." It was impossible to force them onto the reservation as Bratton advocated. He chided the Senator for his narrow approach to the subject, stating that the Navajos were a distinct asset to their community because, like any white man, they had services to offer and money to spend. Bratton's charge that the Indians were reducing the tax revenues of the counties was met by the remind-

---

[30]Roblin to Commissioner of Indian Affairs, April 5, 1929. *Ibid.* To support his last statement, Roblin enclosed an article from the *Gallup Herald* dated April 4, 1929, which showed that 92,800 acres had been filed upon by whites since January 1, 1929; 3,200 acres of it on the preceding Saturday alone.

[31]The necessity for haste was occasioned by the election of Herbert Hoover who favored, as a solution to the overgrazed condition of the public domain, the return of the surface rights of these lands to the states. Bratton and others introduced bills in 1929 which would have enacted this sentiment. As Roblin told the delegates, the day this happened allotments would cease. *Minutes of the Navajo Tribal Council Meeting, Ft. Wingate, New Mexico, September 3-4, 1929.* General Services, 36351-29-054.

[32]*Ibid.*

[33]Hagerman to Rhoads, September 15, 1929. Southern Navajo, 45241-25-313. In this letter Hagerman enclosed an undated item from the *Santa Fe New Mexican* which pooh-poohed the white fear of Indian allotments, stating that the citizens of New Mexico should be more concerned over Rhoads' attempts to gradually ease the Indians into the role of taxpayers, at which time they would gain the right to vote.

er that the federal government, not the counties, paid for the Indian health and educational expenses.[34] When Congressman Albert G. Simms (Rep., New Mexico) protested the Bureau's allotment policy in a press dispatch, Roblin replied in this manner: "Your position reflects the sentiment of a considerable part of the people of New Mexico, which, I believe, is based on an erroneous understanding of the situation." He then advised Simms that he was not assisting the Navajos because they were Indians, but because, as citizens, they deserved assistance from the government to obtain rights under the laws.[35]

In the end the opposition in New Mexico won out, as it always had. Writing to the Secretary of the New Mexico Cattle Growers' Association on May 5, 1930, Rhoads advised her that the allotment policy had been suspended.[36] In reply to the questions asked by the delegates at the 1930 council meeting as to why the work had been suspended and Roblin transferred, the Commissioner stated that the policy had interfered with the success of the program to purchase and exchange lands, and he asked the council not to "press us" until those transactions had been consummated.[37] At the time the allotment work was stopped Hagerman estimated that of the approximately 8,000 Navajos on the public domain, most of them in San Juan and McKinley counties, New Mexico, only about 3,700 were residing on allotted lands.[38]

UNOPPOSED ADDITIONS

With the passage of the act authorizing the expenditure of $1,200,000 for Navajo land in 1928, plans were formulated for systematic purchase. It appears probable, however, that because the Bureau had no representative in the area after Hagerman was transferred in December, 1927, what work was done in the last months of the Burke administration never got beyond the planning stages. It was not until

---

[34]Rhoads to Bratton, October 26, 1929. *Ibid.*

[35]Roblin to A. G. Simms, November 6, 1929. *Ibid.* This file also contains the protests of the New Mexico Cattle Growers' Association and the New Mexico Wool Growers Association.

[36]Rhoads to Bertha Benson, May 5, 1930. *Ibid.*

[37]*Minutes of the Navajo Tribal Council Meeting, Ft. Wingate, New Mexico, July 7-8, 1930.* General Services, 24619-30-054.

[38]Hagerman memorandum, February 10, 1930. Navajo, 1359-30-059. A breakdown made in 1931 showed 490 unallotted Navajos in San Juan County, and 2,500 in McKinley. *Senate Survey,* part 18, p. 9628.

Commissioner Rhoads took office and Hagerman was reappointed on March 4, 1930, that real action began.

The first plan laid before the Tribal Council in 1929 contemplated the expenditure of $217,000 on five separate tracts. One was the purchase of 20,000 acres in the Western Navajo jurisdiction south of Cameron, Arizona, an area owned by the Babbitt Brothers Company known as Tappan Springs. A second tract of 9,000 acres in the vicinity of Ramah, New Mexico, was urged for the use of the Navajo who lived there.[39] The third and fourth tracts were located within the Castle Butte area of Arizona, east of Leupp. The Bailey holdings of 147 acres were recommended because they contained a spring which controlled large areas of pasture. The Marty ranch of 10,240 acres was likewise strategically located within the area. The fifth proposal was for the purchase of 94,000 acres of land owned by the Santa Fe Pacific Railroad Company in New Mexico and Arizona.[40] The council unanimously passed a resolution to purchase all the land possible, and even Jacob Morgan introduced a resolution to urge upon the Commissioner the necessity of immediate use of the $1,200,000 before prices went up.

Prior to the 1930 council meeting, the Bureau, through Hagerman, consummated these transactions and made preliminary arrangements for the expenditure of the remaining authorization. From the Santa Fe it was proposed to purchase 295,534 acres in the Leupp-Western Navajo area, the remainder of the lands which the Santa Fe had deeded to the government in 1912; a second purchase of 233,440 acres scattered over New Mexico and Arizona would acquire the balance of the Santa Fe holdings in the Navajo country. An additional 11,485 acres were sought from the Babbitt Brothers' holdings around Tappan Springs. From the New Mexico and Arizona Land Company, it was proposed to purchase 123,678 acres in New Mexico. In addition to these extensive purchases, the Bureau, with the backing of the new Secretary of the Interior Ray Lyman Wilbur, was attempting to secure the transfer of 600,000 acres in Utah (the Paiute Strip) from the public domain

---

[39]The Navajos, though not on record officially, had generally opposed the government's recommendations to do something for the Navajos at Ramah, Cañoncito, and Puertocito. The Navajo populations at these sites in April, 1931, were 366, 233, and 201 respectively. In 1930 the problem was partially solved by a gratuitous appropriation by Congress of $125,000 which Hagerman suggested be spent on these groups. *Senate Survey,* part 18, p. 9625.

[40]Individual prices were: Babbitt Brothers, $60,000; Vogt Sheep Co. (Ramah), $22,000; Bailey, $7,000; Marty, $34,000; and Santa Fe, $94,000. *Minutes of the Navajo Tribal Council Meeting, Ft. Wingate, New Mexico, September 3-4, 1929.* General Services, 36351-29-054.

and 82,000 acres from the Forest Service in the Tusayan National Forest in Arizona.[41]

The request to incorporate certain lands in the Tusayan National Forest was first recommended by the superintendent of the Western Navajo jurisdiction in the days of the Burke administration. Commissioner Burke had given the request no support, but with the change of administration, Secretary Wilbur began to push the transfer. He first secured the approval of the Forest Service. He then turned to the county supervisors of Coconino County, Arizona, who in time also supported the measure, provided that the small portion of private land included within the proposed transfer area be compensated by lieu lands within the county.[42] With all parties agreed, Senator Lynn Frazier (Rep., North Dakota), introduced a bill embodying these provisions. The original bill was later amended to embrace an additional 116,000 acres of the Tusayan Forest and 5,760 acres of public domain.[43] The bill became law in May, 1930 (46 Stat., 378-70), but because Frazier had failed to include a recommendation by Hayden that all the lands in the area belonging to the Campbell-Francis Company be also included, it was necessary next year to amend the act by adding 23,000 acres of this company's holdings to the original transfer.[44]

Progress on the Paiute Strip measure was slower than on the Tusayan Forest. This area, it will be recalled, had been administered under the Navajo agency from 1884 to 1892, when it was restored to the public domain. In 1908 it was once again withdrawn from the public domain for the use of various Indians, only to be restored again in 1922 at the time that Secretary Fall made his important decision in the Harrison case. When it was determined in 1929 that there was no oil to be found in the region, the oil operators abandoned their sites. Few homesteaders were located within the area because of its generally forbidding and sterile nature. The strip was temporarily with-

---

[41]Hagerman memorandum, February 10, 1930. Navajo, 1359-30-059. *Minutes of the Navajo Tribal Council Meeting, Ft. Wingate, New Mexico, July 7-8, 1930.* General Services, 24619-30-054.

[42]The story of the Bureau's part in this transaction is contained in Western Navajo, 20818-29-304.3, parts I and II.

[43]U. S. Senate, Committee on Indian Affairs, *Transfer of Certain Land from Tusayan National Forest,* 71st Cong., 2d sess., 1930, Rept. 443, pp. 1-4.

[44]Hayden to D. W. Campbell, February 25, 1930. Western Navajo, 20818-29-304.3. Campbell was anxious to sell the land because he could not fence his holdings and the Navajo sheep were already encroaching on it. Earlier he had trouble over this same tract with agent Simington when a conflict developed over some Navajo allotments on the land. At that time, with the support of Hayden, he succeeded in having the Navajo claims voided. Navajo, 45130-22-313.

drawn from all forms of entry in 1929 when the Navajos evidenced a desire to incorporate it within their reservation.[45] Although the transfer was delayed for several years by an inability to satisfy all the factions in Utah, it was finally completed in 1933 when the governor of Utah gave his consent with the proviso that the royalties from any oil discovered in the strip be divided between the state of Utah and the Navajos, with the former receiving 37.5 percent of the total[46] (47 Stat., 1418). Thus these two large areas passed into the Navajo hands in a relatively easy fashion. Such was not the case where white interests of any magnitude were involved.

SUCCESS AND FAILURE

The Bureau's purchase of the Bailey and Marty tracts in the Castle Butte area of Arizona was made with the express intention of controlling the resources of the entire area for Indian use. However, when the Bureau proceeded to lease an additional 187,000 acres surrounding these tracts until such time as the area could be purchased outright, the people of Arizona decided that things had gone far enough. The supervisors of Apache, Navajo, and Coconino counties wired their protests to Washington and, for good measure, included a resolution for the removal of the public-domain Indians to the reservation.[47]

Faced with the possible disruption of the expansion plan, Rhoads, Hagerman, and Senator Hayden met with the county supervisors at Winslow, Arizona, for a two-day discussion in 1930. As a result of this meeting, Hayden introduced a bill to permit relinquishments and reconveyances of private lands in Arizona to the federal government, in trust for the Navajos, along lines similar to those contained in the act for New Mexico in 1921.[48] Although the bill failed to pass, Hayden

---

[45]H. E. Williams, "Report on the Western Navajo Reservation, 1929." Western Navajo, 40373-29-150. U. S. House, Committee on Indian Affairs, *Permanently Set Aside Lands in Utah as an Addition to the Navajo Indian Reservation,* 72d Cong., 2d sess., 1933, Rept. 1883, p. 2.

[46]*Minutes of the Navajo Tribal Council Meeting, Tuba City, Arizona, October 30-November 1, 1933.* Navajo, 9659-E-1936-054. Although the situation is not precisely the same as the conflict over the executive-order reservation, it is interesting to note that this settlement is exactly the same as that favored by Commissioner Burke in the Hayden bill of 1926, even to the requirement that the money thus obtained be spent on schools and roads for the Indians. This act was passed during Collier's administration without a fight.

[47]U. S. Senate, *Improvement of Conditions on Indian Reservations in Arizona,* Doc. 16, 71st Cong., 1st sess., 1929, p. 80.

[48]Hagerman to Rhoads, August 1, 1931. General Services, 35878-31-054.

continued to introduce similar bills into succeeding Congresses. In 1932, with the aid of Bratton, he was successful in obtaining approval for a thorough study of the entire Navajo land problem. The job of preparing the study was entrusted to Hagerman.

The Hagerman report was essentially the same plan which the Bureau had been implementing since Commissioner Rhoads took office. By purchase, consolidation, and exchange, it proposed to add 3,000,000 acres, including the Paiute Strip and the Tusayan National Forest, to the Navajo reservation as a permanent solution to the land problem. Although the utility of this report was partly negated by the decision of Hayden and Bratton to introduce separate bills for each of their states rather than the single bill recommended by Hagerman, this document nevertheless provides an excellent and thorough statement of the land problem as it existed in 1931. Bills incorporating the major recommendations of the report were introduced in 1931, 1932, and 1933, but were defeated each time.[49]

In 1934 separate bills sponsored by the new Democratic administration were once again introduced. Essentially these proposed new boundaries for the reservation on the west, south, and east. They provided for the relinquishment of privately owned lands within the enlarged reservation boundaries, the owners of such lands to be permitted to select other public lands within the same counties. In addition, the Navajos would be permitted to buy certain privately owned lands in each state within the new boundaries. For this purpose, $482,136 for New Mexico and $481,879 for Arizona, reimbursable from

---

[49]The opposition to these first bills came apparently from two sources. John Collier opposed the Hayden bill of 1931 because, if enacted, the bill would not give enough land to the Navajos in New Mexico; since this was so, Collier reasoned, to give up the right to future Indian allotments, as the bill specified, was tantamount to a denial of the entire expansion plan. *Senate Survey*, part 18, pp. 9650-51. The two Senators from New Mexico, Bratton and Cutting, were accused by Hagerman of "direct or sinuous opposition" to any extension of the Navajos in New Mexico. Hagerman to Wilbur, May 7, 1932. Special Agents file, Hagerman, #145. In this letter Hagerman likewise accused Collier and the Senate Sub-Committee on Indian Affairs of "insidious, mischief making propaganda" through which "the whole picture [of the land program Hagerman was working on] has been befuddled." The conflict between Collier and Hagerman here is similar to that which occurred between Burke and Collier earlier. Collier's argument was based on principle: the Indians needed more land, therefore, the right to allotment must not be compromised. Hagerman's was based on a compromise between the Navajo land needs and the stark reality of the bitterly powerful New Mexican opposition. In light of later developments (Collier got no more land for the Navajos than Hagerman had anticipated and he stirred up a great deal of ill-will against them), it is necessary to admit, I believe, that Hagerman's position on the issue was the wiser one.

the Navajo tribal treasury, were authorized.[50] The new Secretary of the Interior, Harold Ickes, stated that the new boundaries were "the ultimate line to which the Indians can hope to expand the reservation," and he encouraged the Congress to approve both bills so that the checkerboard could be eliminated and an effective program of soil conservation inaugurated.[51] The Arizona bill was signed into law (48 Stat., 960), but the New Mexico bill was defeated in the House after securing Senate approval.[52]

The successful passage of the Arizona bill meant the addition of approximately 1,000,000 acres to the Navajo reservation in that state and the cessation of the white-Indian land strife. The failure of the New Mexico bill meant continued strife in the area of greatest Navajo need and eventually defeat for the Indian cause there.

By 1935 all the holdings of the Santa Fe Pacific Railroad Company within the proposed reservation boundaries had either been bought by the Navajos or exchanged with them for lands elsewhere. Including the sales previously discussed, the Santa Fe, between 1920 and 1935, sold 388,161.25 acres to the Navajos for one dollar per acre. The remainder of its holdings were exchanged: 245,898.73 acres in New Mexico under the act of 1921, and 185,015.45 acres in Arizona under the Arizona boundary extension act.[53] Between 1930 and 1933 the New Mexico and Arizona Land Company sold the Navajos 123,678.29 acres, nearly all of it in McKinley County, New Mexico, at an average price of $1.67 per acre.[54] In 1932 when the New Mexico and Arizona

---

[50]U. S. Senate, Committee on Indian Affairs, *Define the Exterior Boundaries of the Navajo Indian Reservation in New Mexico, and for Other Purposes,* 73d Cong., 2d sess., 1934, Rept. 1074.

[51]U. S. House, Committee on Indian Affairs, *Boundaries of Navajo Reservation in Arizona,* 73d Cong., 2d sess., 1934, Rept. 1602. No solution to the overgrazing and soil erosion problems could be reached, Ickes claimed, until the dispute over the land in the checkerboard area was solved. With the holdings of Indians and non-Indians segregated and consolidated, the government could then enforce a policy of conservation on both alike. The Navajos had previously agreed to reduce their flocks in an effort to demonstrate good faith, the Secretary said, and he hinted that it was now time for the states to do likewise. See the comments of James Stewart, Chief of the Bureau's Land Division, before the Navajo Tribal Council, March 12, 1934, for a clear statement of how the Department used the land-acquistion argument to secure approval for the sheep-reduction and soil-conservation program. Navajo, 00-34-054.

[52]Mosk, *Land Tenure Problems in the Santa Fe Railroad Grant Area,* p. 48.

[53]William S. Greever, *Arid Domain* (Stanford: Stanford University Press, 1954), pp. 133-135. According to this account, the Santa Fe had, prior to 1920, swapped 788,898 acres in the Navajo reservation and sold 11,520 acres for a grand total of 1,619,493.43 acres.

[54]New Mexico and Arizona Land Company, file #117.

Land Company was experiencing difficulties as a result of the Depression, Hagerman arranged an agreement whereby the company, whose policy had heretofore opposed exchange, would relinquish all its holdings in the Leupp and Castle Butte districts of Arizona for lieu lands if the government would purchase all of the company's holdings in the Thoreau, New Mexico, district—89,918 acres—for $150,000. When the Congress refused to appropriate funds for this purchase, the New Mexico and Arizona Land Company returned to its former position. Nothing more was done until the Arizona extension act was passed.[55]

In 1935, after the Taylor Grazing Act made consolidation advisable, the New Mexico and Arizona Land Company sold all of its holdings in Coconino County—21,095.67 acres—to the Navajos for $1.67 an acre. At the time of this negotiation an agreement was reached whereby the company would sell an additional 22,968.04 acres of land in Arizona to the Navajos for the same price and exchange the remainder of its Arizona holdings, 124,449.51 acres, for 168,493.30 acres elsewhere in Navajo County. This final transaction was delayed until October 23, 1940, because the federal government refused to accept the company's lieu selections and the Congress refused to appropriate the sum necessary for purchase. In the end, the company was forced to accept an acre-for-acre exchange for its remaining holdings.[56]

CONCLUSION

In addition to the traditional policy of opposition to Navajo expansion in New Mexico, in itself enough to defeat any boundary extension bill, the passage of the Taylor Grazing Act (48 Stat., 1269) in 1934 ended serious negotiations along this line.[57] Henceforth, the use of the

---

[55]T. W. Cabeen to Hagerman, March 22, 1932. *Ibid.*, file #133, 1st part.

[56]T. W. Cabeen to Messrs. Brosnan, Koch and Thomas, June 20, 1939; Cabeen to J. M. Kurn, October 15, 1940; Cabeen to W. H. Burnett, November 2, 1938; U. S. General Land Office to N. M. & A. Land Co., March 1, 1940. *Ibid.* The government's intransigence in a similar matter caused its program for the purchase of land near Ramah for the Navajos to be defeated. The government wanted 67,228.36 acres of land in this area belonging to the New Mexico and Arizona Land Co., but refused to pay the price asked. In time, Cabeen arranged to sell the tract in two parts to the Pueblo Indians of Pojoaque and Picuris for $111,-224.88 on June 3, 1944. A curious situation existed until 1956, whereby the Navajos at Ramah leased the land from their Pueblo neighbors. *Ibid.*, file #117. See also United Pueblos Agency, active files, 300.21-2.

[57]After 1934 the opposition to the New Mexico boundary extension bill was led by Senator Dennis Chavez (Dem., New Mexico), who appears to have had even less sympathy for the Navajos than his predecessors. See Collier's comment on Chavez, June 7, 1937. Navajo, 36599-37-066.

public domain for grazing purposes would be carefully regulated by the Department of the Interior. Conservation of the remaining grass-lands and the prevention of soil erosion would replace chaotic and unrestrained exploitation of the public lands. It was obvious that the number of animals previously grazed on these lands would have to be reduced, and under these circumstances white stockmen were unwill-ing to give up any new lands to the Navajos. In addition, the act also ended the practice of allotting non-reservation Navajos on the public domain, for all public lands were removed from private entry prepara-tory to the creation of federally regulated grazing districts.

As Sanford Mosk indicated in his excellent study of the Santa Fe land grant area, white stockmen in New Mexico now believed they could "gain the upper hand" over the remaining public domain Nava-jos. Under the terms of the Taylor Act, federal officials were to be guided in the issuance of regulations for each grazing district by a local advisory board made up of stockmen within the district. Board members were to be elected by secret ballot, but all persons voting were required to write in the name of their candidates. Since few Navajos could write, they could not in effect vote, thus permitting the whites to dominate the first boards created under the act.[58]

---

[58]Mosk, *Land Tenure Problems in the Santa Fe Railroad Grant Area*, p. 54. Also *Senate Survey*, part 34, p. 17620.

CHAPTER 8

Transition

Attempts to abolish the Bureau of Indian Affairs and to solve the Indian problem finally and for all time have been endemic in American history almost since the founding of the Bureau. At irregular intervals, but at least once in the history of each generation, the American Red Man has been "discovered" by his white countrymen and his plight displayed before the public. When such an interest in the Indian takes place, it is inevitably the Bureau of Indian Affairs which receives the full brunt of whatever criticism is offered. The period from 1917 to 1933 was just such an era, and it is against this background that any interpretation of Navajo history must take place.

THE "NEW POLICY"

In 1917 Commissioner of Indian Affairs Cato Sells announced his "New Policy" for the American Indian, a policy which, he said, meant "in short, the beginning of the end of the Indian problem." At greater length he wrote:

> The time has come for discontinuing the guardianship of all competent Indians and giving even closer attention to the incompetent that they may more speedily achieve competency.
>
> Broadly speaking, a policy of greater liberalism will henceforth prevail in Indian administration to the end that every Indian, as soon as he has been determined to be as competent as the average white man, shall be given full control of his property and have all his lands and moneys turned over to him, after which he will no longer be a ward of the government.[1]

---

[1] Commissioner of Indian Affairs, *Annual Report, 1917*, p. 3. In even more appealing language, Sells continued: "This is a new and far-reaching declaration of policy. It means the dawn of a new era in Indian administration. It means that the competent Indian will no longer be treated as half-ward and half-citizen. It means reduced appropriations by the government and more self-respect and independence for the Indian. It means the ultimate absorption of the Indian race into the body politic of the Nation." The desirability of absorbing the Indian into the "body politic" was to be challenged shortly.

132

The distinction made by the Commissioner between competent and incompetent Indians had reference to the provision in the Dawes Act which stated that Indians allotted from tribal lands should remain under the guardianship of the federal government for a period of twenty-five years. In 1906 the Burke Act had amended this provision to permit the Secretary of the Interior to declare certain Indians "competent" before the expiration of the twenty-five year period.

The "New Policy" appealed to a variety of minds which had little understanding of the Indian or his psychology. *The Outlook* magazine nicely summed up this appeal when it stated that although there was no doubt that such a policy would result in the impoverishment and demoralization of some Indians, it was better that some should be lost, rather than deny the majority the opportunities "for that kind of human development which comes only in the atmosphere of freedom and in bearing the burden of responsibility which freedom entails."[2]

Many of these champions of "freedom" and "liberty" did not know, or perhaps they knew but did not understand, that the directives issued by the Indian Bureau to carry out the "New Policy" stated that all able-bodied, adult Indians of less than one-half Indian blood should be given complete control of their property immediately—it being assumed that such half-breed Indians were all competent to manage their own affairs. The regulations further provided that if, after investigation, Indians of more than one-half Indian blood were found to be competent, they, too, could be given control of their property— as later events proved, over their own protestations of incompetency.[3]

Under the "New Policy," 20,000 patents-in-fee were issued to "competent" Indians between 1917 and 1921.[4] The basis for this action seems to have been a report by a Major James McLaughlin who, at the bidding of the Commissioner of Indian Affairs in 1915, had made a tour of all the Indian reservations, in the course of which he compiled a list of all those Indians he and the local superintendent determined to be "competent." On this evidence, 10,000 patents-in-fee were issued in the two years 1919 and 1920. Many of these patents were issued over the protests of individual Indians who maintained that they would be unable to pay the taxes on the land and thus would lose them to

---

[2]"A New Step in our Indian Policy," *The Outlook*, CXVI (May 23, 1917, p. 136).

[3]Board of Indian Commissioners, *Annual Report, 1921*, p. 21.

[4]*Ibid.* This despite the fact that only 9,894 Indians had been declared competent between the time of the passage of the Burke Act in 1906 and 1917.

the tax collector. Although opposition to the forced patenting policy resulted in the program being halted in late 1920, it was later estimated that at least 9,000 Indians whose lands had been patented and thereby freed from Indian Bureau supervision had lost all of their lands and an undetermined number had lost parts of their holdings.[5]

A potentially greater danger to a larger number of Indians was the agitation for the "complete emancipation" of the Indians which arose after the promulgation of the "New Policy." During 1919 and 1920 the House Committee on Indian Affairs investigated nearly every Indian reservation in the country. When all the facts were in, the committee recommended that all persons of any Indian blood, who had received an education equivalent to that attained by white children at the completion of the seventh grade, and who were twenty-one, be made citizens[6] at age twenty-three, be given certificates of competency, have given to them their share in the tribal wealth, and "then be required to work out their own salvation." The committee further recommended that all surplus land "not necessary for the use of the Indians themselves," be leased or sold "for the benefit and in the interest of all the people of the country."[7] Later in this same year, two bills embodying these principles, plus a provision to extend the General Leasing Act to the executive-order Indian reservations, were introduced into the Congress.[8] This wholesale attempt to "emancipate" the Indians from federal control was opposed successfully by both Commissioner

---

[5]*Ibid.* Also U.S. Senate, Committee on Indian Affairs, *Cancellation of Certain Patents in Fee Simple Issued to Indians for Allotments without their Consent,* 71st Cong., 3d sess., 1931, Rept. 1595. Two Coeur d'Alene Indians who refused to accept the patents pressed upon them later succeeded in getting their cases before the Ninth Circuit Court of Appeals. In both cases the Court held that the Secretary had no authority to issue a patent in fee to an Indian allottee during the trust period unless the Indian had applied for it, and that any patent so issued did not transfer title. See U.S. House, Committee on Indian Affairs, *Cancellation of Patents in Fee Simple to Indians for Allotments Held in Trust by the United States,* 69th Cong., 2d sess., 1927, Rept. 1896. As a result of these decisions, legislation was passed in 1927 (44 Stat., 1247) which authorized the Secretary of the Interior to cancel patents-in-fee where the owners had not mortgaged or sold their holdings. In 1931 (46 Stat., 1205) the act of 1927 was amended to apply to portions of the original allotment which were not encumbered.

[6]Only Indians allotted from tribal reservations in accordance with the provisions of the Dawes Act and certain few others were citizens in 1921. In 1924, as a reward for Indian participation in World War I, citizenship was extended to all Indians.

[7]U. S. House, Committee on Indian Affairs, *Indians of the United States, Field Investigations,* 66th Cong., 3d sess., 1920, Rept. 1133.

[8]U. S. House, Committee on Indian Affairs, *Reorganizing the Indian Service,* 66th Cong., 3d sess., 1921, Rept. 1228 and Rept. 1189.

Sells and the Board of Indian Commissioners, which had originally supported the "New Policy" declaration.[9] Such was the state of events when Commissioner Burke took office in March, 1921.

UNDER FIRE

The practice of issuing fee patents to restricted Indians without careful consideration of individual circumstances was almost at a standstill in 1921. Burke discontinued it entirely.[10] The attack on the Bureau growing out of this controversy, however, continued, and very shortly became more pronounced than ever.

Throughout his eight years in office Burke was under attack from two camps. One believed that the "New Policy" was an ideal solution to the age-old Indian problem and that the recommendations of the House committee should be carried out. An able speaker in Congress argued that:

> The reservation system may have served a good purpose in compelling the Indians of other days to forsake their wild, nomadic ways. But its day is long passed. It is today a breeding place of idlers, beggars, gamblers, and paupers. It is a prison pen where human beings are doomed to live amid sad memories of their ancestors and among the ghosts of the dead. The sooner the whole tribal system and the reservation policy is abandoned the sooner we will write *finis* to one of the blackest pages in American history.[11]

On the other hand, there were those opponents of the Bureau who demanded not an immediate break-up of the reservation system, which

---

[9]Commissioner of Indian Affairs, *Annual Report, 1920*. Board of Indian Commissioners, *Annual Report, 1920*. The BIC report acknowledged that the "New Policy" had set off a powerful drive for the abolition of the Indian Bureau. Such agitation, it warned, was "now being organized" and represented a definite threat to the well-being of the full-blood Indians. In 1921 the Board sent letters to eighty-seven Indian Service field agents inquiring into the success of the "New Policy." Of those replying, 81.5% stated that a majority of those Indians "liberated" under the plan had already lost their land.

[10]Laurence F. Schmeckebier, *The Office of Indian Affairs* (Baltimore: Johns Hopkins University Press, 1927), p. 154.

[11]Speech of Representative Melville C. Kelly in *Cong. Record*, Vol. 61, p. 4664. Representative Carl Hayden, in defense of the Bureau on this occasion, offered an excellent statement of the real transformation which was taking place: "It is interesting to note how the opponents of the Indian Bureau have changed front in recent years. The old cries of fraud and graft and of robbing the Indians of their heritage have been largely abandoned. We are now told that the Indians are over-supervised, that their initiative is being destroyed.... The truth lies between these two extremes, and for that reason we will have an Indian problem, and an Indian Bureau at work solving it for many years to come." *Ibid.*, p. 4679.

they agreed would be disastrous, but an enlightened policy of Indian administration. This would remove many of the Bureau's alleged restrictions on the personal rights of Indians, thus ensuring these people equal participation in the civil rights enjoyed by other Americans. The leading spokesman for this camp, in time, was John Collier.

By 1924 the Collier forces assumed command of the greater part of the opposition to the Bureau.[12] This was probably due to the fact that Collier's charge, based as it was on the principle that the Indians were being denied their civil rights, was popular and more easily documented than the claims of the "New Policy" advocates that the majority of Indians were competent to handle their own affairs. Numerous articles on Indian life were published in the early 1920's and gradually a truer picture of the condition of the American Indian emerged than that presented by the "New Policy" proponents. As this picture took hold in the public mind, the proponents of the "New Policy" fell into disrepute. There was, too, a general consensus of opinion among older and less radical Indian protection societies that, since the days of the Dawes Act, the federal government had become so involved in the property rights of the Indians that the average Red Man had become subordinated to his property.[13]

The brunt of Collier's attack was focused on the Bureau's policy toward the Pueblo Indians of New Mexico.[14] From here it branched out through the American Indian Defense Association to attack other abuses which Collier claimed were being perpetrated by the Bureau on other Indians, not the least of whom were the Navajos. Burke and the Bureau came under increasingly heavy fire as the years wore on.

Two of the most serious charges brought against Commissioner Burke concerned his administration of the Indians in Oklahoma. In 1925 Burke and the superintendent of the Five Civilized Tribes were accused of criminal collusion in preventing the approval of a contract

---

[12]See the comments of Commissioner Burke to this effect in U. S. House, Committee on Appropriations, *Hearings on Department of the Interior Appropriation Bill, Fiscal 1926,* 68th Cong., 2d sess., 1924, pp. 685-91.

[13]The Board of Indian Commissioners, which defended the Bureau against the Collier charges throughout the 1920's, in 1923 wrote: "The chief difficulty, we believe, in the carrying out of the government's Indian policy has been caused by the preponderance of attention which has been given to material things, with the result that the real good of the individual men and women has become a subordinate matter. For a generation the emphasis has been placed on the property rights of the Indians." Board of Indian Commissioners, *Annual Report, 1923,* p. 9.

[14]For the best statement of Collier's position in these early years, see John Collier, *Indians of the Americas,* Chapter 13.

made between an Oklahoma lawyer and a committee of the Creek nation, the purpose of which was to bring suit on behalf of the Creeks for certain claims which they had against the federal government. Burke's argument for refusing to approve the contract was that the Indians had been hoodwinked into an agreement whereby large sums from the Creek estate would be siphoned away through legal fees. Both Burke and the superintendent were cleared through investigations conducted by the Board of Indian Commissioners and the House Committee on Indian Affairs.[15]

A more serious charge was brought against the Commissioner in this same year over his relations with a wealthy Oklahoma Indian named Jackson Barnett.[16] The Barnett case, filled as it was with a multitude of bizarre and tragi-comical events, was a *cause célebre* of the newspapers and magazines during the late 1920's. Burke's action in this case, although he was cleared of the charge of corruption, was to dog him until the day he resigned in 1929.

According to the story, Jackson Barnett, an Oklahoma Creek Indian, suddenly became a millionaire through the discovery of oil on his allotment, and in 1922 requested permission from Burke to place $1,100,000 of his savings in two equal trust accounts. The agreement under which these trusts were negotiated stipulated that Barnett should receive the interest from the trusts during his lifetime and at his death one should pass to his wife and the other to the American Baptist Home Mission Society of New York. The trusts were approved by Burke.

In 1925, Barnett's guardian filed suit to have the trusts declared invalid on the ground that under federal law the authority to approve such an arrangement was vested in the court of the county in Oklahoma wherein Barnett resided, and in the guardian appointed by that court, neither of which had been consulted by Burke on the matter. The peculiar law which had given the county courts control over oil-

---

[15]Board of Indian Commissioners, *Special Reports,* Vol. 5 and tray #118. U. S. House, Committee on Indian Affairs, *Indian Affairs in Oklahoma,* 68th Cong., 2d sess., 1925, Rept. 1527, p. 18.

[16]In recounting the story of the Barnett case, I have not attempted to weigh the pros and cons because the case is exceedingly complex and would make a story in itself. I have relied for the narrative primarily upon the information contained in *Senate Survey,* part 4, which, I believe, dredged up most of the previous materials introduced into the case. In addition, I have used materials contained in U. S. House, Committee on Appropriations, *Hearings on Department of the Interior Appropriation Bill, Fiscal 1928,* 69th Cong., 2d sess., 1926, pp. 424-30, and *House Rept. 1527,* 68th Cong., 2d sess., 1925.

rich Oklahoma Indians deemed incompetent to handle their own affairs had been the source of separating many of these Indians from their wealth. The Barnett case was a test of whether these courts had more authority over the Indians than the Bureau of Indian Affairs.

The Department of Justice, representing the Bureau, at first decided that the trusts were illegal but that the money should be returned to the guardianship of the Department of the Interior. Later the Attorney-General sided with the Oklahoma authorities completely, charging that Burke's action was not only illegal but that the Bureau had no jurisdiction in the matter whatever.

While charges and countercharges were flying between these two branches of the federal government and the Oklahoma courts, Barnett himself was residing in California, seemingly oblivious to the conflict that his request had created. When finally subpoenaed to appear for a hearing on the matter, he refused to attend. The Justice Department then instructed a deputy marshal in California to apprehend Barnett on a charge of contempt of court. The Indian was arrested at his home, spirited away to Oklahoma, and from there transported to New York for trial. In New York Barnett was declared mentally incapable of knowing what he was doing when he made the trust. Subsequently, the Justice Department filed a petition in behalf of the Oklahoma guardian, charging Burke and Secretary Work with fraud and corruption. While these charges were later dropped, they continued to crop up frequently and were in part responsible for Burke's resignation. The final decision of the Attorney-General as to the power of the Commissioner of Indian Affairs to delegate control of restricted Indians' funds to trust companies was in the negative.[17]

MERIAM COMMISSION

The mounting crescendo of criticism against Burke reached its highest point in 1926 with the Barnett case, the Lee's Ferry bridge controversy, and the defeat of the Burke-supported Hayden Indian Oil Bill. As he had done in 1923 when the Committee of One Hundred

---

[17]U. S. House, Committee on Indian Affairs, *Hearings on H. R. 6979, Creation of Indian Trust Estates,* 71st Cong., 2d sess., 1930. It was unfortunate that the question of fraud on Burke's part entered into the controversy over the power of the Department to authorize trust estates. Both Burke and his successor pressed for legislation to authorize these trusts, claiming that the Bureau was spending a disproportionate amount of time and money in administrative control over a relatively few wealthy Indians. There were good arguments against the trusts as the best means of solving this problem, but little disagreement as to the necessity for solving it.

had been formed, Secretary Work again sought counsel from a source outside the federal government. On June 12, 1926, he turned to the Brookings Institution, a non-profit and nonpolitical research organization in Washington, D. C.[18] Once Brookings found a patron for the project (the Rockefeller Foundation), and received assurance from the Bureau that all its files would be opened to members of the research team, the offer was accepted. A report on the condition of the Bureau was delivered to Secretary Work on February 21, 1928.

This Meriam report, so named from the director of the project, Lewis M. Meriam, has become a classic in the field of Indian administration. Thoughtful and sober, it was the product of specialists in the fields of education, health, administration, law, and Indian history. In general the report was highly critical of the Bureau but, unlike many of the Bureau's critics, it found the roots of the Bureau's troubles not in the personalities of its leaders but in tradition.

The basic weakness in Indian administration, according to the report, was in the attitude of the federal government toward the Indian. The emphasis in the past had been on the Indian's property rather than on the Indian himself. Training the Indian for self-support in a white civilization had been in the main a failure. The educational philosophy of the Bureau, since the days of Richard Henry Pratt's experiment with the "outing" system at the Carlisle Indian School, had been to separate the individual from his family and his community in the mistaken belief that this would integrate him more quickly into the American way of life. Some Indians preferred to remain Indians, thus the function of enlightened government should be to aid this group in every way the same as that segment which sought incorporation in the dominant white civilization.[19]

The Dawes Severalty Act was severely condemned. The object of this act, the report charged, was seemingly to get the allotment work done and done quickly, rather than to give the Indian a piece of property capable of supporting him according to an acceptable standard of living. A halt must be called to the allotment policy because it was obviously a failure from the standpoint of Indian

---

[18]In his news release the Secretary stated that such a survey was asked on account of harmful attacks and propaganda creating in the public mind the impression that Indian rights and welfare were being disregarded and that the Indians were not being properly dealt with. Board of Indian Commissioners, tray #41.

[19]*Meriam Report*, pp. 16, 88, 100, 548-49.

welfare; there was absolutely no evidence to warrant the conclusion that the federal government could, in the near future, relinquish its guardianship over the property of restricted Indians. The issuance of fee patents, the sale of inherited lands, and the leasing of Indian lands to whites should be prohibited by law. As a solution to the fractionalizing of Indian estates, the "sounder plan" would individualize Indian property through a corporate organization whereby tribal lands would remain intact, but the interests of individual Indians would be recognized through the issuance of shares of stock in the corporation thus formed.[20] A special plan should be formulated "at once to solve the land problem of the Navajos."[21]

Health and educational standards among the Indians were particularly low, the report stated. Tuberculosis and trachoma were prevalent, especially among the Indians of the Southwest. The theory that it was necessary to remove the child as far as possible from his home environment in order to teach him the white man's ways was brutal and too often merely separated him from the ameliorating influences of family life, taught him skills unsuited to his natural environment, and accustomed him to tastes impossible to fulfill and habits incapable of being practiced upon his return to the reservation. The most fundamental need in the field of education was "a change in the point of view" which would place more emphasis on the Indian as a human being in a given environment, rather than on the teaching of conventional subjects according to a standard study guide emanating from Washington. The most important objective, and one to be "vigorously pressed," was the elimination of preadolescent children from boarding schools.[22]

---

[20]*Ibid.*, pp. 88, 463, 470, 473. Whereas the Dawes Act had assumed that the desirable course of action was to integrate the Indians into the mainstream of American life, the Meriam report assumed that it was more desirable, in some cases, to permit the Indians to live apart. This basic clash of ideologies will be discussed at greater length in the chapter on the Wheeler-Howard Bill.

[21]*Ibid.*, pp. 467-68. The Meriam Report recommended that the Navajo reservation be enlarged. Consolidation as a solution was opposed because it meant the loss of one-half the land. The government should buy the necessary lands immediately and give them to the Indians, the cost to be reimbursed if the Navajo mineral resources produced sufficient revenues. The railroad land-grant companies should be allowed to exchange their holdings in the checkerboard for other lands on the public domain. The Meriam Report, as this recommendation indicates, was throughout based on a concept of justice and equity which made no provision for human passions and greed. No attempt was made to grapple with existing prejudices or to compromise with political realities.

[22]*Ibid.*, pp. 32, 35, 346.

Having criticized the present state of affairs, the report also plotted a course for remedial action. Basic to success was more money: "The overwhelming administrative difficulty has arisen from the efforts to operate the Service on an exceptionally low salary scale."[23]

The majority of Indian Service personnel, although generally devoted and hard-working, were simply not qualified for the jobs which they were entrusted to perform. The differential between salaries in the Indian Service and other branches of the executive department was so great as "doubtless" to render the federal officials involved unwilling to make "so drastic a recommendation" for their increase. Brookings' investigators uncovered a marked tendency within the Bureau to establish the salary for a given position, not on the basis of the ability or training required to adequately fulfill the duties of the position, but on the wages earned by the last incumbent, who might not have been technically qualified to hold the position. The obvious result of this practice was to make the replacement of one individual by another more qualified decidedly difficult. This practice was particularly reprehensible in that when a man died or resigned, "the salary thus fixed operates to get another like him." For a number of years, the report indicated, appropriations of at least ten million dollars annually in addition to current appropriations would be needed to raise the standards of the Indian Bureau to those of the Department of Agriculture or the Public Health Service. After that, when the plant, equipment, and personnel standards had been raised, these expenses would materially decrease.[24]

By way of summary, the report made three fundamental recommendations. First, there should be created a professional and scientific Division of Planning and Development. Secondly, there should be a "material strengthening" of those school and field personnel who were in direct contact with the Indians. A minimum of one-third to one-half salary increases for superintendents was requisite. Thirdly, there must take place the "maximum practical decentralization of authority" for the greatest degree of initiative and responsibility in the qualified personnel thus attracted to the Service. Specific recommendations were made in the fields of health, education, and general welfare, but without these basic reforms no real progress could be expected.[25]

---

[23]*Ibid.*, p. 155.
[24]*Ibid.* pp. 8, 50, 106, 155.
[25]*Ibid.*, p. 113.

BUREAU OF THE BUDGET

When the Meriam Report stated that greatly increased appropriations would be needed for the Indian Bureau for a number of years, it stepped boldly into a controversy which had been agitated for a long time. Many of Commissioner Burke's enemies had long maintained that the Commissioner was personally responsible for the low appropriations granted to the Indian Bureau: he had not asked for sufficient funds and as a result had not been given them. Burke, on the other hand, maintained that recommendations for sufficient funds had been made by his office each year, but had not been accepted by the Bureau of the Budget. The Meriam Report made no attempt to fix the blame for the insufficient funds accorded the Indian Bureau, but it did indicate that the Bureau of the Budget had, since its creation, appeared to regard itself as "merely a restraining agency" rather than as a constructive organ of the executive branch.[26]

The Bureau of the Budget was created by act of Congress in 1920. Burke was thus the first Commissioner of Indian Affairs to contend with its activities. Representing the fiscal-policy recommendations of the executive to the Congress, the Bureau, during the eight years of Burke's administration, reflected the financial views of the Harding and Coolidge administrations. The major consideration was a reduction of taxation which was "imperative to our industrial recovery" following World War I. Such a reduction could only be accomplished, the administration felt, by the success of the strictest federal economy imposed through the budget system.[27]

Prior to the creation of the Bureau of the Budget, each department, bureau, and agency of the government had presented and defended its requests for appropriations directly before the appropriate committees of the two Houses. After 1921 these requests were funneled through the Bureau of the Budget to the Congress. Only the recommendations of the Budget Bureau were considered, not the estimates originally proposed by the individual departments or agencies.

When the House Subcommittee on Appropriations for the Department of the Interior met in 1921 for the first time under the new

---

[26]*Ibid.*, p. 433.

[27]See Representative Cramton's paraphrase of the Harding-Coolidge position on the role of the Budget in U. S. House, *Hearings on Department of the Interior Appropriation Bill, Fiscal 1930*, p. 669.

policy, its Chairman, Louis C. Cramton, made some interesting comments about the function of his subcommittee under the budget system. The general attitude of the subcommittee, he said, was to be based on "the very strictest economy." As though to serve notice that the lobbying days of the executive-department bureaucrats were over, he remarked that:

> This bill comes to us from the Director of the Budget, immediately from the President . . . we maintain that right [to report items not in the budget] but the likelihood of our reporting any item that has not been recommended in the budget is so limited that it will not be wise to devote any great time on the part of the department to an effort to secure inclusion of items that are not in the budget . . . .[28]

Each year thereafter Cramton made a similar statement at the opening of hearings on the appropriation bill.

The Secretary of the Interior worked hand-in-hand with the administration and with Congress in the paring of costs within his department. When, in 1924, Cramton stated that since 1921 there had been a constant annual reduction in the cost of administering the Department of the Interior, Secretary Work in turn informed the committee that the appropriations for fiscal 1925 were some $35,400,000 less than those for fiscal 1924 and, in addition, the Department of Interior was requesting $22,690,000 less in fiscal 1926 than had been granted for fiscal 1925.[29] The following year, Work proudly announced to the committee that his department had returned to the treasury over $35,500,000 of the fiscal 1924 appropriation, and that the Bureau of the Budget had again cut the department's appropriation for fiscal 1927 by $11,300,000 from that of 1926. In all, Work said, the expenses in his department had been trimmed by more than $82,000,000 in the two years of his administration, and he predicted that by the close of 1927 he would have saved the federal government some $129,000,000.[30]

The evidence is that the curtailing of Indian appropriations after 1921 was the combination of many factors, not the least of which was the attitude of the President, the House Appropriations Com-

---

[28]U. S. House, Committee on Appropriations, *Hearings on Department of the Interior Appropriation Bill, Fiscal 1923*, 67th Cong., 2d sess., 1921, pp. 1-2.

[29]U. S. House, *Hearings on Department of the Interior Appropriation Bill, Fiscal 1926*, p. 1.

[30]U. S. House, *Hearings on Department of the Interior Appropriation Bill, Fiscal 1927*, pp. 2-3.

TABLE II

COMPARISON OF RECOMMENDATIONS, APPROPRIATIONS, AND
EXPENDITURES OF INDIAN BUREAU FUNDS, FISCAL 1922-1930

Fiscal Year	Burke Recommendations[1]	Bureau of Budget Recommendations[2]	Congressional Appropriations[2]
1922	$	$11,135,000	$10,042,554
1923	13,089,863	10,632,000	9,817,702
1924	15,311,604	10,967,155	12,617,655
1925	14,378,028	12,151,496	12,320,220
1926	18,339,049	13,427,027	12,968,270
1927	15,319,119	12,901,744	13,886,160
1928	20,312,074	13,551,265	13,629,685
1929	20,190,839	14,614,009	15,144,509
1930	23,637,737	16,810,815	17,523,215

[1]U. S. Senate, Committee on Appropriations, *Hearings on Department of the Interior Appropriation Bill, Fiscal 1933,* 72d Cong., 1st sess., 1932, p. 26.

[2]The figures in these groupings are taken from *The Messages of the President Transmitting the Budget for Fiscal Years 1923-1930* (Washington: G.P.O., 1921-1928). They have been checked against similar figures in U. S. Treasury Department, *Annual Report of the Secretary for Fiscal Years 1923-1930* (Washington: G.P.O., 1924-1931).

mittee, the Bureau of the Budget, and the Secretary of the Interior. Within such an atmosphere it would have been extremely difficult for Burke to have attempted to breast the tide. It is true, nevertheless, that the Commissioner did recommend consistently throughout his term of office more appropriations than were approved by the Bureau of the Budget. Time and time again Burke testified in the hearings before the House Committee that he accepted the estimates of the Budget Bureau because under presidential directive he was required to do so, but that the budget estimates did not necessarily reflect his true judgment of the situation. Driven to an extreme position by his critics, he clearly stated his stand in 1928:

> We have been assailed repeatedly . . . with not asking for suf-
> ficient money to meet the ends of the Indian Service. I want to
> say to this committee that the estimates as transmitted do not
> represent the amounts that we originally asked for; that our
> estimates, both last year and this year, have been very materially
> reduced by the Bureau of the Budget. . . . Recognizing that
> situation we accept the estimates without protest.[31]

The plain facts were that with the introduction of the budget system, directives had been issued by the President that positively forbade members of the executive branch of the government to ask for any-

---

[31]U. S. House, *Hearings on Department of the Interior Appropriation Bill, Fiscal 1930,* p. 669.

thing not approved by the Bureau of the Budget.[32] The validity of Burke's position is borne out by the figures contained in Table II.

Burke's attitude toward the Meriam Report was of a mixed nature. As the field reports of the survey team presented evidence that the fiscal policy pursued in the preceding five or six years had resulted in disastrous consequences for his office, Burke, in 1927, for the first time, began to admit that all was not well in the Indian Service. The Bureau he said, "has not kept pace with the progress elsewhere along health, educational, · industrial, and social lines." Underrating the requirements of the Indian Service in financial matters had "become a habit difficult to control." Capable young people no longer sought positions in the Service because it "offered a restricted social life and little opportunity for a successful career." In discussing employment problems, he gave statistics for the turnover in personnel in fiscal 1927: physicians, 57 percent; nurses, 122 percent; teachers, 48 percent; all permanent employees, 67 percent.[33] And yet, when the report was finally published, he defended the Budget Bureau and the House Appropriations Committee.[34] As on other occasions, it appears that while his actions were never so dastardly as Collier and other critics would make out, Burke was always the politician, temperamentally incapable of being a reformer. Working within the framework of the possible and in the tradition of a generation soon to be discarded, he did what he could and never advocated what he believed to be the impossible.

SENATE INVESTIGATION

Even before the Meriam Report was made public, the growing opposition to the Burke administration had resulted in action by the United States Senate which authorized its Committee on Indian Affairs to begin an intensive survey of Indian conditions. Composed of Senators Lynn J. Frazier (Rep., North Dakota), Robert M. LaFollette, Jr., Burton K. Wheeler, and Elmer Thomas (Dem., Oklahoma), a special subcommittee set out to visit nearly every Indian reservation, school, hospital, and agency in the nation. The subcom-

---

[32]*Ibid.* See also Meritt to Senate Investigating Sub-Committee, March 8, 1928. Hagerman Papers, Indian Office, January-July, 1929. In this letter Meritt states that the Bureau's estimates for the past two years totaled $12,000,000 more than the estimates transmitted to the Congress but, under the presidential directive, the Bureau could not ask for any of it before the committee.

[33]Commissioner of Indian Affairs, *Annual Report, 1927*, pp. 1-2.

[34]U. S. House, *Hearings on Department of the Interior Appropriation Bill, Fiscal 1930*, p. 638.

mittee was continued in action until 1943 and its printed hearings grew into thirty-seven volumes.

Opposition to the subcommittee was quick to form. In the Senate its principal opponent was Senator Carl Hayden of Arizona, long a friend of the Indian Bureau, who labeled the subcommittee a "kangaroo court" and charged that it heard all the "soreheads" who presented themselves before it, while refusing a hearing to the officials of the Indian Bureau. Senator Wheeler, however, who emerged as the major prosecutor at the hearings, maintained that such charges had also been made at the time that he and Senator Walsh had begun the Fall and Daugherty investigations, and the opposition failed to halt the subcommittee's work.[35]

Commissioner Burke was the chief target of the committee. He misjudged the tenacity of the committee in its early stages, confiding to Hagerman in July, 1928, that "the investigation will not amount to much because the members . . . will not devote the time necessary to make anything more than a superficial inquiry even if it does that much."[36] His failure to recognize the seriousness of the committee's intent and the political pressures which called out for a scapegoat after the Meriam Report was published, caused him to treat the committee in an often contemptuous and cavalier fashion. In the end the committee played a major role in his decision to resign.

One of the first issues investigated was the Jackson Barnett case. All the previous witnesses were called and ultimately Burke himself was summoned. Under heavy-handed and sometimes brutal examination by Wheeler, Burke at last lost his self-control and publicly vented his spleen by accusing a member of the Senate, W. B. Pine (Rep., Oklahoma), with conspiracy to "destroy" him because he had not appointed a political friend of Pine's to the post of Superintendent of the Five Civilized Tribes. It was Pine, Burke charged, who had through his political appointees in the Department of Justice, turned the Justice Department against him in the Barnett case.[37] He further

---

[35]*Cong. Record*, Vol. 70, 71st Cong., 1st sess. pp. 4366 and 4539. Hayden was often supported in many of his criticisms by Senator Thomas.

[36]Burke to Hagerman, July 23, 1928. Hagerman Papers, Commissioner's file, January-December, 1928.

[37]*Senate Survey*, part 3, p. 1348. The Special Assistant to the Attorney-General, a Mr. Selby, had stated publicly at the close of the Barnett trial in New York that Burke's testimony before the court warranted his indictment for malfeasance, and Selby further stated publicly that if the Commissioner were indicted, he would be convicted. Burke charged that Selby had secured his post through the influence of Senator Pine.

accused John Collier, whom he labeled "a notorious Indian agitator," of being a party to the conspiracy.[38]

No sooner had Burke made this accusation than Wheeler took up the gauntlet and demanded that Burke produce his evidence. The Commissioner attempted to modify his charge by claiming that he had not accused Pine of criminal conspiracy as Wheeler maintained, but had merely stated that "in his opinion" Pine and Collier had been working together to discredit him. Although he attempted to retreat from his accusation against Pine, he resolutely maintained that John Collier was out to destroy the Indian Service.[39] His protestations, however, were futile in view of the serious charges he had made and was unable to substantiate. Within a month he resigned from office.[40]

Burke's foes later claimed that it was this incident which caused his resignation.[41] There is evidence, however, that he was on his way out even before this. President-elect Hoover, who was very greatly interested in Indian Affairs, was known to favor the recommendations of the Meriam Report which Burke had failed to implement. The rumor that Burke would not be a member of the Hoover administration was known to field men in the Indian Service even before his blunder.[42]

Malcolm MacDowell, secretary to the Board of Indian Commissioners, wrote in January, 1929, that aside from the Senate-Collier opposition, there was another movement on foot to oust Burke on the ground that he was "too old, too sick, and too obstinate" to carry out the recommendations of the Meriam commission. MacDowell quoted Lewis Meriam himself as having said that the only way to reform the Indian Service would be to "get rid of Burke," and MacDowell, who had supported the Bureau and Burke through many trying days, appeared to be in sympathy with this criticism.[43]

---

[38]*Ibid.*, pp. 1071-72.

[39]*Ibid.*, pp. 1344 and 1359.

[40]Writing to Flora Warren Seymour, a member of the Board of Indian Commissioners and an outspoken critic of Collier, Malcolm MacDowell had said on January 23, 1929: "Yesterday the committee exonerated Senator Pine which apparently puts Mr. Burke in a pretty bad situation. Of course, neither he nor anyone else could prove conspiracy, but you know and I know and we all know that Senator Pine and his men in the Department of Justice ... have been after Burke with the firm intention of 'breaking him.'" Board of Indian Commissioners, tray #8.

[41]Collier, *Indians of the Americas,* pp. 257-58.

[42]Interview with Mr. James Stewart, former superintendent of the Navajo reservation.

[43]MacDowell to Seymour, January 23, 1929. Board of Indian Commissioners, tray #8.

When Hoover was corresponding with Charles J. Rhoads, the president of the Indian Rights Association, in an attempt to interest him in filling the position created by Burke's resignation, Rhoads also made reference to Burke's weakening physical condition as the reason for his decision to quit.[44]

The truth of the matter is, I believe, that irrespective of the Senate committee's charges, Burke realized, finally, that at sixty-eight and in poor health, he was no longer qualified for the post which he had held for eight years. He probably was aware that true or not, the many charges which had been leveled against him and his administration had discredited him and his future effectiveness. As the politician he had always been, he also realized that in the Hoover administration his ideas would be anachronistic.

THE HOOVER YEARS

When Burke announced in March, 1929, his intention to resign, he received shortly thereafter a letter from Hagerman which it would have been well for his successor to have read:

> Whoever he may be, I certainly do not envy him the job. I think that any new man who takes the position after your long years there will soon appreciate the stupendous difficulties with which you have had to contend, and that he will find it no simple matter to bring about any radical reorganization of the Service along lines which have been very frequently discussed, unless there is an entirely new disposition on the part of Congress itself.[45]

The "stupendous difficulties" of which Hagerman spoke were eventually to call down upon the new commissioner much of the same kind of abuse which Burke had experienced.

When President Hoover was casting about for a new Secretary of the Interior, his choice ultimately rested on an old friend from

---

[44]C. J. Rhoads to Herbert Hoover, March 12, 1929. National Archives, Record Group 48, file 22-23, C. J. Rhoads. Writing to Roberts Walker on June 26, 1926, Hagerman had this to say of Burke's position and his health: "It must be said for him that his job is about the rottenest in the whole government. He is heckled day after day, month after month, and in fact his hands are tied a good deal. He suffers constantly with rheumatism and it is just a question of what degree of suffering he is in at any time. Under such circumstances it is remarkable that he maintains his equanimity as well as he does. I think that this whole government game is absolutely impossible anyway." Dietrich Collection, Roberts Walker personal file, 1925-26.

[45]Hagerman to Burke, March 18, 1929. Hagerman Papers, Indian Office, January-July, 1929.

Stanford, Ray Lyman Wilbur. Like Hoover, Wilbur had worked his way through college and up the ladder of success. While his profession was medicine, Wilbur's interest early turned to teaching and research rather than practice; at thirty-six he became the dean of the newly founded medical college at his alma mater and, at forty, president of Stanford.[46] Also like Hoover, the new Secretary believed that many of the Indian reservations could be broken up within a generation by training young Indians to handle their own affairs. Shortly before Burke's resignation, Wilbur prophesied that under new leadership, the reservation system would be obsolete in twenty-six years.[47]

The new Indian Commissioner, Charles J. Rhoads, wrote his own ticket for the post. A wealthy Philadelphia banker and Quaker philanthropist, Rhoads had formerly been president of the Indian Rights Association. In this capacity, upon request, he had nominated Henry J. Scattergood, another Quaker active in Indian work, for the post of Indian Commissioner. Hoover's interest, however, soon centered on Rhoads himself and through Secretary Wilbur the Philadelphian was persuaded to take the job. Rhoads was to have journeyed to Washington in late March, 1929, to discuss the matter with Wilbur but he became ill with the flu and was confined to bed. Writing instead, he informed Wilbur that he was willing to accept the post under certain conditions. The items which he had wished to discuss with the Secretary and for which he demanded assurance of administrative backing were spelled out in his letter:

1. Is your plan for the Bureau substantially the one outlined in the Meriam Survey?

2. If so, how much assurance can be had of securing from Congress the new legislation and larger appropriations to carry out the plan?

3. Pending legislation by Congress, can the Bureau obtain the needed expert advice and competent personnel to make a start on the plan?

4. How much of the existing personnel must be retained under civil service rules?

---

[46]National Archives, Record Group 48, Biographies and Portraits, file 1-105, part 2, pp. 6-12.

[47]*New York Times*, July 7, 1929, p. 9. See also Ray Lyman Wilbur, *Memoirs of Ray Lyman Wilbur, 1875-1949*, ed. Edgar E. Robinson and Paul C. Edwards (Stanford: Stanford University Press, 1960).

> I am exceeding interested in the work but would not wish to undertake it unless there was reasonable assurance we could carry out the necessary reforms . . . .[48]

Rhoads' terms were met and he accepted the position, naming Scattergood to the office of Assistant Commissioner. These appointments were widely hailed as the beginning of a new era in Indian history.[49]

As indicated in the letter above, Rhoads' policy was primarily an implementation of the Meriam Report. The fundamental aim of the Indian Service, he said, was to make the Indian "a self-supporting and self-respecting citizen," and not a ward of the government. To solve the problems of administration, two principles must be held uppermost: (1) the federal government must be divorced from its supervision over the Indian person through the gradual break-up of the reservation system; (2) modern business methods and tools such as the corporation, joint stock company, and the trust must be applied to the handling of Indian property. The entire policy of allotment and reimbursable loans called for review and reconsideration by the Congress.[50]

To implement these guiding principles, the Indian Service got financial backing from the Congress. From $18,880,000 in 1930, the gratuity appropriations grew to $24,290,000 in 1931; $27,500,000 in 1932; and $22,160,000 in 1933 when the Depression began to turn the tide in the opposite direction.[51] Compared to the $12,000,000-$14,-000,000 appropriations of the Burke era, the increase was considerable. Most of the money went for health, education expenses, and salaries for better trained personnel.[52]

In education, the Rhoads administration threw out the standardized study programs, giving more initiative to the local teachers. Special emphasis was placed on vocational training designed to prepare the Indian child for making a living within his particular environment. Attendance at local public schools was fostered. A special study of the major reservations was initiated to develop a specific home-

---

[48]Rhoads to Wilbur, March 28, 1929. National Archives, Record Group 48, file 22-23, C. J. Rhoads.

[49]See comments of Harold Ickes and John Collier, *Cong. Record,* Vol. 71, p. 3182 and Vol. 72, p. 2497.

[50]Commissioner of Indian Affairs, *Annual Report, 1929, 1930, 1931.*

[51]U. S. House, Committee on Appropriations, *Hearings on Department of the Interior Appropriation Bill, Fiscal 1933,* 72d Cong., 1st sess., 1932, pp. 209-19.

[52]Secretary of the Interior, *Annual Report, 1930,* p. 44 and p. 60.

and-farm program for each. Boarding schools were deemphasized and more attention was given to day schools. To help the young graduate find employment, a guidance and placement division was formed. Better-paid physicians were hired and new, modern hospitals constructed. A retirement policy for older personnel resulted in the voluntary retirement of 25 percent of the permanent employees within the first two years of the new administration.[53] On March 30, 1931, after a year's study and planning, the Bureau was reorganized administratively. Two assistants to the Commissioner, one in charge of human relations, and the other in charge of property, were appointed to head five new field divisions: health, education, agriculture and industry, forestry, and irrigation.[54] The purpose of reorganization on the Washington level was to free the Commissioner from the pressure of paper work, giving him the time necessary for policy decisions and, on the agency level, to give the superintendent the opportunity for integrated planning by equipping him with a staff of specialists.

Despite these impressive advances and reforms, the Bureau was not invulnerable to attack. The policy of decentralization brought in its wake problems of as serious a nature as those it intended to remove. General Hugh L. Scott of the Board of Indian Commissioners made a special report to his colleagues in late 1931 in which he expressed deep concern over the lowering of morale in the field service as a result of the new policy. Too often, he explained, the emphasis on superior personnel meant simply that the new employee had a college degree. He deplored the "indecent haste" with which the new Commissioner was replacing men of long and ripe experience with others who held diplomas "and nothing else." Bitterness and insecurity were haunting the field-service personnel who felt that Washington had abandoned interest in their welfare.

Nor did Scott find that decentralization was having the desired effect in practice. The creation of the five specialized divisions was resulting in an increasingly impersonal bureaucracy, he wrote. Local representatives were reporting directly to their division chiefs in Washington, with only information copies of their programs going to the local superintendent. Instead of an agency having one head, Scott explained, "it has many." He branded the entire system as vicious because coordinating control was being lost by the superin-

---

[53]M. K. Sniffen, Secretary of the Indian Rights Assn., "Progress in Indian Affairs," March 10, 1931. Board of Indian Commissioners, tray #41.

[54]Commissioner of Indian Affairs, *Annual Report, 1931*, pp. 3-4.

tendent at the very time that he was being charged with increased responsibility. At its worst the system led to competition among the divisions which resulted in a loss of interest in the Indians for whose purpose the divisions had originally been created. Too often the superintendent, now shorn of much of his power, was the only one left with "the real interest of the Indians at heart."[55]

If General Scott's remarks are to be taken as the natural reaction of the old guard, we need but turn to the comments of John Collier and the Senate subcommittee to learn that there were others who thought that Rhoads was dragging his feet in the matter of reform. By 1931 Collier was openly accusing Rhoads of "blocking the policy enunciated by Secretary Wilbur when he took office." The actual policy of the Bureau, he charged, was a reactionary one which, while it had ameliorated some of the worst abuses of the Burke regime, had not pushed basic reforms enough. The more experience Rhoads acquired in office, the more reluctance he displayed for bold and radical action. The Commissioner claimed that he was baffled by the intricacies of the Indian problem and by the conflicting mass of statutes which he was called upon to enforce. Collier in turn charged that the problem lay not in the statutes but in the multitude of inherited office holders whom Rhoads refused to unseat. The Commissioner, he maintained, had aligned himself with the old guard in the Indian Bureau.[56]

Throughout the last two years of his administration, Rhoads was continually subjected to attack from the Senate Indian Affairs Committee and the Collier forces. After the 1932 election, Senator King of Utah, the sponsor of the original resolution creating the Senate investigating committee, rose in the Senate to deliver a blistering attack on the Rhoads administration. The hopes of the nation, he declared, had been "sorely disappointed." The Bureau was "a petrified, crystallized machine, indifferent to criticism, hostile to reforms,

---

[55]Board of Indian Commissioners, *Special Reports*, Vol. 10, pp. 180-85 and 661-63.

[56]U. S. Senate, Committee on Indian Affairs, *Hearings on H. R. 15498, Revision and Codification of the Statutes Affecting American Indians*, 71st Cong., 3d sess., 1931, pp. 58-60. Collier's insistence on this alignment of Rhoads with the old guard eventually resulted in an attack on Herbert Hagerman whom Collier identified as one of the most prominent of the Burke entourage. Acting through the Senate subcommittee, Collier succeeded in having Hagerman removed. Rhoads and Scattergood steadfastly stood by Hagerman and were discredited in the eyes of many by their stand.

ambitious for authority, demanding increased appropriations and a rapidly expanding personnel."[57] The vituperation of the Burke era had returned.

It was Rhoads' unfortunate experience to accept a position for which he was not qualified except by his idealism and humanitarian interests. His innate conservatism made him no match for the more colorful and radical Collier, who by this time had the Senate investigating committee on his side. When Rhoads balked at a reform backed by the committee or Collier, he was accused of being reactionary; when he attempted to implement the Meriam Report he was accused of radical action. In retrospect, it appears that the conflict between the older, traditional, and paternalistic policies of Burke, and the new, revolutionary, and libertarian policies of Collier was too much for any one man to breach. Rhoads placed the major recommendations of the Meriam Report into action, but beyond that he was unwilling or unable to go. As his administration neared its close, the Collier bandwagon picked up steam. With the election of Franklin D. Roosevelt, Collier became Commissioner of Indian Affairs.

---

[57]U. S. Senate, *Conditions of Indians in the United States*, 72d Cong., 2d sess., 1933, Doc. 214.

CHAPTER 9

New Deal for the Navajos

On March 4, 1933, Franklin D. Roosevelt became President of the United States. Roosevelt knew little about Indians and apparently had few ideas concerning the man for the post of Commissioner of Indian Affairs. He trusted implicitly the recommendations of his new Secretary of the Interior, Harold L. Ickes, a political maverick from Chicago.

Harold Ickes was a progressive Republican who, disillusioned by the failure of the Progressive Movement, had assumed an independent position in politics since the election of Warren Harding in 1920. A man of action and pragmatic temperament, he had been dismayed at Hoover's reluctance to act decisively in the face of the Depression. After a period of doubt concerning Roosevelt, he enthusiastically embraced him and the Democratic cause in 1932. From Chicago he headed an "Independents for Roosevelt" organization in the West. When the western vote was delivered, Ickes decided to ask for a post in the new Democratic administration.

At first he thought of the position of Commissioner of Indian Affairs, which he considered an important one.[1] His qualification for this office was mainly one of interest, although he was an officer of the American Indian Defense Association, of which John Collier was Secretary.[2] Before he left Chicago for Washington, however, Ickes decided to seek the post of Secretary of the Interior.[3]

---

[1]As did certain other prominent Americans who wired the President-elect on January 28, 1933: "so great is the Indian distress in many tribes and so rapid is the shrinkage of Indian property held in trust by the government, that we do not believe that we are exaggerating when we suggest that your administration represents almost a last chance for the Indians." The telegram was signed by 600 notables including Robert M. Hutchins, John A. Ryan, Lewis Meriam, Oliver LaFarge, and John Collier. *Senate Doc. 214*, 72d Cong., 2d sess., p. 26.

[2]Oliver LaFarge, *As Long as Grass Shall Grow* (New York: Longmans Green and Co., 1940), p. 68.

[3]Harold Ickes, *The Secret Diary of Harold Ickes*, Vol. 1: *The First Thousand Days, 1933-1936* (New York: Simon and Schuster, 1953), p. viii and pp. 1-10.

Successful in his quest, Ickes found himself face to face with a formidable problem when he sought to have John Collier appointed Commissioner of Indian Affairs. The problem was not so much Collier as it was his rival for the office, Edgar B. Meritt, who had served as Assistant Commissioner of Indian Affairs from 1913 to 1929 when he was ousted from his job shortly after Burke's resignation. He was also the brother-in-law of Joe T. Robinson, the powerful Senate majority leader from Arkansas. Meritt and Robinson fought hard, but in the end Roosevelt sided with Ickes.[4] The showdown, as Ickes described it, was dramatic.

At 5:30 P. M. on April 11, 1933, Ickes went to the White House to discuss the post of Commissioner with the President. He found that Robinson had preceded him. Roosevelt began the conversation by stating that he had received many letters of protest to Meritt's candidacy. He then turned the conversation to other topics. Later he returned to the subject and asked Ickes for his opinion. The new Secretary stated he had documentary proof which showed that Meritt was totally unqualified for the job. When Ickes finished his talk, Roosevelt turned to Robinson and said, "Well, Joe, you see what I am up against. Every highbrow organization in the country is opposed to Meritt and Secretary Ickes, under whom he would have to work, doesn't want him."[5] With that Collier was appointed Commissioner. For twelve years he and Ickes worked closely together in the conduct of Indian affairs.

NEW PHILOSOPHY

John Collier had been a vociferous and unyielding critic of the Indian Bureau since the attempted passage of the Bursum bill in 1922. He was at last to have the opportunty to translate some of his ideas into actions. In many ways Collier was more favored than his immediate predecessors. He knew more personally about the Indians than had either Burke or Rhoads. He had almost complete backing from both the Secretary of the Interior and the President, and he had far greater sums of money at his disposal. Yet there were drawbacks to his appointment. In the course of eleven years of lobbying for the Indian cause, Collier had made friends in the Senate, but he had

---

[4]See Edgar B. Meritt folder (National Archives, Record Group 48) for the letters promoting and protesting Meritt's appointment. Several of these letters indicate that Meritt had become mentally unbalanced following his ouster in 1929. He died shortly after losing to Collier.

[5]Ickes, *The First Thousand Days*, p. 19.

also made powerful enemies in the House of Representatives which by 1935 would seriously limit his freedom of action. There was also his philosophy for Indian betterment which called for a radical break with the past. Collier charged that the allotment policy and bureaucratic control of Indian lives had proven a failure in integrating the Indians into the white civilization. He concluded from this that allotment must not only cease, but that more land must be given to the Indians, a policy which stepped on the toes of many vested interests. To replace the centralized control of the Bureau over the Indian, he favored local self-government and economic self-sufficiency. To some this concept appeared to be tinged with Communism,[6] or at best to represent a regression in Indian policy.

Many critics of John Collier have, through oversimplification of his statements, created a straw man easy to attack. One of the major criticisms is that he envisioned an Indian society completely separated from the whites: a "glass cage" society preserved for tourists and anthropologists, in which the Indian lived much as he had centuries ago. This type of criticism fails to grasp the essence of the Collier reform, which aimed essentially at working out a pattern of living for a minority group in a pluralistic society,[7] as Collier stated in 1935:

> Modernity and white Americanism are not identical. If the Indian life is a good life, then we should be proud and glad to have this different and native culture going on by the side of ours. . . . America is coming to understand this, and to know that in helping the Indian to save himself, we are helping to save something that is precious to us as well as to him.[8]

Neither complete separation nor complete integration was desirable. The goal was a blending of cultures which, from the Indian viewpoint, would enable him to select from the dominant culture what he believed to be helpful and good without, in the meantime, having to sacrifice those good and desirable aspects of his native culture.

---

[6]In April, 1935, the House Committee on Indian Affairs which almost from the outset had opposed Collier, attempted to place him in a bad position by associating him with Roger Baldwin of the American Civil Liberties Union. The implication was that by association, Collier was shielding Communism and advocating the overthrow of the government, thus not fit to be Commissioner. See U. S. House, Committee on Indian Affairs, *Hearings on H. R. 7781, Indian Conditions and Affairs*, 74th Cong., 1st sess., 1935. And "The Fight on the New Indian Policy," *The Nation*, CXL (April 24, 1935), p. 479.

[7]See Collier's essay on the Indians in J. B. Gittler (ed.), *Understanding Minority Groups* (New York: John Wiley and Sons, Inc., 1956).

[8]*New York Times*, July 14, 1935, part vii, p. 10.

To implement this philosophy, to make it possible for the Indian to partake of some aspects of the white culture which surrounded him, Collier believed a program of rehabilitation was necessary:

> How then should we reorient Indian Land Policy? It is clear that the allotment system has not changed the Indians into responsible, self-supporting citizens. . . . As a starting point for a rational policy, we can categorically say that the immediate problem is not that of absorbing the Indians into the white population, but first of all lifting them out of material and spiritual dependency and haplessness.[9]

A three-point program to effect this goal was outlined. (1) Consolidate allotted lands into tribal or corporate ownership, acquire new lands for 90,000 landless Indians, extend financial credit to these newly formed corporate organizations so that they might develop their own natural resources. (2) Further reduce the boarding schools and accelerate the construction of day schools to educate a greater number of Indian children in their home environments. (3) Decentralize administrative control over the Indian.[10]

The translation of this program into specific recommendations for the Navajo country came in late 1933. Testifying before the House Appropriations Subcommittee, Collier presented his program. He expected first to abolish the six jurisdictions, consolidating them into one superintendency to be located at Window Rock, Arizona. A single superintendent would be given adequate power to guide the Navajos effectively without undue recourse to Washington. Decentralization was to be further achieved by dividing the newly consolidated reservation into twenty-five subareas instead of the traditional six. Collier expected a grant of $1,000,000 from the Public Works Administration to set up a demonstration area on the reservation for the control of soil erosion. The reduction of sheep and goats to the carrying capacity of the range was necessary. Funds had already been received from the Public Works Administration to provide for the construction of seventy new day-school, community-center units.[11] Despite the fact that the Appropriations Committee awarded him considerably less money than it had given his predecessor Rhoads, Collier's physical improvement program was not hampered. The

---

[9]Commissioner of Indian Affairs, *Annual Report, 1933*, pp. 108-09.

[10]Secretary of the Interior, *Annual Report, 1933*, p. 68.

[11]U. S. House, Committee on Appropriations, *Hearings on Department of the Interior Appropriation Bill, Fiscal 1935*, 73d Cong., 2d sess., 1933, pp. 372-73.

Bureau of Indian Affairs received from various "New Deal" organizations more money than it did from its own apppropriations. From 1933 to February 5, 1935, it received $44,475,000 from these agencies.[12]

SHEEP REDUCTION

The Navajo sheep-reduction program got an unexpected boost from Mother Nature during the winter of 1932-1933. A series of "unprecedented" storms and blizzards occurred on the reservation during the months of November and December. At one time an estimated 16,000 Navajos and 500,000 sheep were completely snowbound. Over 150,000 sheep starved or froze to death during the winter.[13] John Collier, who was not yet Commissioner at this time, initiated an intensive campaign in Washington to aid these people. In all, $410,000 in relief appropriations were approved by Congress; $150,000 went to replace the animals that had died. Collier at this time was unaware of the overstocked range conditions[14] and, while he later publicly admitted his error, the stock-reduction program which he instituted a few months later was handicapped by his action in this instance.

Collier set out quickly after assuming office to rectify his mistake. At the Tribal Council meeting held October 30-November 1, 1933, he stated the need for stock reduction and soil conservation, and laid before the council a seemingly reasonable program for accomplishing

---

[12]U. S. House, Committee on Appropriations, *Hearings on Department of the Interior Appropriation Bill, Fiscal 1936,* 74th Cong., 1st sess., 1935, p. 626. PWA funds were used to construct the new day schools, the Window Rock offices, and to develop irrigated land. The Indian Emergency Conservation Administration undertook the construction of roads, the drilling of deep water wells, reservoir construction, spring development, rodent control, and fencing of the reservation. The Federal Surplus Relief Administration (FSRA) put up the money for the sheep purchasing program. The Soil Conservation Service (SCS) administered the range-control program. *Senate Survey,* part 34, p. 17578. Also Northern Navajo, "Annual Narrative Report, 1934," p. 3. Appropriations for the Indian Bureau had reached their height in 1932 with $27,030,046. In 1933 they dropped to $22,140,098; in 1934 to $18,966,545; and in 1935 to $16,275,185. Secretary of the Interior, *Annual Report, 1933,* p. 71; *Annual Report, 1934,* p. 117.

[13]*Cong. Record,* Vol. 75, 72d Cong., 1st sess., pp. 1167-69. Commissioner of Indian Affairs, *Annual Report, 1933,* p. 3.

[14]Collier told the Navajo Tribal Council in March, 1934, that at the time he had begun the campaign to get them money to replace their sheep, he ignored advice from various people that the range was overstocked. He went on to state: "Well, later on, I have found that I was mistaken. That there were too many stock." *Minutes of the Navajo Tribal Council Meeting, Ft. Defiance, Arizona, March 12-13, 1934.* Navajo, 00-34-054. In testimony before the House in 1935 he stated: "There had been only a vague awareness of this condition [overgrazing] which had crept upon them until a year and a half ago, or shortly after I became Commissioner. I myself did not know it." U. S. House, *Hearings on H. R. 7781,* 74th Cong., 1st sess., p. 358.

both. To save the Navajo range he proposed a reduction of 400,000 animals: 200,000 sheep and 200,000 goats. The loss of income incurred by the reduction would be offset by an income from wages paid by the federal government to Navajos who engaged in the soil-erosion and conservation programs. When the wage program ended in four or five years, the range would be restored and the Navajos could return to their sheep industry which would then produce, from reduced herds, an income "at least 50% greater than in the past ten years." One hundred thousand sheep should be sold immediately. The Commissioner, moreover, had a buyer ready: Harry Hopkins' Federal Surplus Relief Administration had allotted $100,000 to purchase the Navajo sheep and goats.[15]

The Navajos in the council, however, did not take kindly to the stock-reduction suggestion, and finally avoided the topic completely. Nal Nishi, delegate from Leupp, expressed the basic Navajo fear that to pass a resolution favoring the reduction plan at this time would be to move too quickly into an area about which the delegates knew too little. His hesitancy was seconded by Jim Shirly and Billy Pete, delegates from Southern Navajo and Hopi respectively, who voiced a reluctance to embrace the wage economy offered by the government during the interim period. For the Navajos, sheep were wealth, and money was a poor and unsatisfactory substitute.[16] After much debate, the council resolved that it was in favor of the other government proposals: land purchases and exchanges in Arizona and New Mexico, the Window Rock centralization plan, the building of the day schools, the soil-erosion program, and an improved irrigation program. But no action was taken on the stock-reduction proposal other than to promise that such a program would be urged upon the people.[17]

Thus, at the close of the meeting, no more than a vague promise to reduce the flocks at a later date had been elicited from the

---

[15]*Minutes of the Navajo Tribal Council, Tuba City, Arizona, October 30-November 1, 1933.* Navajo, 9659-E-1936-054. Collier even had quotas prepared for the reduction. According to the schedule, the Northern Navajo jurisdiction was to dispose of 20,000 animals; Southern Navajo, 32,000; Eastern Navajo, 15,000; Western Navajo, 15,000; Hopi, 10,000; and Leupp, 8,000. The allocation of FSRA funds was subsequently advanced to $200,000. Bureau of Indian Affairs, *The Progress of Indian Affairs from 1933 to 1936* (Washington: mimeographed, 1937), pp. 57-58.

[16]*Minutes of the Navajo Tribal Council, Tuba City, Arizona, October 30-November 1, 1933.* Navajo, 9659-E-1936-054.

[17]*Ibid.* The Window Rock centralization plan was strongly opposed by J. C. Morgan and his Shiprock delegation, but it passed over their opposition.

Navajos. Despite this lack of cooperation, the Bureau still had funds on hand with which to begin, so an attempt was made through the local superintendents to gain compliance with the government program. Sometime after the council meeting, Superintendent Balmer of the Western Navajo jurisdiction attended a Yeibichai dance west of Tuba City, Arizona. Here he made the first definite offer to buy. According to a government source, his offer was flatly refused by the large stock owners who felt that they did not need government relief and were definitely opposed to reduction. After an all-night session the large owners agreed to an across-the-board reduction of 10 percent for all Navajos in the immediate area. This pattern spread throughout the reservation so that by the spring of 1934, $200,000 of Federal Surplus Relief Administration funds had been expended for 86,517 head of sheep.[18]

This first attempt at reduction was statistically a success, but psychologically a failure. It produced suspicion and resentment against the government[19] because it took desirable stock from small owners who lived on a subsistence level and merely culled undesirable stock from the large owners. No real reduction was accomplished in the areas where the need was imperative and much harm was done in others. Nor did the $1,000,000 being spent for rehabilitation seem to trickle down to those most in need of the wage income. The Navajos were becoming opposed to further sheep reduction.

In March, 1934, the Bureau again went before the Tribal Council seeking Navajo approval of the sheep-reduction program. The argument was stronger this time. James Stewart, Chief of the Indian Office Land Division, told the council bluntly that he was sure that the New Mexico and Arizona boundary-extension bills would fail if the Navajos did not enact a program of stock reduction and soil conservation. Moreover, he threatened the withdrawal of $2,000,000 in soil-conservation wages if they did not approve the Bureau's program. After lengthy discussion the council unanimously agreed in principle to both the stock-reduction and soil-conservation plans; the details were to be worked out after the delegates had had a chance to confer with their people. To avoid the criticism that had been leveled at the earlier voluntary reduction program, however, the delegates insisted that families with herds of 100 sheep and/or goats or less must not

---

[18]Bureau of Indian Affairs, *The Progress of Indian Affairs from 1933 to 1936,* pp. 57-58. E. R. Freyer, "A History of the Stock Reduction Program," *Senate Survey,* part 34, p. 17985.

[19]Freyer, "A History of the Stock Reduction Program," *ibid.*

be required to take part in the reduction program. Those in this group who possessed herds in which goats comprised more than 50 percent of the herd were, however, required to sell these animals and use the money thus obtained to purchase sheep from the large owners.[20] One month later another council was held at Crownpoint, New Mexico. Here the delegates agreed to the sale of 150,000 goats. The Indian Bureau promised to return in July with a formal contract for the Tribal Council to sign.[21]

This contract was to contain the following promises. The Navajos would agree to sell 150,000 goats in 1934 and, in addition, they would be allowed to sell 50,000 sheep. For this purchase the FSRA would set aside $250,000. The Navajo subsistence herds would not be affected by the agreement. Until reduction was accomplished, the Navajos would sell 80 percent of their lamb crop annually. All goats remaining after this sale would be castrated or sterilized in return for eventual replacement by milk goats furnished by the government.[22]

Even before the meeting broke up there were signs of discontent over the reduction agreement. Becenti Bega, delegate from the Eastern Navajo jurisdiction, confronted Collier with the fact that despite the Bureau's insistence on the relationship between stock reduction and the boundary-extension proposal, the New Mexico boundary bill had been defeated in Congress. It was his understanding, he said, that if the Navajos agreed to reduce their flocks, "we would have that additional boundary line. . . ." In view of Collier's failure to produce, he went on, "I think we have a right to withhold half of our goat reduction too."[23] There is no clearcut evidence to indicate how powerful Bega's argument was in the final Navajo decision to fight the reduction measure. But even without it, there were other good reasons that led to this position.

The original plan for the disposal of the goats called for the government to can the meat and return it to the reservation for use at the new schools. When it proved difficult to get the goats to the packing plants, however, orders were given to slaughter the animals

---

[20]*Minutes of the Navajo Tribal Council Meeting, Ft. Defiance, Arizona, March 12-13, 1934.* Navajo, 00-34-054. See also Ickes to Wheeler, June, 1934 (Navajo, 19189-1934-013), for a statement that the Navajos had been frequently informed of the intimate connection between stock reduction and land expansion.

[21]*Minutes of the Navajo Tribal Council Meeting, Crownpoint, New Mexico, April 9-11, 1934.* Navajo, 00-34-054.

[22]*Minutes of the Navajo Tribal Council Meeting, Keams Canyon, Arizona, July 10-12, 1934.* Navajo, 00-34-054.

[23]*Ibid.*

on the reservation after purchase. Some of the goats were dried or jerked for food but others were merely shot and left to rot. A government document tells how 3,000 head were shot at one time in Navajo Canyon. The Navajos, who viewed their sheep and goats as subsistence itself, were incapable of understanding this "inexcusable waste."[24]

As if this were not enough, the government agents violated even the letter of their agreement. In the checkerboard area to the east of the reservation in New Mexico, the government purchasing agents bought sheep and goats from many Navajos who owned only subsistence flocks. The result was to impoverish many families, forcing them onto relief and, even worse, to allow the white men in the area to overrun the now-vacant Navajo range. When the Taylor Grazing districts were formed, the Navajos in this area lost priority to the land.[25] It was bureaucratic blunders of just this type that Collier had so bitterly criticized during the Burke administration.

It is not surprising that in 1935, when the FSRA again allotted $362,500 for the purchase of 200,000 Navajo sheep and goats, the council refused to bind itself to an agreement. Only 14,317 sheep and 14,185 goats were purchased under this appropriation; the remainder of the funds were diverted for a similar purchase at the Pueblo reservations of Laguna and Acoma.[26]

The sheep-reduction program was a sorry spectacle although some alleviation of the range was accomplished. It was an expensive blunder in terms of overall results. The total expenditure of $476,000 for 315,000 sheep and goats through 1935 reduced the Navajo herds by only 212,000 animals. This came about as a result of a declining lamb market. Despite the Navajo promise in the contract, the lamb market was so bad in these years that buyers could not be found for the 80 percent of the lamb crop which was to be sold annually. Nor were the remaining goats castrated. The Bureau simply could not find the milk goats it had promised to provide in their stead. The formula outlined at the Keams Canyon council meeting in 1934, Collier stated in 1935, "has been incompletely carried out."[27]

---

[24]*Senate Survey*, part 34, pp. 17985-88.

[25]U. S. House, Committee on Indian Affairs, *Hearings on H. R. 8360, Conditions of Indians in the United States*, 74th Cong., 2d sess., 1936, p. 51.

[26]Bureau of Indian Affairs, *The Progress of Indian Affairs from 1933 to 1936*, p. 57.

[27]U. S. House, *Hearings on H. R. 7781*, 74th Cong., 1st sess., pp. 354-55. See also *Senate Survey*, part 34, pp. 17537-58.

Even worse was the resentment which the program built up in the Navajos as the years progressed. A range rider hired by the Bureau to enforce the reduction program was set upon and severely beaten with heavy clubs as he attempted to deliver notices of reduction quotas. Those who opposed the program, usually the big stock owners, sometimes attempted to incite their followers to murder other government enforcement personnel.[28] Navajos were jailed in an attempt to control these outbursts and to enforce the program. Buck Austin, a Navajo from the western area of the reservation, has left an account of this treatment at Bureau hands in which he maintains that he was transferred from one jail to another for eighty-two days before he was released.[29]

The sheep-reduction program was necessary and, despite Navajo opposition, the Bureau, for the good of the Navajo, had very little choice except to enforce it. It is ironic, however, that the methods and the immediate results were little better than those of the Burke administration.

WHEELER-HOWARD BILL

While the reduction program was underway, plans were made in Washington to present to Congress a bill which would incorporate the major ideas of the Collier administration. Popularly known as the Wheeler-Howard bill for its Congressional sponsors, Senator Burton K. Wheeler and Representative Edgar Howard (Dem., Nebraska), it was granted a hearing in the spring of 1934, and passed into law, with amendments, in June, 1934.

As originally drafted by the Indian Office, the bill contained six major provisions. (1) Indian societies were to be recognized and empowered to undertake political, administrative, and economic self-government. (2) The allotment policy was to cease and landless Indians were to be given new lands. (3) Fractionalized allotted lands were to be consolidated and merged into the tribal estate. (4) An agricultural and industrial credit fund was to be established for Indian use. (5) A system of Indian courts, responsible to the individual tribes, was to be created below the federal jurisdiction. (6) The Secretary of the Interior was to be empowered to waive Civil Service

---

[28]Elizabeth Ward, *No Dudes, Few Women, Life with a Navaho Range Rider* (Albuquerque: University of New Mexico Press, 1951), pp. 77-79.

[29]Robert W. Young and William Morgan (eds.), *Navajo Historical Selections* (Washington: G.P.O., 1954).

regulations for otherwise-qualified Indian personnel.[30] The initial bill was a lengthy and intricately contrived document. As it passed through Congress much of its verbiage and several of its provisions were deleted. It incurred major opposition in the House of Representatives.

The House opposition focused on two of the six major provisions: the Indian courts and the self-governing corporations. For years Collier had opposed the Indian judicial system, charging it with inhumane abuses. Under the law, federal courts had jurisdiction over eight major crimes; minor crimes were either handled by the Indians themselves, where their tribal organization was still intact, or by an administrative tribunal composed of the local superintendent and several Indians appointed by the Secretary of the Interior. It was Collier's contention that the latter system had restricted the Indians' civil rights. He wished, therefore, to free them from Bureau and Department control and to entrust judicial power on the lower levels to the tribe itself.[31] Many Congressmen were opposed to this because they believed that the Indians should be subjected to the same judicial norms as other citizens.

The strongest opposition to the self-governing corporations came from Congressman William W. Hastings (Dem., Oklahoma), himself an enrolled member of the Cherokee tribe. He charged that self-government was a regressive measure which would result in Indian nonparticipation in local and state government.[32] After lengthy hearings the House struck out everything after the enabling clause of the Bureau bill and substituted its own draft which omitted the Indian courts, the self-governing corporations, and "various other provisions which were highly controversial or not urgently required at this time. . . ."[33]

With the exception of one hearing in February, 1934, the Senate did not get around to the Wheeler-Howard bill until late April. The many objections to the bill in the House had led to several major amendments by this time. For one, the original bill made it compul-

---

[30]Collier, *Indians of the Americas,* pp. 264-65.

[31]U. S. House, Committee on Indian Affairs, *Hearings on H. R. 7902, Readjustment of Indian Affairs,* 73d Cong., 2d sess., 1934, pp. 315-16.

[32]*Cong. Record,* Vol. 78, 73d Cong., 2d sess., pp. 9267-68.

[33]U. S. House, Committee on Indian Affairs, *Readjustment of Indian Affairs,* 73d Cong., 2d sess., Rept. 1804.

sory for allotted Indians to transfer their land titles to the chartered communities approved in the bill. This was now made optional. The House also recommended that Collier obtain approval from the tribes to indicate that they favored his program. As a result, meetings were held with the Indians in an attempt to explain the bill to them. About forty separate amendments resulted from this action. A third major change was made when the Bureau agreed to allow any Indian tribe or group to exempt themselves from the Wheeler-Howard bill by a majority vote after it had become law.[34] These amendments placed the bill in a more acceptable position. In addition, Roosevelt himself came to its defense when on April 28, 1934, he addressed identical letters to Wheeler and Howard stating his approval of the bill and expressing his wish that it be passed at the present session of Congress.[35] Howard announced the following day that with the President's backing and the amendments which had been made, he was sure that the bill would now go through.[36]

The opposition that remained was mainly concerned with the Indian court provision. Senator Wheeler, who professed himself baffled at some of the bill's provisions, at last came out in opposition to this measure "absolutely," and it was killed.[37] An amendment sponsored by Howard removing compulsion from the transfer of allotted

---

[34]U. S. Senate, Committee on Indian Affairs, *Hearings on S. 2755 and S. 3645, To Grant to Indians Living Under Federal Tutelage the Freedom to Organize for Purposes of Local Self-Government and Economic Enterprise,* 73d Cong., 2d sess., 1934, pp. 77, 87, 100. Despite Collier's insistence earlier on freeing the Indians from Bureau dictatorship, the many compulsory clauses in the first draft of this bill seem to indicate that his own attitude toward Indian policy was somewhat authoritarian.

[35]U. S. Senate, Committee on Indian Affairs, *Authorizing Indians to Form Business Councils, Corporations, and for other purposes,* 73d Cong., 2d sess., 1934, Rept. 1080, pp. 3-4.

[36]*New York Times,* April 27, 1934, p. 34. There appears to have been some doubt up to the last concerning the probability of the bill's passage. Although Ickes believed the bill would pass if put to a vote, he was concerned as late as June 9, 1934, with the difficulty of getting the bill out of committee. Ickes, *The First Thousand Days,* p. 169.

[37]U. S. Senate, *Hearings on S. 2755 and S. 3645,* 73d Cong., 2d sess., p. 146. In his autobiography Wheeler later wrote that he was "not proud" of having helped to enact the Indian Reorganization Act. As one of Collier's supporters on the Senate subcommittee investigating Indian affairs in the late 1920's and early 1930's, Wheeler introduced the bill at Collier's request "without even having read the bill." When he did read it he found much that he did not like. The special Indian courts he termed "a crazy idea" which he had "thrown out in committee." See Burton K. Wheeler, *Yankee From the West* (New York: Doubleday and Co., 1962), p. 315.

lands to the chartered communities had already practically killed that provision. The other four objectives of the original bill, in somewhat modified but basically the same form, were accepted by the House on June 16, 1934, and the bill was sent to the President. On June 18 it became law (48 Stat., 984-986).

Despite amendments, the Indian Reorganization Act, as it was officially named, was a milestone in Indian history comparable to the Dawes Severalty Act of 1887, but representing a definite break with the tradition and philosophy of the past. It bore the clear stamp of the opposition movements of the 1920's, and incorporated both the major ideas of the Meriam Report and those of John Collier. Its major provisions are paraphrased below.

1. No land on any kind of Indian reservation should in the future be allotted to any Indian.

2. $2,000,000 annually was authorized to provide land for landless Indians.

3. The Secretary of the Interior was empowered to issue regulations to restrict the number of Indian livestock to the carrying capacity of the range.

4. $250,000 annually was authorized for expenses incurred in organizing the chartered Indian corporations.

5. A revolving credit fund of $10,000,000 was authorized for the purpose of promoting economic development among those tribes that chose to incorporate themselves.

6. $250,000 annually was to be made available for Indian children who sought special vocational or trade school education.

7. Civil Service requirements for positions in the Indian Service were waived for Indians.

8. All Indian tribes were empowered to adopt an appropriate constitution and by-laws for their own self-government when approved by a majority of the adult members of the tribe.

9. Charters of incorporation granted to the tribes adopting them the right to purchase, own, manage, operate, or dispose of their property, real or personal.

10. An Indian was defined as any person of Indian descent who was a member of a recognized tribe under federal jurisdiction at the time of the passage of the act, all persons who were descendants of such members and were on June 1, 1934, residing within the boundaries of such a reservation, and all other persons of one-half or more Indian blood.

NAVAJO REJECTION

The Indian Reorganization Act was accepted by more than two-thirds of all the Indians in the United States. One hundred and seventy-two tribes with a total population of 132,426 persons accepted it; seventy-three tribes representing 63,467 Indians rejected it. The vote on acceptance of the act was somewhat closer, however, than these figures indicate, for the actual votes cast show that 38,762 Indians voted for the act, 23,794 against it.[38] On many reservations the vote was close. On the Navajo reservation the act was defeated.

The major aim of the Indian Reorganization Act, to put a end to the allotment policy, came as the result of the Indian experience in Oklahoma and other Plains states, although Oklahoma and Alaska were initially exempted from the act. The second major objective, the establishment of Indian self-government, was derived from the example of the Southwestern Indians, particularly the Pueblos and the Navajos. Throughout the course of the hearings on the Wheeler-Howard bill, Wheeler and Collier both had frequently pointed to the Navajos as the prime example of a tribe which would welcome this aspect of the bill.[39] It was a particularly bitter blow when the Navajos, the largest single tribe in the nation, rejected the act.

The Navajo vote should not, however, have come as a great surprise to the Indian Bureau. Since February, 1934, unfavorable reports had been received from the reservation. On February 11, the superintendent at Shiprock, after holding meetings to explain the bill at various locations on his jurisdiction, reported to Collier that

> at practically every meeting they were of the opinion that with the Tribal Council and community organizations, they were self-governing. I am frank to tell you, Mr. Commissioner, that at none of these meetings did they become enthusiastic over any drastic change.[40]

In an apparent attempt to avoid any argument that might damage tribal unity, Collier recommended in March that each jurisdiction pass on the bill rather than have it brought before the Tribal Council for debate. The Navajos at Fort Defiance, however, opposed this plan

---

[38]*Indians at Work*, July 15, 1935, pp. 1-3. And, Commissioner of Indian Affairs, *Annual Report, 1935*, pp. 115-16.

[39]U. S. Senate, *Hearings on S. 2755 and S. 3645*, 73d Cong., 2d sess., pp. 30, 67, 145. See also Collier to E. R. McCray, March 1, 1934. National Archives, Record Group 75, Wheeler-Howard file, 4894-34-066, part 1-A.

[40]McCray to Collier, February 11, 1934. *Ibid.*

and insisted that the bill be considered in the council.[41] At the March
meeting it was, therefore, discussed but since there was no unanimity,
a vote was not taken. In spite of this lack of enthusiasm, an official
Bureau publication reported that "near unanimous approval was . . .
indicated by the delegates of the Navajo tribe at this session," and
it was freely predicted that the Wheeler-Howard bill "would be approved without any serious opposition when the Tribal Council next
meets April 9."[42]

Despite this optimism, unfavorable reports continued to arrive
at the Washington office. Chester Faris, superintendent of the Santa
Fe Indian School, was sent into the reservation to encourage sentiment for the bill. He reported a few days after the March Tribal
Council meeting that he saw few signs of interest in the bill among
the Navajos:

> . . . it seems there is rather an atmosphere of confusion and be-
> wilderment among them which is difficult to clear. The first
> meeting at Wingate was very discouraging, a second at Shiprock
> little better. . . .
> You will know that I am not often pessimistic in this work, hence
> my hesitancy in giving you this picture of the problems out here.[43]

When the Tribal Council did actually vote on the bill on April 10,
1934, only seven of the twelve delegates voted for it. The three delegates from Shiprock and the two from Tuba City refrained from
voting.[44] The Navajos as a tribe thus went on record favoring the
still-pending Wheeler-Howard bill, but the lack of unanimity on the
vote signified future trouble.

Between the time of the council vote and the Navajo referendum
on the applicability of the Wheeler-Howard bill to their own reservation, more than a year went by. During this period, the second
phase of the detested sheep-reduction program was carried out, the
New Mexico boundary-extension bill was defeated in Congress and
cattlemen, under protection of the Taylor Grazing Act, moved onto

---

[41]Hunter to Collier, February 15, 1934. *Ibid.*

[42]*Indians at Work,* April 1, 1934, p. 7.

[43]C. E. Faris to Collier, March 16, 1934. Wheeler-Howard file, 14499-34-066,
part 1A-1B.

[44]*Minutes of the Navajo Tribal Council Meeting, Crownpoint, New Mexico,
April 9-11, 1934.* Navajo, 00-34-054. In *Indians at Work* (April 15, 1934, p. 8) it
was reported that the vote had been seven for, one opposed, and four favorable
but abstaining.

TABLE III
NAVAJO VOTE ON THE WHEELER-HOWARD BILL BY JURISDICTIONS

	For	Against
Keams Canyon Navajo (Hopi)	1,322	63
Eastern Navajo	1,131	1,917
Southern Navajo	3,272	2,921
Northern Navajo	536	2,771
Leupp	700	74
Western Navajo	834	468
Total	7,795	8,214

Source: *Albuquerque Journal,* June 17, 1935, p. 8 and June 24, p. 6. The *Journal's* analysis of the vote argued that the Navajos believed their original treaty with the federal government provided ample protection without the additional safeguards claimed for the act. The Bureau of Indian Affairs reported the final vote as 7,608 for, 7,992 against. Secretary of the Interior, *Annual Report, 1935,* p. 116.

the Navajo pastures in the Eastern Navajo jurisdiction. All of these events were reflected in the Navajo vote.

On June 17, 1935, the Navajos went to the polls. A week before, Commissioner Collier came to the reservation for a two-day defense of the bill. On June 11, Leo Parker, a Navajo from the Southern Navajo jurisdiction, opposed Collier publicly and charged that the Bureau was coercing the Navajo vote by threatening to withdraw PWA funds from the soil-conservation program. On June 12, Howard Gorman, a Navajo from Ganado, Arizona, accused the Commissioner of being a Communist, a charge to which Collier replied by accusing Gorman of religious prejudice.[45] When the vote was counted, the Navajos had defeated the Indian Reorganization Act by a vote of 8,214 to 7,795.

The breakdown of the voting by jurisdictions contained in Table III indicates several reasons for the defeat of the bill. The Northern Navajo jurisdiction, where the growing influence of J. C. Morgan, the leader of the Tribal Council opposition to the bill, was strongest, overwhelmingly opposed the measure. The Eastern Navajo reservation, whose delegates had voted for the bill at the April, 1934, meeting, now rejected it by a sizeable majority. This was the area most affected by the failure of the New Mexico boundary bill and the region where the sheep-reduction blunders made possible the white invasion under the Taylor Grazing Act. The populous Southern Navajo jurisdiction, whose boundaries had been extended over the public-domain Navajos in the Gallup region in 1928, returned a very close vote despite its

[45]*Albuquerque Journal,* June 11, 1935, p. 1; June 12, p. 1.

earlier united stand in the Tribal Council. In all probability this vote, too, indicates the opposition of the public-domain Indians.

In his annual report for 1935,[46] Collier blamed the Navajo defeat on vested interests in the area who spread "fantastic fictions" about the Indian Reorganization Act, connecting it "falsely" with the sheep-reduction plan. Navajos were told that to accept the act would mean the immediate destruction of their sheep and goats. Although there is no doubt some truth in Collier's statement, there is better reason to believe that the Navajo opposition stemmed from the causes previously discussed. There is also the consideration that the Indian Reorganization Act, so baffling at times to men like Senator Wheeler, seemed to offer very little to the average Navajo. He was in little danger of being allotted. He believed that his Tribal Council had already given him self-government. He was excluded from the land-purchase funds so long as the boundary-extension bills were pending. Only the revolving credit fund was lost. The average Navajo conceivably believed that he could well afford to forego this provision in return for defeating the one empowering the Secretary of the Interior to enforce grazing restrictions on his land. As later events proved, this was not to be the case. The sheep-reduction program progressed over Navajo objections. Despite the vote, the Indian Reorganization Act, with modifications here and there, was essentially applied to the Navajo reservation.

------

[46]Secretary of the Interior, *Annual Report, 1935*, p. 116. See also Collier's statement in *Indians at Work*, July 1, 1935, p. 44.

CHAPTER 10

Education, Health and Politics

Beyond a doubt, the failure of the federal government to recognize the educational and health problems of the Navajos in the 1920's was its most conspicuous shortcoming. Despite reports from the lowest field agents up through the Secretary of the Interior himself, little was done in a constructive way to meet the problems of the Navajos in these areas.

EDUCATION

The Indians of the Southwest had traditionally lagged behind the other members of their race in education. The major reasons were historic and economic. The Southwest was one of the last areas in the continental United States to be populated by the western-moving tide of pioneers. Even as the region began to fill up with immigrants and an interest in the welfare of the Indians grew, there was always the problem of the means to educate a people who were often on the move: children could not complete a school term when their parents were constantly following the flocks. As a result, the only type of school which succeeded in any measure in much of the Southwest was the boarding school, where children were sent to live as well as to learn for eight or more months of the year.

In the Navajo country the problem was particularly acute by the 1920's. Despite the promise made by the Navajos in the treaty of 1868 to compel their children between the ages of six and sixteen to attend school, little interest in education had been evidenced by the tribe. The United States, by the same treaty, had obligated itself to provide a school and a teacher for every thirty children who could be "induced or compelled to attend school."[1] Legally the obligation of the federal government had been satisfied as a result of the Navajo

---

[1] 15 Stat., 667.

171

apathy. In practice, the government also evidenced little interest in Navajo education.

The reports of the Commissioner of Indian Affairs before 1919 indicate little grasp of the educational situation. Commissioner Sells, it is true, had called attention to the lack of schools in the Navajo and Papago country in 1914,[2] but his appeal for expanded facilities apparently had little effect on the Congress.

In 1919, however, both the Congress and the Board of Indian Commissioners inquired into the Navajo school situation and came up with some startling statistics. Of an estimated 9,613 Navajo children eligible for school, the Board of Indian Commissioners found that only 2,089 were actually attending school. The House Indian Affairs Committee in 1920 was taken aback by the comment of Superintendent Paquette that 75 percent of the children in his jurisdiction could not even be given a prevocational education (grades 1-6) because of the lack of facilities. The reason he gave was a shortage of funds for building schools.[3] Paquette also testified that in the absence of vocational schools on the reservation and in the face of Navajo reluctance to allow their children to attend nonreservation schools for vocational training, not only were the greater part of the Navajo children receiving no education but, of those who did receive the basic course, very few went on to trade or vocational schools.[4]

These and similar investigations elsewhere culminated in 1920 in a campaign to educate the Indian in record time. The Secretary of the Interior was charged by law in 1920 "to make and enforce such rules and regulations as may be necessary to secure the enrollment and regular attendance of eligible Indian children who are wards of the Government" (41 Stat., 410). In typical fashion the outgoing administration promulgated regulations which its successor would have to implement. Thereafter, all Indian children were subject to the compulsory school-attendance laws of the states in which they were resident. If the children lived beyond the limits of public school districts and their parents failed or refused to place them in suitable schools, they were to attend boarding schools designated by the Commissioner of Indian Affairs. Those Indian parents who

---

[2]Commissioner of Indian Affairs, *Annual Report, 1914,* p. 7.

[3]Board of Indian Commissioners, *Annual Report, 1919,* p. 23. U. S. House, *Hearings, Indians of the United States,* 66th Cong., 1-3d sess., Vol. 3, p. 731.

[4]U. S. House, *Hearings, Indians of the United States,* 66th Cong., 1-3d sess., Vol. 3, p. 730.

refused to comply with the new regulation were subject to fines and imprisonment. In the Navajo country the previous shortage of schools would be solved at no increase in federal expenditures by sending all Hopi and Pueblo children to enlarged day schools, and then moving the Navajos into the boarding schools vacated by them.[5] It seemed to make little difference that the great majority of Navajos would be forced by this regulation to attend boarding schools which were off their reservation, some at great distances.

In addition to inheriting the directive and the plan to educate Navajos in nonreservation boarding schools, the incoming Burke administration also inherited a Congress which was interested in trimming old expenses and avoiding new ones. Even before the Harding administration came into control of fiscal policy, this penny-pinching attitude had been felt in the Navajo schools. Homer P. Snyder (Rep., New York), Chairman of the House Indian Affairs Committee, informed Superintendent Paquette in 1920 that the "desire of Congress" was that every Indian boarding school in the country should be filled to capacity at all times and that where this could not be accomplished, it was his committee's intention to close those schools. When Paquette complained that even under present conditions he was unable to adequately clothe and feed the children entrusted to his care, Snyder replied that when he could demonstrate the ability to keep his school filled, the necessary funds would be forthcoming.[6]

This attitude of Congress, requiring the local superintendents to fill quotas in order to obtain the necessary funds to run their schools, led to definite abuses in the period of the Burke administration. The year following Snyder's comment, Representative Louis Cramton, the new House Appropriations Subcommittee Chairman, delivered a stern lecture to the Bureau in which he accused it of spending more money on its pupils than was allowed under the law. He warned Burke that henceforth strict compliance with the law would be the order of the day under his chairmanship.[7]

In his first year as Commissioner, Burke inaugurated a "Drive for Education" within the Indian service which employed such slogans

---

[5]Commissioner of Indian Affairs, *Annual Report, 1921*, pp. 7-8.

[6]U. S. House, *Hearings, Indians of the United States*, 66th Cong., 1-3d sess., Vol. 3, pp. 723-24.

[7]U. S. House, Committee on Appropriations, *Hearings on Department of the Interior Appropriation Bill, Fiscal 1923*, 67th Cong., 2d sess., 1921, pp. 326-28.

as "Every eligible Indian child in school every day," and "Every Indian school filled to the limit." In 1922 he announced that within four or five years every Indian child in the Southwest would be provided with school facilities. "As Commissioner of Indian Affairs," he wrote, "I am not willing to longer overlook the failure to provide schools for these native Americans." By 1923 his program was seemingly nearing its goal, for the Board of Indian Commissioners announced that while one-third of all Indian children who were not in school were Navajos, the percentage of unschooled children within this tribe had dropped to 67 percent, as compared with the Board's 1919 figures which showed 78 percent out of school. While much remained to be done, progress was nevertheless evident.[8]

Although the figures were impressive, the methods which made them possible were cruel and reprehensible. Driven by criticism to educate the Navajos quickly and yet hampered by the Congressional reluctance to build the necessary schools, Burke attempted to meet the situation by limiting the reservation boarding schools to the first three grades, transporting all Navajo children in and above the fourth grade to other nonreservation boarding schools throughout the West and Southwest. Opposition to this plan developed quickly.

The Navajos themselves protested through their newly formed Tribal Council in 1924. Hagerman reported to Burke following the meeting that "while it does not so appear in the minutes," the government policy in this matter had been discussed at great length. The Navajos complained of force in the implementation of the new policy, he recounted, and they demonstrated knowledge of a United States statute which prohibited the government from sending the children to nonreservation schools without the voluntary consent of the parents.[9] Almost as serious in the Navajo mind as the forced removal of their children was the threat to their economic existence which the compulsory school-attendance regulation posed — some children were needed at home to tend the sheep. Burke, accordingly, announced in 1924 that the compulsory ruling was not suitable to the Navajo economy. Instead he appealed to the Congress for increased funds with which to conduct a year-round school of two terms of six months each so that those Navajos not in attendance during the

---

[8]Commissioner of Indian Affairs, *Annual Report, 1922*, p. 5; *Annual Report 1925*, p. 1. Board of Indian Commissioners, *Annual Report, 1923*, p. 4.

[9]Hagerman to Burke, August 4, 1924. Hagerman Papers, Commissioner's file July-December, 1926.

regular school year could receive some education.[10] This program failed to materialize and the Bureau returned to its earlier position.

As outspoken on this issue as any critic of the Bureau was the Board of Indian Commissioners. A special report by Flora Warren Seymour on the Navajo school situation stated that "strong objection" to the Bureau's intensive campaign to place all Navajo children in school had been encountered. She deplored the policy of sending Indian children to schools off their reservation, stating that to send children below the sixth grade to a nonreservation school was contrary to general practice and, furthermore, nothing in the curriculum of these schools would prepare even older students for the kind of life to which they would return. Miss Seymour called for a complete re-evaluation of Navajo education:

> If the school has a definite aim at all it is to lead him to an entirely different life, a different stage of culture, a different standard of living. . . . We cannot escape the fact that we are planing to educate him out of his present environment.[11]

Burke also encountered opposition from the local superintendents. His attempts to impress upon them the necessity for filling their quotas in the nonreservation schools by transferring all children who had completed the third grade,[12] resulted in a unanimous statement, signed by the six superintendents and Hagerman, opposing the policy:

> . . . we are unanimously of the opinion, from the investigations we have made, that the quota of children asked of us is altogether too large and we know that to secure them will be a task well nigh impossible. Certainly the full numbers demanded cannot be secured without seriously antagonizing the Indian population as a whole. The parents are already generally bitter and discontented at having so many of their children sent off the reservation to school and the insistence of the Educational Division of the Office that the maximum estimated quota of children be found by the superintendents is antagonizing the Navajo to a very considerable degree to the whole school policy of the Indian Office, and to some extent to the Government itself, . . . a very regrettable situation.
>
> The Navajos are not antagonistic to education, . . . but

---

[10]Commissioner of Indian Affairs, *Annual Report, 1924,* p. 6.

[11]Report of Flora Warren Seymour, July 31, 1924. Navajo, 60291-24-150.

[12]Burke to Paquette, July 22, 1924. Hagerman Papers, Commissioner's file, July-December, 1924.

they do beg and implore, with ever increasing insistence that the educational plans of the Government be so adjusted as to conform to the economic and industrial necessities of their present situation.[13]

In reply to the superintendents, Burke wrote that the present policy was an "emergency measure" and that he had no thought of making any permanent changes in the general policy.[14]

Despite his protestations of the "emergency nature" of the program and despite the fact that he could demonstrate an increased school enrollment, Burke received no support from the Congress. By 1924 the statute limitations per child had been raised to $225 annually versus $200 in 1921. Cramton, however, refused to appropriate more than the former figure. When Assistant Commissioner Meritt protested that out of this sum the Bureau had to pay for tuition, board, clothing, books, medical and dental services, and that comparable costs for such services in the average white school averaged $500, there was no evidence that the committee was impressed. Indeed, it threatened to cut the appropriations for the Fort Mohave school which had not met the enrollment figures specified the year before. Only on Meritt's promise that it would be filled the following year, a statement obviously evoked by sheer desperation, were the funds reinstated. An even more grotesque example of the committee's unwillingness to cooperate with the Bureau came when Meritt presented the attendance figures for the Theodore Roosevelt School at Fort Apache, Arizona. The school buildings had been taken over from the War Department in 1923. Despite the fact that they needed repair and remodeling, the school was opened in April of that same year. The school had been plagued by Navajo "desertions," Meritt explained, because the Navajos were opposed to its location so far from their reservation. The buildings were still in a bad state of disrepair and he estimated that it would take six months to get the physical

---

[13]Superintendents to Burke, April 21, 1924. Board of Indian Commissioners, tray #16. The quotas referred to in this letter had reference to the fact that the superintendents were informed each year by the Educational Division of the Bureau of the number of students they were each to furnish the nonreservation boarding schools. The quotas were nearly always higher than the superintendents thought reasonable, a condition caused in great part by the lack of a census on the reservation until 1929. In time the policy led to child-snatching between jurisdictions.

[14]Burke to superintendents in charge of Navajo, Zuñi, and Hopi reservations, and the Commissioner to the Navajo tribe, May 26, 1924. Hagerman Papers, Commissioner's file, January-June, 1926.

plant up to standards — this despite the fact that Navajo children had been living there for eighteen months. Cramton's comment varied not a bit: fill it or the funds would be cut.[15] Burke's statement before the committee that, with his proposed two-term school program, he could take care of all the Navajo children without additional schools, should perhaps be criticized but, on the other hand, he perhaps realized the futility of requesting additional funds from the committee.[16]

By 1925 Navajo tempers were near the explosion point as a result of the enforced school policy. In April of that year Chee Dodge wrote to Hagerman protesting the policy. He reminded the Navajo Commissioner that the high percentage of desertions from the Theodore Roosevelt School at Fort Apache was an expression of the general Navajo attitude, and he warned Hagerman that the policy was causing great harm to the Navajo sheep industry. He intimated that he personally "smelled a rat" in the whole plan whereby the government might possibly take over the Navajo oil interests in the event that the tribe should openly oppose the program.[17]

Dodge's letter and a rumor to the effect that he was planning a trip to Washington to protest the nonreservation school program prompted a request from Hagerman to Burke for more information on the subject. Burke's reply was of little value, stating only that until schools were available, the students must be transferred to other nonreservation schools.[18] Needless to say, Burke's words were little comfort to the Navajo council which met in July, 1925.

Many Navajos spoke openly against the forced educational policy at this meeting. One of the most eloquent speeches was made by Hosteen Nez of the Hopi agency, who said:

> With a baby in your arms you kiss that baby a lot. We feel the same way about our children. But you want to come in and take

---

[15]U. S. House, *Hearings on Department of the Interior Appropriation Bill, Fiscal 1926,* 68th Cong., 2d sess., 1924, pp. 892-94.

[16]*Ibid.,* p. 694. This is one of the few times that Burke was consulted by the committee on the adequacy of appropriations. He stated that Meritt did not agree with his optimism but that he was "willing to take a chance on it anyway for a while."

[17]Dodge to Hagerman, April 20, 1925. Hagerman Papers, Commissioner's file, January-June, 1925. There is no evidence to support Dodge's supposition, but the very fact that he could conceive of this scheme demonstrates the prevalent Navajo uneasiness and suspicion caused by the forced schooling program.

[18]Hagerman to Burke, May 15, 1925; Burke to Hagerman, June 8, 1925. *Ibid.*

the children and rush these poor children off to school. We have got the same feeling for these children as you people have for yours. We want fair and square treatment. We don't want our children taken by force. About all the children we have left now is one year old, two year old, three year old — you have all the others.[19]

The delegates often repeated their approval of the Bureau's educational goal, but they insisted that primary education be furnished on the reservation and they wanted vocational schools there also. Near the close of the meeting a resolution was unanimously adopted which denounced the transfer of children below the seventh grade and their removal to a lower altitude under any circumstances, requested industrial education on the reservation, and protested the employment of immature teachers.[20] This action by the Tribal Council had no effect on federal policy. Each year the Navajo opposition became more entrenched as conditions worsened.

Superintendent Kneale at Shiprock has left the best account of the problems encountered after 1925. In 1926 he wrote directly to the Commissioner warning him that in his jurisdiction the authority of the government was being openly resisted. The intensity of the opposition, he felt, "could easily assume the magnitude of open revolt." Kneale's description of the conditions which he faced, and the methods which were being employed to enforce the Bureau directives, are illustrative of the proportions which the problem had assumed. In January, 1926, he had ordered his district farmer

to secure pupils for the Mesa school. He was instructed to make a thorough canvass of the territory covered by him. That is to say, he was instructed to visit *every* family in the territory and to secure every available child no matter how much time it might require. Argument and moral suasion were to be the first instruments used by him, but when these failed, he was directed to cause the arrest of the obdurate parent or parents and send them under escort to the agency headquarters.

---

[19]*Minutes of the Navajo Tribal Council Meeting, Ft. Wingate, New Mexico, July 7-8, 1925.* General Services, 37534-25-054.

[20]*Ibid.* The Navajo protest against the transfer to a lower altitude was based on their belief that the lower climate was injurious to the health of their children. In his annual report for 1924, Hagerman stated that the Navajos were strongly convinced that the lower climate was unhealthy and that many of the children were returning with tuberculosis. He went on to warn the Bureau that "the constantly growing difficulty of filling the schools is indissolubly linked up with the question of health and sanitation." Navajo, 61584-24-150.

It is only when we endeavor to transfer to non-reservation schools, pupils of immature age and experience and from the lower grades that we meet with opposition that, so far, seems insurmountable. For when we attempt to do this, we find that we have not the support of the parents, nor of the police, nor of the Headmen, nor of the Tribe. In fact we find ourselves without support of any kind. . . .[21]

Aside from the cruelty of this forced transfer of young children to schools many hundreds of miles from their homes, there was, as time went on, a practical reason for ending the policy. Throughout the many years of insufficient appropriations, the cost of running a boarding school had been materially reduced through the use of child labor. By 1926 the result of the transfer policy had been to greatly reduce the average age of those children who were attending the reservation boarding schools. The work which they had to perform was not, however, materially reduced. Although Kneale protested this practice, there was no remedy forthcoming.[22] Another evil was brought to light when the Meriam Commission arrived on the scene in 1927. Members of its staff were repeatedly informed that schools were enrolling many more students than they could reasonably accommodate so that the average attendance figures would meet the requirements necessary for securing further Congressional appropriations.[23]

An abrupt change in policy came with the Rhoads administration. Pledged to put the Meriam Report into action, the new Commissioner sought to get his Indian wards out of the boarding schools, both reservation and nonreservation, and into the public schools or new day schools. To attain this objective, increased appropriations were obtained so that by 1931 more money was being appropriated for Indian education than had been approved for the entire Indian

---

[21]Kneale to Commissioner of Indian Affairs, January 9, 1926. San Juan, 423-26-150.

[22]Kneale to Hagerman, July 9, 1925. Hagerman Papers, San Juan file. In this letter Kneale wrote: "We have skimmed the cream from these two schools year in and year out and transferred it to non-reservation schools much faster than the children grew up, each year transferring smaller and smaller children until now we have nothing left but small children. . . . I am sure that we require of these pupils tasks that are beyond their years and their strength and that they should not be performing, and further transfers simply intensify a condition already reprehensible."

[23]*Meriam Report*, p. 404.

Service ten years before.[24] By 1932 the total number of students in government boarding schools had been reduced, particularly in the case of smaller children.[25]

The Rhoads administration, however, had little total impact on the Navajo educational problem. The appalling shortage of facilities on the reservation was too large to overcome in four years; in 1934 there were still over 8,000 children in a school-age population of 13,000 who did not attend any schools at all.[26] The major contribution which Rhoads made was a change in the pattern of thinking both in Washington and on the reservation. In this respect he was successful, for in 1930 the Tribal Council, after a long debate which indicated that the Navajo bias toward the day schools had been overcome, unanimously voted to accept the day schools along with some small reservation boarding schools.[27] In another area, that of placing high school graduates in remunerative positions, the Rhoads administration also made great progress through the establishment of placement offices on the various reservations and in neighboring large towns and cities. In this way one of the most frustrating aspects of Indian education, the "return to the blanket," was largely eliminated.[28]

It was not until Collier's administration that the day-school building program really got underway. Sites for forty-seven day schools at points of population concentration were selected in 1935. With PWA and WPA funds, construction began shortly thereafter. Other relief

---

[24]Secretary of the Interior, *Annual Report, 1931,* p. 1. Ray Lyman Wilbur and William A. DuPuy, *Conservation in the Department of the Interior* (Washington: G. P. O., 1931), p. 126.

[25]Secretary of the Interior, *Annual Report, 1932,* p. 44.

[26]*Ibid., 1934,* p. 87.

[27]*Minutes of the Navajo Tribal Council Meeting, Ft. Wingate, New Mexico, July 7-8, 1930.* General Services, 24619-30-054. After many years of dependence upon the government to feed, clothe, and shelter their children while in school, the Navajos were reluctant to take this responsibility upon themselves.

[28]As late as 1929 this "return to the blanket" by educated Indians was one of the chief complaints of the Navajo superintendents. On August 27, 1929, C. L. Walker, superintendent of the Western Navajo jurisdiction wrote to the Commissioner of Indian Affairs: "We educate our children up to a place where, if properly handled, they could make a very good living for themselves, but we do not provide for them after they are released from school. Consequently, we lose the greater portion of what we invest in the education of each one. In many instances they have returned to my office after a year or so on the reservation and I cannot tell them from one of the uneducated, long-haired Indians." Western Navajo, 40373-29-150. The situation was particularly bad in the case of the girls. Walker was so distressed by their plight that he allowed some of his female graduates to live in the school dormitories and work for their board and room only, rather than send them back to their families. Western Navajo, "Annual Narrative Report, 1926," p. 11.

funds were employed to construct the roads that would make these schools feasible. According to Collier, three Indian children could be placed in the day school for the cost of one in a boarding school. Equally important was the fact that the day schools would serve as cultural and educational centers for an entire area. As more Navajos were educated and yet remained at home, the knowledge which they imbibed would be spread to the older members of their families. To facilitate this type of exchange, and also because studies indicated that children learned to read and write a foreign tongue more rapidly if they were well grounded in their own, the teaching of Navajo as a written language was introduced into some of the schools.[29] By 1935 local white opposition to the closing of the boarding schools and Indian opposition to a program which did not feed, clothe, and shelter the children as the boarding schools had done, resulted in a slow-down in the day-school program.

Under Rhoads and Collier a more humane and enlightened educational policy was pursued which represented a significant change from the brutal days of the Burke era. The sheer enormity of the Navajo educational problem, however, prevented its solution prior to World War II when a decline in appropriations once again produced a lapse in educational work.

HEALTH

As pointed out in various places throughout this study, the Burke administration was a particularly vulnerable target for critics of Indian affairs. This was partly because it was the heir to an outmoded and uninspired system at a time when progressive and inspired people were turning their attention to the conduct of Indian affairs; partly because Burke himself was intransigent in the face of criticism; and partly because Congress was reluctant to appropriate the sums necessary to effect desired improvements. Nowhere did these factors add up to more mismanagement than in the field of Indian health. Most of the charges made against the Bureau by its critics in this area were, unfortunately, true.

The argument that low appropriations were a hindrance to Bureau policies, though a major factor in other areas, does not seem to be

---

[29]Secretary of the Interior, *Annual Report, 1934,* p. 87; and *Annual Report, 1935,* p. 128. *Minutes of the Navajo Tribal Council Meeting, Ft. Wingate, New Mexico, July 7-8, 1933.* Navajo, 00-33-054. U. S. House, *Hearings on H. R. 7781,* 74th Cong., 1st sess., pp. 361-63.

the primary cause of the federal government's unenlightened attitude toward its wards in the field of health. It is true that the Burke administration inherited a tradition of inadequate appropriations for health purposes,[30] but it is likewise true that appropriations swelled greatly during this period: from $375,000 in 1922 to $500,000 in 1925, to $948,000 in 1928, to $1,440,000 in 1929.[31] It appears that the House Appropriations Committee and apparently the Budget Bureau were willing to spend money in this area if the requests were made. It is here that the Burke administration seriously failed the Indians, and the reason seems to be that the Bureau had a very inadequate concept of the problem.

For one thing, the physicians employed by the Bureau were substandard. The demand for physicians during World War I resulted in the loss of two-thirds of the Bureau's doctors by the close of the war. Afterwards, great difficulty was encountered in filling these vacancies, both qualitatively and quantitatively, because of the low salary scale, poor living conditions, insecure promotional policies, and general lack of equipment and other facilities. Thus, the personnel recruited under such circumstances were all too often incompetent. Such men could hardly have been expected to supply much advice to their superiors.[32]

The major reason for the backwardness of the Bureau, however, stemmed from the concept which it held of its role. The Bureau had traditionally, the Meriam Report said, considered its role in the field of health to be curative and, as a result, had too often ignored the educational and preventive aspects of a good health program. Its program had "to a great extent been merely palliative in practice."[33] Thus no matter how much money was appropriated, until a change in attitude was effected, health standards among the Indians would continue to be deficient.[34]

---

[30]In 1887 the Medical Division of the Indian Bureau was discontinued; it was not revived until 1909, and not until 1910 was the first appropriation specifically for health purposes made. See Edward Everett Dale, *The Indians of the Southwest* (Norman: University of Oklahoma Press, 1948), pp. 202-204.

[31]U. S. House, *Hearings on Department of the Interior Appropriation Bill, Fiscal 1930*, 70th Cong., 2d sess., 1928, p. 657.

[32]Commissioner of Indian Affairs, *Annual Report, 1929*, p. 30. *Meriam Report*, pp. 229-34. Dr. Haven Emerson, later president of the American Indian Defense Association, reported in 1925 that the average salary for Bureau physicians in 1924 was $1,200 to $1,300 a year. *New York Times*, March 18, 1925, p. 11.

[33]*Meriam Report*, p. 259.

[34]A striking example of the Bureau's inability to comprehend its health responsibilities is demonstrated by the fact that the medical needs of the Service,

Shortly after he assumed office, Burke, in a well-intentioned attempt to acquaint himself with health conditions on the Indian reservations, requested the American Red Cross to undertake a study of the problem. In June, 1924, the study was concluded and its recommendations forwarded to Burke. It was never published and at the height of the criticism against the Bureau in 1925-1926, the opposition forces frequently cited this fact to substantiate their charge that the Bureau, with full knowledge of the "shocking account of Indian health before it," deliberately suppressed the report to hide its own mismanagement of the health program.[35] Although such charges made good propaganda, they did not tell the entire story.

The Red Cross survey was made by Miss Florence Patterson, a Public Health Service nurse. "Health conditions," she stated simply, "are serious." There was an "alarming prevalence" of trachoma and tuberculosis among the Navajos whom Miss Patterson visited and an excessively high mortality rate. Malnutrition, insufficient sleep, an exacting routine, and a high degree of physical defects that were not being attended to, were encountered in most of the boarding school children she inspected. Miss Patterson's major recommendation was the inauguration of a Public Health Service nursing program.

When the Senate Committee on Indian Affairs at last obtained a copy of the Red Cross Report from the Bureau in 1928, it discovered that Commissioner Burke had been advised by the chief medical supervisor of the Bureau against both the conclusions and the evidence presented in the report. The supervisor was apparently most disturbed by Miss Patterson's recommendation that Public Health Service nurses be employed, mainly because, as he pointed out, the Public Health Service which Miss Patterson represented had nothing to do with the United States Public Health Service, as some supposed, but was a nurses' organization designed to improve their professional situation. He obviously regarded the report as a propaganda docu-

---

prior to the Meriam Commission investigation, were presented to the Bureau of the Budget by nonmedical personnel whose ability to impress upon the Budget Bureau the seriousness of the Indian health situation was gravely questioned by the Commission. This subordination of the medical staff to the administrative staff was continued on down to the agency level where the local superintendents exercised total control over the hospitals, sometimes in a manner which worked at cross-currents with the goals of the physician. *Meriam Report*, pp. 225-31.

[35]*Cong. Record*, Vol. 68, 69th Cong., 2d sess., p. 390.

ment for hiring more expensive nurses in the Indian Service.[36] Although Miss Patterson's description of many conditions was later upheld by the Meriam Commission, the comments of his chief medical advisor undoubtedly influenced Burke in his decision not to publish the report.

This action did not imply, however, as Burke's critics unjustly assumed, that the Bureau had closed its eyes to the conditions described. The Meriam Report, despite its criticism of the deplorable health conditions among the Indians, insisted that the Red Cross report had "served a valuable purpose in stimulating the Service to review its work and undertake new and improved efforts," and that the Bureau had attempted to carry out some of the major recommendations, although imperfectly.[37] As a matter of fact, shortly after the report was received, Burke and Secretary Work launched the Southwest Trachoma Campaign in an attempt to root out one of the most prevalent diseases mentioned in the report.

Trachoma, rather than tuberculosis or some other infectious disease, was probably singled out by the Bureau as a result of urgent and frequent letters received from Hagerman. The Commissioner to the Navajos was particularly shocked by the prevalence of this disease among the Southwestern Indians, especially the Navajos. Writing from Gallup in March, 1924, he addressed to Burke "a very strong letter" on the subject. Some of the items discussed in this letter were spelled out at greater length in his annual report for 1924. Here he stated that an estimated 40-50 percent of the Navajo children in the government boarding schools were afflicted with this disease, as were an estimated 25-30 percent of those not in school. At a time when the dust had not yet settled over the Bursum bill, his conclusion must have had a sobering effect in Washington:

> . . . if trachoma, in particular, and health conditions generally are not vigorously and continuously and promptly dealt with in a big way by the government, they will, I doubt not, cause the

---

[36]For the text of the Red Cross Report and the comments of the Bureau medical supervisor, see *Senate Survey*, part 3, pp. 955-1017.

[37]Burke's responsibility in the matter of the Red Cross Report is a difficult one to determine. It is probably true, as the Collier forces charged, that if the report had been published, the result would have been the application of sufficient public pressure to secure the needed appropriations. On the other hand, it is probable that Burke's reluctance to publish the report was based on the concept which he often expressed, that to do so would foster suspicion and distrust toward the Bureau by both Indians and Bureau critics.

office about as much trouble in the not distant future as the Pueblo situation in the recent past.[38]

Less than a month after the receipt of Hagerman's letter, both Commissioner Burke and Secretary Work appeared in the Navajo country to lay plans for a sustained drive to eradicate trachoma from among the Indians of the Southwest. A special Congressional appropriation of $100,000, available July 1, 1924, was obtained and the campaign launched that same month. Because conditions were considered most acute on the Navajo reservation, the traveling clinics were to begin there and then branch out into the Hopi, Pueblo, Zuñi, and Apache reservations.[39]

The Southwest Trachoma Campaign was launched with fanfare and much publicity but it ended ingloriously with little good accomplished and much harm done to individual Indians. The trouble was that the Bureau, in its haste to eradicate the disease, placed its faith in a radical operation which proved to be unnecessarily dangerous and often ineffective. Not until 1938, when sulfanilamide was discovered, would a quickly effective method of treating this disease be found.

Prior to the inauguration of the campaign, trachoma had been treated by a method in use since the time of the ancient Egyptians. The gelatinous cysts, or "follicles," formed by the disease on the under surface of the eyelids, were removed and the infected surfaces then rubbed with a copper-sulfate pencil. This procedure was effective only when repeated at frequent intervals over long periods of time, a requirement almost impossible to achieve among the Indians.

During the 1920's a theory was advanced which argued that since the site of the greatest number of follicles was the tarsus or tarsal plate of the upper eyelid, its removal would effect a quick cure of trachoma. Despite the fact that the theory was unproven and the tarsectomy operation itself a radical and delicate one, the Indian Bureau issued regulations ordering all its physicians, surgeons or not, to familiarize themselves with the tarsectomy technique to the end that "every physician in the Indian Service shall become a trachoma specialist." The result was disastrous, particularly in the Southwest where the greatest effort was made. Thousands of operations were

---

[38]Navajo, 61584-24-150. See also Hagerman's testimony before the Senate Indian Affairs Committee, *Senate Survey*, part 11, p. 4540.

[39]Bureau of Indian Affairs, *Progress in the Handling of Indian Affairs, 1923-1924*, p. 1; Board of Indian Commissioners, *Annual Report, 1924*, p. 20.

performed on Indians, many of whom did not require the radical treatment, many others of whom because of faulty diagnosis did not even have the disease. Some of the physicians who performed the operations were improperly or insufficiently trained in the intricacies of the operation. Nevertheless, it was not until September 20, 1927, after the Meriam Commission denounced the use of the tarsectomy as a routine procedure, that the Bureau rescinded its previous order and prohibited the operation.[40]

The Bureau's one big drive in the field of Indian health during the Burke administration was then worse than unsuccessful — it was irresponsible and unjust to the thousands of Indians who were subjected to the treatment. The Bureau's conduct was not only unscientific but indefensible, especially when it continued to insist upon the operation in the absence of any evidence that it was effecting a cure. Following the decision to abandon the tarsectomy in 1927, the Bureau turned to a policy of segregating trachomatous children in special boarding schools. Here, with the aid of specially trained nurses, it was possible to carry out properly the old copper-sulfate treatment which required months of continuous treatment to be effective. But even in making this admirable move, the Bureau made a tactical blunder; when trachomatous Navajo children were transferred to the special school set up at Fort Defiance, the move was made without notifying the parents. This in turn led to increased Navajo opposition to the Bureau's school policy.[41]

As in the case of education, the Rhoads administration moved quickly and decisively in the field of health. One of the first steps was to increase allowances for food and clothing for Indian children in the government boarding schools, a matter which the Meriam Commission had recommended for immediate attention back in 1927. Statistics were introduced by the Bureau to show that during the 1920's the annual appropriation per capita for these items had steadily dwindled. Although there was disagreement between the House

---

[40]*Meriam Report,* pp. 212-14. Secretary Work reported in November, 1925, that in the past year and a half 41,686 Indians had been examined in New Mexico, Arizona, Utah, and parts of California. Nineteen percent of those examined were found to have trachoma: 4,610 were operated on; 3,416 were treated without operation; and 2,967 were operated on for eye diseases other than trachoma. Work to the International Health Board, November 4, 1925. Board of Indian Commissioners, tray #9, file 732.2.

[41]See *Minutes of the Navajo Tribal Council Meeting Leupp Arizona November 12-13, 1928.* General Services, 20204-30-054.

of Representatives and the Bureau as to whether average food costs in the boarding schools had been eleven cents per day or twenty-five, the Bureau, with Hoover's backing, won the argument that in either case appropriations were too low for the physical well-being of Indian children.[42] Appropriations for Indian health rose to $2,658,-000 in 1930, an increase of $1,218,000 over the previous year, and they continued to rise steadily under both Rhoads and Collier.[43] New hospitals, better physicians, in effect all the major recommendations of the Meriam Report, were implemented, despite lingering opposition in the Congress.[44] As with education, improvements in the matter of Navajo health were to come slowly, but they were at last moving in the right direction by 1935.

VOTING

The Dawes Severalty Act of 1887 had provided that all Indians who were allotted under that act became, at the time of allotment, citizens of the United States. When experience proved that conferring citizenship in this manner often resulted in abuses, the Burke Act of 1906 modified the earlier provision by deferring citizenship until the completion of the twenty-five-year trust period which accompanied allotment. The intimate connection between allotment and citizenship established by these two major pieces of Indian legislation was severed by the Supreme Court in the Nice case in 1916 when it declared that "citizenship is not incompatible with tribal existence or continued guardianship, and so may be conferred without completely emancipating the Indians or placing them beyond the reach of Congressional regulations adopted for their protection."[45]

Many Indians who were not citizens volunteered for service in

----

[42]U. S. House, *Hearings on Department of the Interior Appropriation Bill, Fiscal Year, 1930,* 70th Cong., 2d sess., p. 638. U. S. Senate, Committee on Indian Affairs, *Hearing on Increased Allowances for Food and Clothing for Children at Indian Schools,* 71st Cong., 2d sess., 1930.

[43]Secretary of the Interior, *Annual Report, 1930,* p. 60.

[44]Representative Cramton in 1930 voiced the attitude of the conservatives when, in answer to Secretary Wilbur's request for a $2,500,000 increase in health appropriations, he stated: "The trouble about the situation now is that all over the United States there is this hysterical idea about the Indian with his halo of romance about him, and these people are demanding that every Indian in the United States shall live in just as comfortable a condition as a prosperous white man, and if he will not live in clean surroundings, there must be an inspector there to force him to live so . . . ." U. S. House, *Hearings on Department of the Interior Appropriation Bill, Fiscal 1932,* 71st Cong., 3d sess., 1930, p. 7.

[45]*U. S. v. Nice,* 241 U. S., 598, in *Meriam Report,* p. 753.

World War I; many others contributed to the war bond issues. These patriotic actions led to a demand for citizenship for all Indians regardless of allotment status. Since the Nice case had declared that citizenship was not incompatible with wardship, many Indian protective societies, which had earlier feared that citizenship would mean the throwing off of government protection, joined the cause. Others who resented the tax immunity granted the Indians under the Dawes and Burke Acts and the existence of the large, nontaxed unallotted Indian reservations in the Southwest, attempted to use this sentiment to break up the reservations and to impose taxes on all Indians as a concession for the grant of citizenship.

In 1919 a bill conferring citizenship on every Indian who had fought against Germany and had received an honorable discharge became law (41 Stat., 350). A second bill which would have linked allotment, taxation, and separation from federal control with citizenship, was defeated.[46] In 1924 "all non-citizen Indians born within the territorial limits of the United States" were given full citizenship (43 Stat., 1255). Some 125,000 Indians, including the Navajos, were now advanced to legal equality with their white countrymen.

However, as the Southern Negro in the 1890's had learned, citizenship did not necessarily confer the right to vote. In the case of the Navajos, both Arizona and New Mexico had laws designed to keep Indians from voting. In Arizona the law restricted "wards of the Government" from the voting booths, and in New Mexico the state constitution withheld the right from "Indians not taxed."

The Indian Citizenship Act of 1924 was passed in June, 1924, just a few months before the national election. Under Hagerman's guidance a test case was arranged to determine the implications of the act on the voting restrictions in New Mexico, since some Indians there had been allowed to register before opposition set in. The test took place in the San Juan jurisdiction where Superintendent Kneale was advised by Hagerman to send those Navajos who had been allowed to register "to cast their votes so that the issue might be defined in case it proves necessary to so define it." Kneale, accordingly, accompanied Deshna Clah Chischillige when he demanded his ballot. The election judge, according to Kneale, replied to Deshna's request: "In view of a recent opinion rendered by the Attorney-

---

[46]U. S. House, Committee on Indian Affairs, *Indian Citizenship*, 66th Cong., 1st sess., 1919, Rept. 144.

General, we refuse to give you a ballot."[47] The issue was closed for the time being.

In 1928 test cases were brought in both New Mexico and Arizona. In the latter, the Arizona Supreme Court decided several days prior to the election that since reservation Indians were wards of the government, they had no right to vote.[48] In New Mexico, in Hagerman's absence, Commissioner Burke himself instructed Kneale to select one of his "most intelligent and progressive Indians who pays no taxes but is otherwise qualified" and have him present himself for registration. On August 29, 1928, Kneale informed Burke that he had selected Deshna again, and again he had been denied the right to vote and the right to register "on the sole ground that he is a non-taxpaying Indian." This time Burke requested the Secretary of the Interior to press for an opinion from the Attorney-General of the United States.[49]

On October 10, 1928, the Attorney-General replied that his department would take no action in a test case for the reason that "the Government has not such legal interest in this matter as would entitle it to maintain a suit in the federal courts in behalf of the Indians." If Deshna "feels aggrieved by reason of the provision in the state constitution which excludes him from the right to vote because he is a non tax-paying Indian," the thing for him to do was to "apply either to the state or federal courts, as he may see fit and proper, like any other citizen of the United States. . . ."[50]

The question of the Navajo right to vote was apparently dropped after this rebuff. Not until 1947 when, with the backing of the Indian Bureau two cases were successfully waged, one in Arizona and one in New Mexico, was the issue at last resolved. As a result of these two test cases, Indians who could demonstrate their literacy were henceforth permitted to vote.[51]

---

[47]Kneale to Hagerman, November 6, 1924. Hagerman Papers, San Juan file. I have not been able to locate this opinion or even to determine if the reference was to the Attorney-General of the United States or the State of New Mexico.

[48]*New York Times,* November 4, 1928, part ii, p. 1.

[49]Kneale to Burke, August 6, 1928; Burke to Secretary of the Interior, August 29, 1928. National Archives, Record Group 48, 5-1, Northern Navajo, General.

[50]Attorney-General to Roy O. West, October 10, 1928. *Ibid.*

[51]Underhill, *The Navajos,* p. 257.

CHAPTER 11

Navajo Tribal Council

By 1935 the Navajo Indians had progressed greatly from the position they occupied in 1922 when oil sparked a national interest in their affairs. Much of this progress was made possible by legislative victories won for them by others. It is nevertheless true that a great transformation had taken place among the Indians themselves. The Navajo Tribal Council, created in 1923 to grant the federal government power to make oil leases in the Navajo name had, through the years, made itself an articulate and outspoken, although not always representative, organ of the Navajo people. This is not, however, generally recognized in most studies of the Navajos.

THE MYTH

Since the days of John Collier's administration it has come to be accepted as fact that the Navajo Tribal Council, prior to its reorganization in 1938, was largely a "yes-man's" organization, subservient to the government.[1] Quite the opposite was true. Since the anthropologists have simply posited this concept without reference to sources, it is possible that they have not availed themselves of the documents that recorded Navajo sentiments at the various council meetings. A careful reading of the minutes shows that while the Tribal Council was rarely listened to by the powers-that-be in Washington, the delegates, nevertheless, often had strong opinions of their own which they expressed clearly and forcefully. That their sentiments were not heeded was no fault of the delegates. This is a very different thing from stating that the council was composed of "yes-men."

The origin of this unsupported myth devolves in all probability, from the salutary but often biased imprint which John Collier has left on recent Indian history. Collier's initial attack on the Bureau, it

---

[1]Alexander and Dorothea Leighton, *The Navaho Door*, p. 49; Clyde Kluckhohn and Dorothea Leighton, *The Navaho*, p. 101.

will be recalled, developed as a result of the Bursum bill. To fight this scheme which he claimed would deprive the Pueblo Indians of their ancient land grants, Collier and others defying the Indian Bureau organized the Council of All of the New Mexico Pueblos in 1922 to fight the government. The success of the Pueblo experiment led Collier to demand self-government for all Indian groups and ultimately led to the incorporation of this principle in the Wheeler-Howard Bill. In the case of the Navajos, however, their Tribal Council had been organized prior to Collier's entrance upon the scene. As he became embroiled in Navajo affairs, especially as a result of the legislation which culminated in the Indian Oil Act of 1927, Collier gradually worked out a theory concerning the Navajo Tribal Council which placed it in the category of a "yes-man's" council. The anthropologists have simply adopted his view.[2]

Collier's attitude toward the Indian problem was based in large measure on the premise that most of the adverse Indian legislation of the 1920's was intimately tied in with the evil genius of Albert B. Fall. Fall and Bursum had worked out the Bursum Bill. Fall's had been the guiding hand in the formulation of the Indian Omnibus Bill of 1923 which attempted to individualize all remaining Indian tribal property and to withdraw all federal responsibility from the Indians.[3] It was Fall who had issued the decision which withdrew temporarily all the executive-order reservations from Indian ownership. There is some truth in all these charges and there is little doubt but that Fall would have despoiled the remaining Indian estates if he could have done so. But when Collier began to charge that Commissioner Burke's administration was simply a continuation of the Fall schemes, especially in its support for the Hayden Oil Bill and the Lee's Ferry bridge, and ultimately to charge the Special Commissioner to the Navajos, Herbert J. Hagerman, with being a partner to similar attacks on the Indian estate, he permitted his zeal for reform to get the best

---

[2]It is evident in all of Collier's writings that he viewed the Pueblo Council as a showcase of Indian self-government. As I hope to demonstrate in another work, there was in reality little self-government in the much-vaunted Pueblo experiment. The Council was a mouthpiece for Collier and few if any of the reforms which it endorsed originated with the Indians. Because of the hostility which existed between Collier and Hagerman after 1930, it became necessary for Collier to belittle the Navajo Commissioner's work and the council which he had helped to create.

[3]For a copy of this bill see U. S. House, Committee on Indian Affairs, *Authorizing the Secretary of the Interior to Appraise Tribal Property of Indians*, 67th Cong., 4th sess., 1923, Rept. 1429. See also Collier, *Indians of the Americas*, pp. 246-47.

of his judgment. Burke and Hagerman may have lacked Collier's vision for a better life for the Indian but there is no evidence to support Collier's thesis that they were attempting to carry out some nefarious plot originally hatched by Fall. Here it is enough to demonstrate that Collier's interpretation of the Navajo Tribal Council, because of his bias, was also wrong.

A CORRECTION

It was not until 1931 that Collier began to find things wrong with the Navajo Tribal Council. In the course of an attack on Hagerman before the Senate Committee on Indian Affairs, he hammered away at the thesis that the order promulgated by Fall giving birth to the Navajo Council in 1923 had "retired from official existence the then existing Navajo Council and ordered the formation of a new 'Navajo Tribal Council.'" The tribal councils which had been in existence on several of the Navajo jurisdictions "for many years," he charged, had been abolished by the order "without a pretext of consulting the Indians and without reference to the existing tribal organization."[4]

As with many of Collier's statements there is a good deal of truth in what he says, but the tenor of the charge is quite misleading. The council at San Juan was indeed abolished by the Fall order, but for the purpose of extending the lease-making power and ultimately all the tribal powers to all of the Navajos, not just a segment of the tribe. The San Juan council had been organized peremptorily in 1921 in reply to the requests of certain oil companies to drill on the reservation. With the discovery of oil, the attitude of the Bureau changed and it was decided that all the Navajos should be represented on the council under the terms of the law passed in 1891. To abolish the San Juan council was not a regressive measure depriving these Navajos of their rights, but rather a progressive one which, for the first time, bound all the Navajos together into one deliberative body. Nor had there been any councils in existence "for many years." Only at Leupp was there a council before 1921, and it was patently controlled by the local agent.

It was true that the orders for the Navajo Tribal Council were formulated in Washington "without a pretext of consulting the Indians," but it was likewise true that the regulations for the new

---

[4]*Senate Survey*, part 11, p. 4377.

council were amended to a large extent by Hagerman and the six superintendents after consultation with Navajo leaders. As a result, membership on the council was made more representative by the addition of six more delegates and the power of the Secretary of the Interior to remove delegates was withdrawn. True, the council could not meet except in Hagerman's presence, but the reason for this was the fear that Collier would proceed to stir up the Navajos as he had the Pueblos. The clause authorizing the Secretary of the Interior to appoint delegates if they were not elected was not designed to force an unwelcome council on all the Navajos, but merely to insure that the San Juan Navajos, who for obvious reasons might oppose the arrangement, would not boycott the new assembly.

If these examples are not enough, contemporary records indicate the freedom with which the Navajo Tribal Council was elected and its permission obtained to grant the oil-leasing power. In a letter to Superintendent Estep, only a month after the decision in Washington to revamp the council, Commissioner Burke wrote that if the Navajos declined to grant Hagerman power of attorney at the coming council, "It will probably mean that there will be no leases, and the oil will remain in the ground, if there is any. There is one thing very certain — it will keep."[5] The only election of delegates which Hagerman could not attend was the one on the Pueblo Bonito reservation. When it was certain that he could not be present, he wrote Superintendent Stacher:

> It is very important that at your meeting at Crown Point, you give the Indians themselves every opportunity to exercise the freest choice in selecting from among their own members, the delegates and alternate delegates apportioned to your jurisdiction.[6]

Just before the council met Hagerman wrote to Burke that he as yet had no idea who might be elected chairman, but in any case he was satisfied that the choice would be a good one for the delegates were all responsible men.[7]

As time went on, Collier's account of the origins of the first Navajo Tribal Council became more fanciful. Several times during the hearings on the Wheeler-Howard Bill he referred to the council

---

[5]Burke to Estep, February 7, 1923. Hagerman Papers, Commissioner's file, January-June, 1923.

[6]Hagerman to Stacher, June 1, 1923. *Ibid.*, Pueblo Bonito file.

[7]Hagerman to Burke, June 12, 1923. *Ibid.*, Commissioner's file, January-June, 1923.

as a good example of what the Bureau dictatorship could accomplish.
In one account he stated:

> In January 1923, when it had already become known that there
> was great oil wealth on the Navajo reservation, the Secretary of
> the Interior by one fiat smashed the Navajo tribal government.
> It ceased to exist. It had gone on over a long time successfully
> and peacefully. He wiped it out and dictated a new Navajo
> Tribal Council.[8]

In the Senate, he said:

> They had their own self-government once. They were getting
> along very well back in 1922. The Secretary of the Interior, acting
> under the boundless powers that he had and has, just simply
> smashed their government by an order, set up a fiat council to
> govern them, prohibited them from acting except in the presence
> of his commissioner.[9]

Because of his tendency to see evil in every action of Albert Fall
and later of Commissioner Burke and Hagerman, Collier sometimes
misrepresented the facts and consequently distorted the true picture.
His interpretation of the Navajo Tribal Council as a body created to
serve the will of the Indian Bureau is a case in point. The council
was often ignored by the Bureau and it was not as representative
of the Navajo people as it might have been, but it was not simply
a "yes-man's" organization.

---

[8]U. S. House, *Hearings on H. R. 7902*, 73d Cong., 2d sess., pp. 37-38.

[9]U. S. Senate, *Hearings on S. 2755 and S. 3645*, 73d Cong., 2d sess., p. 106.

CHAPTER 12

Epilogue

In the years since 1935, the pace of Navajo adjustment to modern American life has quickened. This adjustment has not been easy and the cost in terms of cultural values has often been high. Especially during the 1930's and 1940's, primarily as a result of the sheep-reduction program, the clash between cultural values and economic reality was most severe. The passions stirred by this conflict threatened to disrupt the progress toward tribal unity made since 1922 and to permanently embitter the relationship between the Navajos and the federal government. Fortunately, the storm was weathered and since 1950 their gradual but steady accommodation to modern life has continued.

As we have seen, the Navajo struggle for land reached its climax in 1935. The defeat of the boundary-extension bill in New Mexico and the passage of the Taylor Grazing Act ended the likelihood of future land additions. Both the Navajos and the federal government were then forced to face squarely the problems created by a steadily growing population confined to a fixed land base.

It was John Collier's fervent hope that the problems created by land restriction could be used to strengthen the Navajo sense of corporate unity and tribal responsibility. Their defeat of the Indian Reorganization Act was a distinct disappointment for him but he continued to emphasize the importance of tribal self-government by securing approval from the existing council for all measures proposed by the government, especially the livestock-reduction program. Instead of enlisting tribal support for these programs, however, this strategy eventually resulted in turning the Navajos against their Tribal Council.

In 1936 Collier proposed once again to grant self-government to the Navajos. He hoped to reorganize the Tribal Council, thereby making it more representative of all the people and investing it with a larger role in the determination and execution of programs designed to improve Navajo life. A second opportunity was to be offered the tribe to draft a constitution providing for limited self-government and to throw off the shackles allegedly imposed by the Burke regulations promulgated in the 1920's. The call for a constitutional assembly was issued by the Secretary of the Interior in the spring of 1937.

Once again the stock-reduction program blocked the movement toward self-government. Jacob Morgan of Shiprock, long a dissident member of the Tribal Council and now a leader of the forces opposed to stock reduction, protested the dissolution of the old Tribal Council and refused to take part in the formulation of a constitution despite the fact that he was named chairman of the committee appointed to draft the document. As a result of his opposition, the government, fearing a permanent split among the Navajos and even greater hostility to the stock-reduction program, abandoned the attempt to establish self-government. Instead, it recognized the constitutional assembly as the new Tribal Council and in 1938 promulgated regulations for its guidance.

Collier's plan for self-government was thus administered a second defeat. Morgan's election as chairman of the new Tribal Council in 1938 ended discussion of further reorganization and killed any hope for a viable solution to the problems of the overgrazed range. The regulations issued in 1938 remain today the basis of Navajo tribal government and while they are responsible for such beneficial innovations as the enlargement of representation on the Council to seventy-two delegates and the use of a secret ballot, they do not define the jursidiction or authority of the Tribal Council any more clearly than the previous regulations.

No acceptable solution for reducing the number of livestock was ever agreed upon between the Navajos and the federal government. In 1937 a committee of the Tribal Council approved regulations which called for the issuance of grazing permits based on the estimated carrying capacity of the range and a livestock-ownership census taken in 1937.

During the 1940's these regulations were sometimes enforced by the Secretary of the Interior through court orders, at other times the regulations were relaxed. After years of wrangling and strife the punitive provisions of the grazing regulations were suspended in 1948 and the burden of devising an adequate range-management program was placed entirely upon the Navajo Tribal Council. Not until 1956 did the Council come up with revised grazing regulations and enforcement continued to be difficult. Meanwhile, as a result of continuous overgrazing, it was estimated that 676,000 acres of land formerly used for grazing were now completely depleted and an additional 5,500,000 acres had been severely damaged.[1]

The failure of the stock reduction program was caused mainly by the reluctance of the Navajos to abandon their traditional way of life. Despite the obvious necessity of the program, the reduction of sheep and goats meant abandoning old ways and values; it meant a cultural transformation as well as an economic one. The inexorable laws of nature would eventually force a change, especially since the Navajo population was constantly growing,[2] but whether the inevitable change would prove beneficial or whether it would reduce the Navajos to hopeless despair depended in large part on the availability of alternative methods of livelihood. During the Collier years a start was made in providing these alternatives.

Through various New Deal agencies — the Civilian Conservation Corps (Indian Division), Works Progress Administration, and the Soil Conservation Service — large sums of money were funneled into the reservation. Navajos were employed on a variety of local projects where they learned new skills and gradually wage income began to lessen the previous dependence on subsistence stockraising. With the outbreak of World War II the reliance upon wage income increased. Thousands of Navajo men left the reservation for the armed services and their families grew accustomed to monthly dependency checks. Others left to take positions in war industries, and still others found employment on the railroads. By 1945 wage work had definitely begun to replace sheep raising as the major source of Navajo income.

It had long been recognized that if the Indian was to be brought into the mainstream of American life, his educational level would have to be markedly improved. During the twenties the Indian Bureau had forced the Navajos to attend school. Many of the schools were located far away from the reservation and the fruits of this policy were resentment and stubborn resistance. Under John Collier an attempt was made to provide educational facilities at day schools located on the reservation near existing population centers. During the thirties fifty combination day schools and community centers were constructed and seats provided for an additional 3,500 Navajo children. The day-school theory was excellent but it did not ade-

---

[1]Robert W. Young, *The Navajo Yearbook, 1951-1961* (Window Rock, Arizona, 1961), p. 163.

[2]In 1930 the census estimate for Navajos under the jurisdiction of the Bureau of Indian Affairs was 39,064. In 1940 the estimate was 49,185. By 1950 the official census listed 62,167 Navajos and in the 1960 census the figure was 73,614.

quately take into consideration the primitiveness of the Navajo road system over which school buses had to travel. When the war came the day-school system broke down almost completely because of gasoline and tire-rationing difficulties.

Nevertheless, a thirst for education had been planted. In some areas on the reservation, parents who refused to see the education of their children curtailed by the war constructed make-shift dormitories near the existing day schools and voluntarily took over the chores of supervising the children after school hours. When the war was over, servicemen and war workers, their horizons considerably broadened by the experiences of the last few years, returned to the reservation and advocated a greatly expanded educational system. In 1946 a delegation of the Navajo Tribal Council formally called upon the Secretary of the Interior to present a petition that education be recognized as the number one need of the tribe.

The immediate post-war years brought renewed hardship to the Navajos. Dependency allotments were cancelled as servicemen were discharged. The men themselves returned to a reservation where work was unavailable. War workers were discharged as contracts were cancelled and they too drifted back to the reservation, swelling the tide of the unemployed. By 1947 the attention of the entire country was being directed to the Navajo plight. Congressional committees visited the reservation and held hearings in Washington. As a result, a long-range rehabilitation program was formulated and finally enacted into law in 1950 (64 Stat., 44). During the interval between discussion and enactment of this act, Congress provided relief appropriations and inaugurated a work-relief program to combat the most extreme cases of deprivation.

The Navajo-Hopi Long Range Rehabilitation Act of April 19, 1950, was recognition on the part of the federal government that massive aid was necessary to assist the Navajos in "promoting a self supporting economy and self reliant communities, and to lay a stable foundation on which these Indians can engage in diversified economic activities and ultimately attain standards of living comparable with those enjoyed by other citizens. . . ." The act basically provided for an appropriation of $88,570,000 to be expended over the next ten years for school construction, road improvement, hospital and health facilities, irrigation construction and improvement, soil conservation, and the resettlement of Navajos who voluntarily chose to leave the reservation. In addition, the act authorized the tribe to adopt a tribal constitution, entrusted the existing Tribal Council with control over all tribal funds and future income, and through agreements with the states of Utah, Arizona, and New Mexico, extended the benefits of Social Security to the Navajos for the first time.

The effects of the Long Range Rehabilitation Act are observable throughout the reservation today, but it would be a mistake to attribute the material and economic gains of the past fifteen years entirely to this legislation. Almost simultaneously with the passage of the act, private industry began to extract sub-soil riches from the reservation. Oil exploration resumed in the early 1950's has resulted in new discoveries surpassing the dreams of the most optimistic speculators of the 1920's. Over $100,000,000 from oil alone had flowed into the tribal treasury by 1960, and in that same year the royalties and rentals from oil were averaging over $1,000,000 a month. In addition, natural gas, uranium, and coal have all found markets. Sizeable sums of money have come to the tribe from these new sources and individual Navajos have found good employment opportunities with the companies that exploit the resources. The responsibility of administering and investing these large sums has resulted in invigorating the Tribal Council in a manner which no amount of government prodding or assistance could have accomplished.

Despite many problems which continue to exist, it seems clear today that the Navajos have successfully met the challenge of the twentieth century. In 1900 they were an almost exclusively agricultural and pastoral people who lived much as they had since their arrival in the Southwest centuries before. The relentless advance of white stockmen and the discovery of oil on their preserve rudely awakened them to the realities of a rapidly changing world. Out of the struggle to preserve their traditional way of life and their land came the first glimmerings of real tribal organization and solidarity, the determination of their title to land additions made by presidential order, and an expansion of their reservation boundaries which, while amounting to almost 3,000,000 acres, nevertheless fell short of the requirements for subsistence stock-raising. Confused, embittered, and bewildered, the Navajos struck back by defeating the Indian Reorganization Act and stubbornly refused to accept the stock-reduction program. For fifteen years their willingness to adapt to modern life was in doubt, but since the early 1950's it is evident that as a result of governmental assistance, the development of reservation resources and their own mature decision, the Navajos are emerging once again as a proud and self-reliant people.

Bibliography

MANUSCRIPT AND ARCHIVAL SOURCES

The National Archives of the United States:

Record Group 75, Indian Records Office, 1907-1939:

Annual Narrative Reports: Leupp, Western Navajo, Southern Navajo, Navajo, Eastern Navajo, Pueblo Bonito, Northern Navajo and San Juan Agencies.

Central Classified Files: Leupp, Western Navajo, Southern Navajo, Navajo, Eastern Navajo, Pueblo Bonito, Northern Navajo, and San Juan Agencies.

General Services File: Correspondence and reports on a variety of topics, collected without regard to Indian agency or jurisdiction. Most of the minutes of the Navajo Tribal Council are contained in this file.

Hagerman Papers: some forty packages of correspondence from the files of Herbert J. Hagerman.

Special Agents File: Herbert J. Hagerman reports.

Wheeler-Howard File.

Board of Indian Commisisoners File: the *Special Reports* of the Board and over 100 trays of miscellaneous materials.

Record Group 48, Secretary of the Interior Records Office, 1907-1939:

1-105: Leupp, Western Navajo, Southern Navajo, Navajo, Eastern Navajo, Pueblo Bonito, Northern Navajo, and San Juan Agencies.

5-18: Portraits and Biographies of the Secretaries of the Interior.

22-23: Personal Records of the Commissioners of Indian Affairs.

The Dietrich Collection:

When he died in 1935, Herbert J. Hagerman entrusted his private papers to Mrs. Charles H. Dietrich of Santa Fe, New Mexico.

This collection consists of some of the public papers which Hagerman did not forward to the Indian Bureau when he left office, some papers pertaining to the Pueblo Lands Board, Walapai Indians, the Middle Rio Grande Conservancy District, and a large collection of private correspondence. Mrs. Dietrich graciously opened these papers to me for use in this study. When she died in 1961, the bulk of the papers was deposited with the National Archives while those of regional interest were deposited with the University of New Mexico Library.

Huntington Library:

Albert B. Fall Papers: The Fall Papers did not prove to be particularly helpful in this work, although they do contain valuable information on Secretary Fall's overall Indian policy. Most of these papers have been microfilmed by the University of New Mexico and are available in its Library.

New Mexico and Arizona Land Company Files:

The files of the New Mexico and Arizona Land Company were useful in tracing the consolidation of the Navajo reservation during the 1920's and the early 1930's. The company's offices are located in Albuquerque, N. M.

Library of Congress:

Hugh L. Scott Papers: General Hugh L. Scott served with the United States Army in the West from 1876 until 1897. His lively interest in the Indians and their culture resulted in his frequent appointment as federal troubleshooter in times of crisis. In all his dealings with the Indians he was sympathetic, firm, and just. As numerous letters in these papers indicate, he was regarded by the Indians as one of their most trusted advisors. Scott served as Chief of Staff of the Army from 1914 to 1917 but was retired before the United States entered World War I. In 1919 he was chosen to succeed Edward E. Ayer on the Board of Indian Commissioners.

PUBLISHED GOVERNMENT DOCUMENTS

U. S. Board of Indian Commissioners. *Annual Reports of the Board of Indian Commissioners, 1913-1933.* Washington: G.P.O., 1914-34.

U. S. Bureau of Indian Affairs. *Annual Reports of the Commissioner of Indian Affairs, 1900-1936.* Washington: G.P.O., 1901-37.

U. S. Bureau of Indian Affairs. *Progress in the Handling of Indian Affairs, 1923-1924.* Washington: mimeographed, 1924.

———. *Minutes of the Meeting of the Advisory Council on Indian Affairs, December 12-13, 1923.* Washington: mimeographed, 1924.

———. *Indian Policies, Comments on the Resolutions of the Advisory Council on Indian Affairs by Hubert Work.* Washington: mimeographed, 1924.

———. *The Progress of Indian Affairs from 1933 to 1936.* Washington: mimeographed, 1937.

U. S. *Congressional Record.* Vols. 38-78.

U. S. Department of the Interior. *Annual Reports of the Secretary of the Interior, 1912-1936.* Washington: G.P.O., 1913-37.

———. *Decisions of the Department of the Interior in Cases Relating to the Public Lands,* Daniel M. Green (ed.), Vol. 49. Washington: G.P.O., 1923.

U. S. Department of Justice. *Official Opinions of the Attorneys General of the United States,* Vol. 34. Washington: G.P.O., 1926.

U. S. Geological Survey. *Water Supply Paper 380, The Navajo Country,* by Herbert E. Gregory. Washington: G.P.O., 1916.

U. S. House of Representatives, Committee on Appropriations. *Hearings, Department of the Interior Appropriation Bills, Fiscal Years 1923-1936.* Washington: G.P.O., 1921-35.

U. S. House of Representatives, Committee on Indian Affairs. *Metalliferous Minerals on Indian Reservations.* Report No. 533, 64th Cong., 2d sess., 1916.

———. *Metalliferous Minerals on Indian Reservations.* Report No. 730, 65th Cong., 2d sess., 1918.

———. *Indian Citizenship.* Report No. 144, 66th Cong., 1st sess., 1919.

———. *Hearings, Indians of the United States,* 3 Vols. 66th Cong., 1-3d sess., 1919-20.

———. *Indians of the United States.* Report No. 1133, 66th Cong., 3d sess., 1920.

———. *Reorganizing the Indian Service.* Report No. 1189, 66th Cong., 3d sess., 1921.

_____. *Hearings on H. R. 11687, Leasing Unallotted Navajo Lands.* 67th Cong., 2d sess., 1922.

_____. *To Provide for Exchanges of Government and Privately Owned Lands in Navajo Indian Reservation, Arizona.* Report No. 1249, 68th Cong., 2d sess., 1925.

_____. *Indian Affairs in Oklahoma.* Report No. 1527, 68th Cong., 2d sess., 1925.

_____. *Oil and Gas Mining Leases Upon Unallotted Lands.* Report No. 763, 69th Cong., 1st sess., 1926.

_____. *Hearings on H. R. 8823, Leasing of Allotted Indian Lands.* 69th Cong., 1st sess., 1926.

_____. *Hearings on H. R. 15021, Leasing of Executive Order Reservations.* 69th Cong., 2d sess., 1927.

_____. *Oil and Gas Mining Leases Upon Unallotted Lands.* Report No. 1791, 69th Cong., 2d sess., 1927.

_____. *Cancellation of Patents in Fee Simple to Indians for Allotments Held in Trust by the United States.* Report No. 1896, 69th Cong., 2d sess., 1927.

_____. *Hearings on H. R. 6979, Creation of Indian Trust Estates.* 71st Cong., 2d sess., 1930.

_____. *Permanently Set Aside Certain Lands in Utah as an Addition to the Navajo Indian Reservation.* Report No. 1883, 72d Cong., 2d sess., 1933.

_____. *Readjustment of Indian Affairs.* Report 1804, 73d Cong., 2d sess., 1934.

_____. *Boundaries of Navajo Reservation in Arizona.* Report No. 1602, 73d Cong., 2d sess., 1934.

_____. *Hearings on H. R. 7902, Readjustment of Indian Affairs.* 73d Cong., 2d sess., 1934.

_____. *Hearings on H. R. 7837, Indian Claims Commission.* 74th Cong., 1st sess., 1935.

_____. *Hearings on H. R. 7781, Indian Conditions and Affairs.* 74th Cong., 1st sess., 1935.

_____. *Hearings on H. R. 8360, Conditions of Indians in the United States.* 74th Cong., 2d sess., 1936.

U. S. House of Representatives, Committee on Public Lands. *Exploration for and Disposition of Coal, Oil, Gas, etc.* Report No. 668, 63d Cong., 2d sess., 1914.

_____. *Exploration for and Disposition of Coal, Phosphate, Oil, Oil Shale or Gas.* Report No. 563, 65th Cong., 2d sess., 1918.

_____. *Mining of Coal, Phosphate, Oil, Gas, and Sodium on the Public Domain.* Report No. 600, 66th Cong., 2d sess., 1920.

U. S. President. *Messages of the President Transmitting the Budget for Fiscal Years* 1923-1930. Washington: G.P.O., 1921-28.

U. S. Senate. *Indian Affairs, Laws and Treaties,* 5 Vols., Charles J. Kappler (ed.). Washington: G.P.O., 1904-38.
Vol. 1: Senate Document 452, 57th Cong., 1st sess.
Vol. 2: Senate Document 319, 58th Cong., 2d sess.
Vol. 3: Senate Document 719, 62d Cong., 2d sess.
Vol. 4: Senate Document 53, 70th Cong., 1st sess.
Vol. 5: Senate Document 194, 76th Cong., 3d sess.

_____. *Message from the President of the United States Returning Without Approval the Bill (S. 4152) to Authorize Oil and Gas Mining Leases Upon Unallotted Lands Within Executive Order Indian Reservations, and for Other Purposes.* Document 156, 69th Cong., 1st sess., 1926.

_____. *Improvement of Conditions on Indian Reservations in Arizona.* Document 16, 71st Cong., 1st sess., 1929.

_____. (Herbert J. Hagerman) *The Navajo Indian Reservation.* Document 64, 72d Cong., 1st sess., 1932.

_____. *Condition of Indians in the United States.* Document 214, 72d Cong., 2d sess., 1933.

U. S. Senate, Committee on Indian Affairs. *Hearings, Indian Appropriation Bills, Fiscal 1914 and 1915.* 63d Cong., 1st-2d Sess., 1913-14.

_____. *Metalliferous Minerals on Indian Reservations.* Report No. 880, 64th Cong., 2d sess., 1916.

_____. *To Provide for the Disposition of Bonuses, Rentals, and Royalties from Unallotted Lands in Executive Order Indian Reservations.* Report No. 669, 68th Cong., 1st sess., 1924.

_____. *Hearings on S. 1722 and S. 3159, Development of Oil and Gas Mining Leases on Indian Reservations.* 69th Cong., 1st sess., 1926.

_____. *Hearings on S. 3159 and S. 4152, Development of Oil and Gas Mining Leases on Indian Reservations*. 69th Cong., 1st sess., 1926.

_____. *To Authorize Oil and Gas Mining Leases Upon Unallotted Lands Within Executive Order Indian Reservations*. Report 1240, 69th Cong., 2d sess., 1927.

_____. *Hearings on S. 4893, Development of Oil and Gas Mining Leases on Indian Reservations*. 69th Cong., 2d sess., 1927.

_____. *Hearings, Survey of Conditions of Indians of the United States, 1928-1943*, 43 Vols. Washington: G.P.O., 1928-43.

_____ *Cession, Transfer of Certain Land from Tusayan National Forest*. Report 443, 71st Cong., 2d sess., 1930.

_____. *Hearings on Increased Allowances for Food and Clothing for Children at Indian Schools*. 71st Cong., 2d sess., 1930.

_____. *Cancellation of Certain Patents in Fee Simple Issued to Indians for Allotments Without Their Consent*. Report No. 1595, 71st Cong., 3d sess., 1931.

_____. *Hearings on H. R. 15498, Revision and Codification of the Statutes Affecting American Indians*. 71st Cong., 3d sess., 1931.

_____ *Hearings on H. R. 8898, Authorizing the Secretary of the Interior to Adjust or Eliminate Reimbursable Debts of Indians*. 72d Cong., 1st sess., 1932.

_____. *Survey of Conditions of the Indians of the United States, Charges of Misconduct Against Herbert J. Hagerman*. Report No. 25, part 3, 72d Cong., 1st sess., 1932.

_____. *Authorizing Indians to Form Business Councils, Corporations, and for Other Purposes*. Report 1080, 73d Cong., 2d sess., 1934.

_____. *Define the Exterior Boundaries of the Navajo Indian Reservation in New Mexico, and for Other Purposes*. Report 1074, 73d Cong., 2d sess., 1934.

_____. *Hearings on S. 2755 and S. 3645, To Grant to Indians Living Under Federal Tutelage the Freedom to Organize for Purposes of Local Self-Government and Economic Enterprise*. 73d Cong., 2d sess., 1934.

U. S. Senate, Committee on Public Lands. *Mining of Coal, Phosphate, Oil, Gas, Phosphate, and Sodium on the Public Domain*. Report 116, 65th Cong., 1st sess., 1917.

U. S. *Statutes At Large*. Vols. 15-48.

U. S. Treasury Department. *Annual Reports of the Secretary of the Treasury for Fiscal Years 1923-1930*. Washington: G.P.O., 1924-31.

BOOKS AND MONOGRAPHS

Bates, J. Leonard. *The Origins of Teapot Dome; Progressives, Parties, and Petroleum, 1909-1921*. Urbana: University of Illinois Press, 1963.

Brayer, Herbert O. *Pueblo Land Grants of the "Rio Abajo."* Albuquerque: University of New Mexico Press, 1939.

Collier, John. *The Indians of the Americas*. New York: New American Library, 1961.

———. *From Every Zenith: A Memoir*. Denver: Sage Books, 1963.

Dale, Edward Everett. *The Indians of the Southwest*. Norman: University of Oklahoma Press, 1949.

Giddens, Paul H. *Standard Oil Company (Indiana): Oil Pioneer of the Middle West*. New York: Appleton-Century-Crofts, 1955.

Gittler, J. B. (ed.). *Understanding Minority Groups*. New York: John Wiley and Sons, Inc., 1956.

Greever, William S. *Arid Domain*. Stanford: Stanford University Press, 1954.

Hill, Willard H. *The Agricultural and Hunting Methods of the Navaho Indians*. ("Yale University Publications in Anthropology," No. 18). New Haven: Yale University Press, 1938.

Hobson, Richard. *Navaho Acquisitive Values*. ("Papers of the Peabody Museum of American Archaeology and Ethnology," Vol. XLII, No. 3). Cambridge: Harvard University Press, 1954.

Ickes, Harold L. *The Secret Diary of Harold Ickes, Vol. 1: The First Thousand Days, 1933-1936*. New York: Simon and Schuster, 1953.

Ise, John. *The United States Oil Policy*. New Haven: Yale University Press, 1926.

Kappler, Charles J. *Indian Affairs, Laws and Treaties*. Washington, G.P.O., 1904-38. (See U. S. Senate above.)

Kluckhohn, Clyde, and Leighton, Dorothea. *The Navaho*. 2d ed. revised. Garden City, N.Y.: Doubleday and Co., Inc., 1962.

———. *Children of the People*. Cambridge: Harvard University Press, 1948.

Kluckhohn, Clyde, and Vogt, Evon Z. *Navaho Means People*. Cambridge: Harvard University Press, 1951.

LaFarge, Oliver. *As Long as Grass Shall Grow*. New York: Longmans Green and Co., 1940.

Landgraf, John L. *Land Use in the Ramah Area of New Mexico*. ("Papers of the Peabody Museum of American Archaeology and Ethnology," Vol. XLII, No. 1). Cambridge: Harvard University Press, 1954.

Leighton, Alexander H. and Dorothea C. *The Navaho Door, An Introduction to Navaho Life*. Cambridge: Harvard University Press, 1944.

Lindquist, G. E. E. *The Red Man in the United States*. New York: George H. Doran Co., 1923.

Meriam, Lewis (ed.). *The Problem of Indian Administration*. Baltimore: Johns Hopkins University Press, 1928.

Mosk, Sanford A. *Land Tenure Problems in the Santa Fe Railroad Grant Area*. Berkeley: University of California Press, 1944.

Newcomb, Franc J. *Hosteen Klah, Navaho Medicine Man and Sand Painter*. Norman: University of Oklahoma Press, 1964.

Northrop, F. S. C. (ed.). *Ideological Difference and World Order*. New Haven: Yale University Press, 1949.

Priest, Loring B. *Uncle Sam's Stepchildren*. New Brunswick: Rutgers University Press, 1942.

Rinehart, Ira. *Reference Book on the Four Corners Area*. Dallas: Rinehart Oil News Co., 1955.

Roberts, Harold D. *Salt Creek, Wyoming: The Story of a Great Oil Field*. Denver: W. H. Kistler Stationery Co., 1956.

Sanchez, George Isidore. *The People*. Lawrence, Kansas: Haskell Institute Press, 1948.

Schmeckebier, Laurence F. *The Office of Indian Affairs*. Institute for Government Research, Service Monographs of the United States Government, No. 48. Baltimore: Johns Hopkins University Press, 1927.

Spicer, Edward H. *Cycles of Conquest: The Impact of Spain, Mexico, and the United States on the Indians of the Southwest, 1533-1960.* Tucson: University of Arizona Press, 1962.

———. (ed.) *Perspectives in American Indian Culture Change.* Chicago: University of Chicago Press, 1961.

Thompson, Laura. *Personality and Government; Findings and Recommendations of the Indian Administration Research.* Mexico, D. F.: Ediciones del Instituto Indigenista Inter-Americano, 1951.

Underhill, Ruth. *Here Come the Navaho!* Lawrence, Kansas: Haskell Institute Press, 1953.

———. *The Navajos.* Norman: University of Oklahoma Press, 1956.

Ward, Elizabeth. *No Dudes, Few Women; Life With a Navaho Range Rider.* Albuquerque: University of New Mexico Press, 1951.

Weber, Anselm. *The Navajo Indians, A Statement of Fact.* St. Michaels, Arizona: St. Michaels Press, 1915.

Wheeler, Burton K. *Yankee From the West.* New York: Doubleday and Co., 1962.

Wilbur, Ray Lyman. *The Memoirs of Ray Lyman Wilbur, 1875-1949.* Edited by Edgar E. Robinson and Paul C. Edwards. Stanford: Stanford University Press, 1960.

Wilbur, Ray Lyman, and Du Puy, Atherton. *Conservation in the Department of the Interior.* Washington: G.P.O., 1931.

Wilbur, Ray Lyman, and Hyde, Arthur M. *The Hoover Policies.* New York: Charles Scribner's Sons, 1937.

Wilken, Robert L. *Anselm Weber, O.F.M., Missionary to the Navaho.* Milwaukee: Bruce Publishing Co., 1953.

Young, Robert W. *The Navajo Yearbook, 1961.* Window Rock, Arizona, 1961.

Young, Robert W., and Morgan, William (eds.). *Navajo Historical Selections.* Washington: G.P.O., 1954.

ARTICLES

Borgman, Rev. Francis, O.F.M. "Henry Chee Dodge, The Last Chief of the Navajo Indians," *New Mexico Historical Review,* XXIII (April, 1948), 81-93.

Haile, Berard. "Návaho or Navajó," *The Americas,* VI (July, 1949), 85-90.

Hewitt, Edgar L. "Origin of the Name Navaho," *American Anthropologist,* VIII (n.s., 1906), 193.

Hill, Willard W. "Some Aspects of Navaho Political Structure," *Plateau,* XIII (October, 1940), 23-28.

Reeve, Frank D. "Federal Indian Policy in New Mexico, 1858-1880," *New Mexico Historical Review,* XII (July, 1937), 218-69.

_____. "Federal Indian Policy in New Mexico, 1858-1880," *New Mexico Historical Review,* XIII · (January, 1938), 14-62.

_____. "The Government and the Navaho, 1846-1858," *New Mexico Historical Review,* XIV (January, 1939), 82-114.

_____. "Early Navaho Geography," *New Mexico Historical Review,* XXXI (October, 1956), 290-309.

_____. "Seventeenth Century Navaho-Spanish Relations," *New Mexico Historical Review,* XXXII (January, 1957), 36-52.

_____. "Navaho-Spanish Wars, 1680-1720," *New Mexico Historical Review,* XXXIII (July, 1958), 205-31.

_____. "The Navaho-Spanish Peace, 1720's-1770's," *New Mexico Historical Review,* XXXIV (January, 1959), 9-40.

_____. "Navaho-Spanish Diplomacy, 1770-1790," *New Mexico Historical Review,* XXXV (July, 1960), 200-35.

Vogt, Evon Z. "Navaho," in *Perspectives in American Indian Culture Change,* edited by E. H. Spicer, which see.

Index

Allotment policy
Albert Fall opposes application to
public-domain Navajos, 29-31
ended by Wheeler-Howard Act,
163-66
failure of public-domain allotment,
34-35
Indian Bureau renews attempt to
allot public-domain Navajos,
122-24
limitations imposed on public-domain
Navajos, 31-34
not applied to Navajo tribal lands, 16
public-domain allotment ended by
Taylor Grazing Act, 101
special application of for public-
domain Navajos, 23-28
American Indian Defense Association,
77, 136, 154
American Red Cross studies Indian
health, 183-84
Andrews, William H., 24
Apache, origin of the name, 1
Arizona
agrees to present Navajo boundary
in Arizona, 128-29
defeats appropriation for Lee's Ferry
Bridge, 86
opposes Navajo expansion, 33-34
opposes purchase by Navajos in
Castle Butte area, 127
permits Navajo expansion, 24
refuses Indians right to vote, 188-89
supports opening of Indian
reservations to mining, 42
Ashurst, Henry F.
opposes Navajo allotment on public
domain, 30-31

Ashurst, Henry F. (Cont.)
proposes opening of executive-order
Indian reservations to mining,
40-42
sponsors bill permitting Navajos to
buy land with oil royalties, 121
supports bill forbidding creation of
executive-order reservations, 34
supports Lee's Ferry Bridge, 86
Athabascan migration, 1
Atlantic and Pacific Railroad, land
grant in Navajo reservation, 21
Austin, Buck, 163
Aztec Land and Cattle Company,
holdings in Navajo reservation,
21

Babbitt Brothers Company, 125
Bailey ranch, 125
Ballinger, Richard A., 38
Balmer, John E., 160
Baptist Home Mission Society of New
York, 137
Barboncito, in raid on Ft. Defiance,
5
appointed head chief, 14
Barnett, Jackson, 137-38, 146
Bega, Becenti, 161
Benavides, Alonso, 1
Board of Indian Commissioners
abolishment of, 33 (n. 36)
clears Commissioner Burke of
criminal-collusion charges, 137
creation of, 33 (n. 36)
reports on Navajo school situation,
172, 174-75
supports and then opposes "New
Policy," 135

211

Board of Indian Commissioners (Cont.)
  urges solution of checkerboard
    problem, 33
Bratton, Sam G.
  opposes Lee's Ferry Bridge, 86-87
  opposes legislation to free executive-
    order Indian reservations from
    Fall ruling, 91-92
  opposes Navajo allotments on public
    domain, 123
Brookings Institution, 139-41
Bureau of Animal Husbandry,
    107, 109-10
Bureau of the Budget
  economy drive ousts Evan Estep, 68
  federal employees prohibited from
    opposing appropriation
    recommendations of, 87, 144-45
  attitude toward Indian appropriations,
    142-45
  increases appropriations for Indian
    health, 182
Bureau of Indian Affairs
  agrees to restrict allotment of public-
    domain Navajos, 30-31
  and Bureau of the Budget, 142-45
  announces "New Policy" in Indian
    affairs, 132-35
  appropriations for, 144, 157-58
  attacked by critics, 132, 135-41,
    145-48, 151-53
  attempts to allot Navajos on public
    domain, 23-25, 27-30, 122-24
  attitude toward Navajo Tribal
    Council prior to 1923, 49-50
  attitude toward reimbursable debts,
    83-85
  calls for investigation of Navajo land
    problem, 30-31
  educational policy, 173-79, 179-81
  failure to exchange land with Santa
    Fe railroad, 22
  health program, 181-87
  launches scabies eradication program
    on Navajo reservation, 107
  opposes application of Dawes Act, 17
  reforms proposed by Meriam
    Commission, 141
  reforms under Commissioner Rhoads,
    150-53

Bureau of Indian Affairs (Cont.)
  role in passage of Wheeler-Howard
    Act, 163-66
  seeks Navajo approval for stock
    reduction, 158-63
  status of executive-order reservations
    debated within, 73-74
  urges expansion of Navajo
    reservation, 23-25
  urges program of land purchase for
    Navajos, 125-31
Burke Act (1906), 133, 187
Burke, Charles H. (Commissioner of
    Indian Affairs)
  attacked by critics, 135-41, 145-48,
    191-94
  attacks John Collier, 99, 147
  attitude towards Lee's Ferry bridge,
    96-99
  biographical sketch, 56 (n. 30)
  blocks legislation to apply General
    Leasing Act to executive-order
    reservations, 78
  decides against further leasing of
    Navajo reservation, 101
  discontinues forced patenting of
    Indian lands, 135
  Indian education under, 173-79
  Indian health under, 181-86
  mentioned, 51, 55, 109, 115
  opposes Fall's application of General
    Leasing Act to executive-order
    reservations, 65
  quoted on Indian title to executive-
    order reservations, 73-74
  rebukes Hagerman for Lee's Ferry
    bridge stand, 87
  relations with Bureau of the Budget,
    142-45
  resigns from office, 147
  seeks vote for Navajos, 189
  states policy for Navajo oil
    development, 52-53
  supports Bursum bill, 59
  supports Hayden bill, 79, 89, 93-99
  vacillates on reimbursable debt
    policy, 84-85, 98-99
Bursum Bill, 59, 61 (n. 38), 191
Bursum, Holm O., 59, 191

California State Immigration and
  Housing Commission, 60
Cameron, Ralph H.
  opposes Lee's Ferry Bridge, 86-87
  sponsors bill to free executive-order
    reservations from Fall ruling,
    90-92
Campbell-Francis Company, 126
Carleton, James Henry, Brigadier
  General, organizes expedition
  against Navajos, 5-7
Carlisle Indian school, 139
Carson, Christopher (Kit), leads
  Navajo expedition, 6
Castle Butte, included in executive-
  order withdrawal, 24-25
  failure of allotment on public domain
    in, 33
  purchase of Bailey and Marty
    ranches, 125
Chaco Land and Cattle Company sells
  12,000 acres to Navajos, 35
Checkerboard
  consolidation of in Arizona, 118-19
  consolidation of in New Mexico,
    34-36, 115-17
  development of artesian water in,
    23-25
  final solution of, 124-30
  legislation to eliminate, 22, 32, 36,
    115-17
  origin of, 21
Chischillige, Deshna Clah, attends
  Cong. hearings on leasing of
  executive-order reservations, 93
  denied right to vote, 188-89
Citizenship for Indians, 187-88
Civilian Conservation Corps, 197
Clans, function of, 9
Collier, John (Commissioner of
  Indian Affairs)
  and Navajo rejection of Wheeler-
    Howard bill, 167-70, 195
  and Wheeler-Howard bill, 163-66
  appointed Commissioner of Indian
    Affairs, 153-55
  assumes leadership of forces opposing
    Bureau of Indian Affairs, 136
  attacked by Commissioner Burke,
    99, 147

Collier, John (Cont.)
  biased interpretation of Navajo Tribal
    Council, 190-94
  biographical sketch, 59-60
  criticizes Rhoads administration,
    152-53
  education and health programs for
    Navajos, 180-81, 187
  Indian reform philosophy, 156-58
  leads opposition to Fall's decision
    applying General Leasing Act to
    executive-order reservations,
    76-77, 80-81, 89-92
  Navajo livestock reduction program,
    158-63, 196-97
  Navajo policy after 1934, 195-98
  opposes Hagerman plan for Navajo
    expansion, 128 (n. 49)
  opposes Lee's Ferry Bridge, 86-87
Committee of One Hundred, 72, 138
Coolidge, Calvin, 92-93, 142
Council of All the New Mexico
  Pueblos, 59, 63 (n. 41), 191
Cramton, Louis C.
  claims responsibility for passage of
    bill permitting Navajos to
    purchase land from oil revenues,
    122 (n. 27)
  parsimonious attitude toward Indian
    appropriations, 143, 173, 176-77

Daniels, Josephus, 38
Dawes Severalty Act (1887)
  amended by Burke Act, 133, 187
  criticized, 136, 139-40, 166
  description of, 16-17
  not applied to Navajo tribal lands, 16
  special application of for public-
    domain Navajos, 23-28
  Supreme Court severs allotment-
    citizenship link, 187
Department of Justice
  defeated in first attempt to overrule
    Fall decision, 81-82
  attacks Commissioner Burke, 138
Dodge, Henry Chee
  emergence as Navajo spokesman,
    66-67
  favors imposition of excess grazing
    fees, 112

Dodge, Henry Chee (Cont.)
   opposed by Estep and San Juan
      Navajos, 67-68
   present for Congressional hearings on
      leasing of executive-order
      reservations, 93
   proposes expenditure of oil money for
      land, 120
   protests forced schooling policy, 177
Dodge, Henry Linn, first Navajo
      agent, 5
Dourine epidemic, 109-10

Eastern Navajo agency
   allotment urged upon Navajos
      residing there, 123
   creation of, 27 (n. 17)
   eradication of scabies on, 108
   extent of overgrazing on, 114
   rejects Wheeler-Howard Act, 169
   Taylor Grazing Act results in loss of
      control of public domain, 162
   see also Pueblo Bonito agency
Estep, Evan W.
   attitude toward oil development,
      51-55
   ill-will toward Chee Dodge, 66-68
   opposed to prospecting, 48
   ousted as San Juan superintendent,
      67-69
   reports on absence of Indian Council
      at San Juan agency, 49
   role in San Juan Council, 51-55
Executive-order Indian reservations
   Attorney-General rules against Fall
      decision, 74-75
   compromise on creation of in New
      Mexico, 23-24
   creation of forbidden by Congress,
      33-34
   E. H. Harrison attempts to apply
      General Leasing Act to, 57-58
   Fall decision calls into question
      Indian title to, 58
   Fall decision upheld by Utah District
      Court, 81-82
   Indian title to upheld, 99-100
   legislation to free from Fall decision,
      78-81, 88-93, 99-100

Executive-order reservations (Cont.)
   legislation to permit exchange of
      private land within, 22, 32, 36,
      115-17
   Navajo additions of 1900 and 1901,
      21-23
   opened to mining for metalliferous
      minerals, 39-42
   status of debated in Bureau of Indian
      Affairs, 73-74
   test case to determine legal status
      postponed, 23
   vague status of, 20

Fall, Albert B.
   appointed Secretary of Interior,
      55-56
   appoints Hagerman commissioner to
      Navajos, 61
   attacked by John Collier, 191-94
   opposes allotment of Navajos on
      public domain, 28-31
   resigns as Secretary of Interior, 64
   supports bill to open executive-order
      Indian reservations to mining,
      41
   supports Bursum bill, 59
   upholds E. M. Harrison on
      application of General Leasing
      Act to executive-order Indian
      reservations, 57-58
   withdraws Indian claim to executive-
      order reservations, 58
Faris, Chester, 168
Farmington, N. M., oil boom town, 55
Federal Surplus Relief Administration,
      159-62
Finney, E. C., 94-95
Fort Defiance, establishment of, 5
Fort Wingate, purchase of by Navajos,
      119
Four Corners, 48
Frazier, Lynn, 126, 145
Frear, James, 76-77, 80-81, 86-88

Ganado Mucho appointed chief of
      western Navajos, 14
General Federation of Women's Clubs,
      77

General Leasing Act (1920)
  Albert Fall applies to executive-order
    Indian reservations, 57-58
  applies leasing system to public
    domain, 43-47
  Attorney-General asked to rule on
    application to executive-order
    Indian reservations, 72-75
  Division of opinion on in Interior
    Department, 76
  E. H. Harrison attempts to apply to
    executive-order Indian
    reservations, 57-58
  legislative attempts to modify Fall
    ruling applying General Leasing
    Act to executive-order Indian
    reservations, 77-81, 88-93
  significance of legislation blocking
    application of to executive-order
    Indian reservations, 99-100
  Solicitor of Department of Interior
    rules against Fall decision, 65
  Western arguments in opposition to,
    43-44
Geological Survey reports on
    prospecting in Four Corners
    area, 49
Gorman, Howard, 169
Grand Canyon National Park, 84, 86
Gregory, Thomas W., 38
Guadalupe Hidalgo, treaty of, 58

Hagerman, Herbert J.
  agrees with Fall interpretation
    applying General Leasing Act
    to executive-order reservations,
    63, 73-74, 76
  appointed Special Commissioner,
    61-63
  biographical sketch, 62 (n. 40)
  calls attention to Navajo trachoma
    problem, 184-85
  comments on Burke's resignation, 148
  disappointment over Santa Fe
    auction, 71-72, 100
  given authority to negotiate Navajo
    oil leases, 69
  instructed to prepare study of
    Navajo land situation, 128

Hagerman, Herbert J. (Cont.)
  opposes Lee's Ferry Bridge, 87, 97
  opposes reimbursable debt policy,
    84-86
  organizes support for scabies
    eradication, 107
  ousted from office, 152 (n. 56)
  plan to obtain land for Navajos
    defeated, 115-17
  prepares for first Navajo Tribal
    Council, 66-69
  proposes land purchases from Navajo
    oil revenues, 119
  protests transfer of Navajo
    school children, 175-76
  reappointed Commissioner to the
    Navajos, 125
  recommends changes in directive
    creating Navajo Tribal Council,
    64
  relieved as Commissioner to the
    Navajos, 101
  role in development of Navajo Tribal
    Council, 191-94
  seeks Navajo voting rights, 188-89
  supports Hayden bill to lease
    executive-order Indian
    reservations, 90
  urges limited leasing of treaty
    reservation, 70
  willingness to share Navajo oil
    revenues with states rebuked by
    Navajo Tribal Council, 85
Hall, J. J. *see* Lockhart, W. E.
Harding, Warren G., 55, 142
Harrison, E. M., attempts to apply
    General Leasing Act to
    executive-order Indian
    reservations, 57-58
  Utah District Court upholds
    position, 81
Hastings, William W., 164
Hayden, Carl
  attempts to open Navajo reservation
    to mining, 40-42
  defends Indian Bureau against Senate
    investigating committee, 146
  recommends special commissioner
    for Navajos, 61

Hayden, Carl (Cont.)
    sponsors bill to permit Navajo
        expansion in Arizona, 127-28
    sponsors legislation to modify Fall
        ruling on executive-order Indian
        reservations, 78-81, 88-93
    supports Lee's Ferry Bridge, 86
Herrero, in raid on Ft. Defiance, 5
Hinkle, James F., 116-17
Hogback lease
    granted to Midwest Refining
        Company, 51
    oil struck on, 54
    production declines, 102 (n. 72)
Hoover Dam, 105
Hoover, Herbert
    appoints Charles J. Rhoads
        Commissioner of Indian
        Affairs, 148-49
    favors return of public domain to
        states, 123 (n. 31)
    supports Meriam Commission
        report, 147
    suspends oil prospecting on public
        domain and Indian reservations,
        102
Hopi agency, creation of, 27
    eradication of scabies on, 108
Howard, Edgar, 163, 165-66
Howe, Frederick C., 59
Ickes, Harold
    appointment as Secretary of the
        Interior, 154-55
    urges bills enlarging Navajo
        reservation, 129
    warns against overgrazing on
        Navajo reservation, 105
Indian Affairs Committee (House)
    amends Wheeler-Howard bill,
        164-66
    approves opening of executive-order
        Indian reservations to mining, 41
    clears Commissioner Burke of
        criminal-collusion charge, 137
    investigates conditions on Indian
        reservations in 1919-1920,
        134, 172
    opposes Hayden bill for leasing of
        executive-order Indian
        reservations, 79-80

Indian Affairs Committee (Cont.)
    recommends "emancipation" of
        Indians, 134
Indian Affairs Committee (Senate)
    amends Wheeler-Howard bill,
        165-66
    approves opening of executive-order
        Indian reservations to mining,
        41-42
    attacks Rhoads administration,
        152-53
    investigates Indian affairs, 145-48
    prohibits federal funds for Navajo
        allotment on public domain, 30
Indian citizenship, 187-88
Indian education
    abuses in during 1920s, 173-79
    compulsory school attendance
        inaugurated, 172
    criticized by Meriam Commission,
        140-41
    improvement in under Rhoads and
        Collier, 179-81
    reforms under Commissioner
        Rhoads, 150-51
Indian health
    blunders during Burke administration,
        181-86
    efforts of Rhoads administration to
        improve, 151, 186-87
    improvement under Collier, 187
    Meriam Commission criticizes
        Bureau administration of, 140-41
Indian mineral deposits
    Albert Fall applies General Leasing
        Act to, 57-58
    Attorney-General rules against Fall
        decision, 74-75
    executive-order reservations opened
        to mining for metalliferous
        minerals, 42
    guaranteed to Indians, 90-93, 99-100
    treaty lands opened to exploitation,
        39
Indian Oil Leasing Act (1924)
    amends act of 1891 for leasing
        of treaty reservations, 77-78
    sought as guide for leasing
        executive-order reservations,
        79, 95

Indian Oil Leasing Act (1927)
  passage of, 92-93
  significance of, 99-100, 191
Indian Omnibus Bill (1923), 191
Indian Reorganization Act (1934)
  see Wheeler-Howard Act
Indian Rights Association, 149

Janus, Stephen, 33
Johnson, Tillman D., 81-82
Johnston, Rev. W. R., attempts to
  secure title for Navajos at
  Leupp, 21
Jones, Andrieus A., 88-89, 92, 116
Jones, Howell, 118
Joseph case, 58

Kinney Oil and Refinery Company,
  50, 52-53
Kluckhohn, Clyde, cited on Navajo
  philosophy, 11-13
Kneale, Albert H., 87, 178-79, 188-89

LaFollette, Robert M., Jr., 90-91, 145
Lane, Franklin K., opposes withdrawal
  of oil lands on public domain,
  38
Lawrence, D. H., 60
Lee's Ferry Bridge, 82-88, 100, 138
Leupp, Francis E. (Commissioner of
  Indian Affairs), attempts to
  secure more land for Navajos,
  23, 25
Leupp Reservation
  allotment urged upon Navajos
    residing there, 123
  consolidation of checkerboard
    approved, 118-19
  creation of, 21-22, 27
  existence of Indian Council, 49
  extent of overgrazing on, 114
  failure to solve checkerboard
    problem, 23, 32-33
  horse reduction on, 110
  scabies eradicated on, 108
Lockhart, W. E., and J. J. Hall
  lease, 54, 65, 71
Luhan, Mabel Dodge, 60
MacDowell, Malcolm, 147

Manuelito, in raid on Ft. Defiance, 5
  appointed chief of eastern Navajos,
  14
Marty ranch, 125
McLaughlin, James, 133
Meriam Commission, 139-42, 145,
  149-50, 166, 179, 182, 184,
  186-87
Meriam, Lewis M., 139, 147
Meritt, E. B. (Assistant Commissioner
  of Indian Affairs)
  advises against continued leasing
    of Navajo oil lands, 101
  agrees to restrict Navajo allotment
    on public domain, 30-31
  defeated in bid for Commissioner
    of Indian Affairs, 155
  forces vote in Navajo Tribal Council,
    113 (n. 32)
  requests more money for Indian
    education, 176
Metalliferous Minerals Act (1919),
  39-42
Midwest Refining Company
  angers Navajos, 53
  appeals for lease renewal on
    Hogback, 97
  obtains lease to Hogback, 51
  origin and importance of, 50-51
  strikes oil on Hogback, 54
  waterhole adversely affects Navajo
    auction, 71
Missionary activity, failure under
  Spaniards, 3
Morgan, Jacob C., 70, 86, 120-21,
  125, 169, 196
Morrow, John, 116, 122 (n. 27)
Navajo agency
  creation of, 27
  extent of overgrazing on, 114
  rivalry with San Juan agency,
    66, 120-21
  scabies eradication on, 108
  see also Southern Navajo agency
Navajo-Hopi Long Range
  Rehabilitation Act (1950),
  198-99
Navajo Indians
  education, 171-81, 197-98
  history from 1626 to 1911, 2-7

Navajo Indians (Cont.)
  morality concepts, 12
  oil development, 48, 54, 57-58,
    70-72, 100-103, 199
  origin of name, 1-2
  population growth, 104, 197 (n. 2)
  religious ceremonies, 13
  social organization, 7-15
  voting rights, 187-89

Navajo Reservation
  additions to by land purchase, 119-29
  creation of sub-agencies, 26-27
  creation of treaty reservation (1868),
    7
  discovery of oil on, 54
  E. H. Harrison attempts to open
    executive-order portions to
    General Leasing Act, 57-58
  executive-order additions, 17-25, 33
  executive-order additions forbidden
    by Congress, 33-34
  expansion of tied to oil
    development, 69
  Fall withdraws title to executive-
    order portion, 58
  free from white land-hunger until
    1900, 16-17
  oil development on, 48, 54, 57-58,
    70-72, 100-103, 199
  overgrazed condition of, 104-105,
    114, 196-97
  physical description of, 8
  problem of checkerboard, 20-36

Navajo Tribal Council
  adopts excess grazing fee, 112-13
  adopts resolution for horse
    reduction, 110
  attitude toward Collier's stock
    reduction plan, 159-61
  calling of first council, 65-66, 69
  Collier's biased interpretation of,
    190-94
  endorses reservation day schools, 180
  grants Hagerman lease-making
    power, 69
  Jacob Morgan challenges land
    purchase, 120-21
  lack of unanimity in approving
    Wheeler-Howard Act, 167-68

  membership based on natural
    communities, 9
  nonexistence prior to 1923, 49
  opposes Lee's Ferry Bridge
    appropriation, 85-86
  post-1934 development, 195-99
  protests against educational policy
    under Burke, 174, 177-78
  protests halt in allotment work, 122
  provisions of directive creating, 62-64
  refuses to extend lease of Midwest
    Company, 97
  resolves to purchase land with oil
    royalties, 119
  urges land purchase speed-up, 125

New Mexico
  approves consolidation of
    checkerboard, 36
  calls for allotment of Navajo
    reservation, 28
  defeats plan to consolidate
    checkerboard, 117
  opposes allotment of Navajos on
    public domain, 33-34
  opposes bill authorizing Navajo land
    purchase, 121
  opposes Navajo expansion, 23-25,
    28, 123-24
  refuses Indians right to vote, 188-89
  uses Taylor Grazing Act to halt
    Navajo allotment on public
    domain, 130-31

New Mexico and Arizona Land
    Company
  land holdings in Navajo
    reservation, 21
  Navajos purchase land from,
    125, 129-30
  refuses to exchange lands in
    checkerboard, 32
  subsidiary of Saint Louis and San
    Francisco Railroad, 21

New Mexico Cattle Growers'
    Association, 124

New Mexico Wool Growers
    Association, 117

New Policy, 132-36

Nez, Hosteen, 177-78

Nice case, 187

Nishi, Nal, 159
Northern Navajo agency, creation of, 27 (n. 17)
   rejects Wheeler-Howard Act, 169
   see also San Juan agency

Overgrazing, problem of, 104-105, 112-14, 158

Paiute Strip, 125-27
Paquette, Peter, 67, 172-73
Parker, Leo, 169
Patterson, Florence, 183-84
Peoples Institute, 59-60
Pete, Billy, 159
Pine, W. B., 146-47
Placer Mining Act (1870), applied to oil, 37-38
   replaced by General Leasing Act, 43-47
Pratt, Richard Henry, 139
Producers and Refiners Corporation, 54, 71
Public Health Service, 183
Public Works Administration, 157, 180
Pueblo Bonito agency, creation of, 27
   failure of public-domain allotment at, 32
   proposed land addition to, 116
   see also Eastern Navajo agency
Pueblo Indians
   cultural exchange with Navajos, 3
   effect of Bursum bill on, 59
   focal point for Collier's reforms, 136, 191-93
   legal controversy concerning ward status, 58
   resistance to white culture, 15
   revolt against Spanish rule, 2-3

Rattlesnake lease, sold at Santa Fe auction, 71
   discovery of oil on, 84 (n. 22)
   decline of production on, 102
Reimbursable loan policy, origin of, 83
   comes under attack, 83-85
   questioned by Rhoads administration, 150

Rhoads, Charles J. (Commissioner of Indian Affairs)
   administration of Indian affairs, 150-53
   appointed Commissioner of Indian Affairs, 148-50
   criticized by John Collier, 152-53
   meets with Arizona officials to discuss Navajo land purchase, 127
   opposes free dipping for Navajo sheep, 108
   reforms Indian education, 179-80
Robinson, Joseph T., 155
Roblin, Charles E., 122-24
Rockefeller Foundation, 139
Roosevelt, Franklin D., 154-55, 165

Salmerón, Gerónimo Zárate, coins the name "Navaho," 1
Sandoval case, 58
Santa Fe auction, 70-72, 100
Santa Fe railroad
   attacked by Senator Henry Ashurst, 31
   discovery of artesian water increases land value of, 23
   federal government refuses offer to exchange land, 22, 117
   land holdings in Navajo reservation, 21
   Navajos purchase land from 125, 129
   refuses to exchange lands in checkerboard, 32, 118
San Juan agency
   Council abolished, 62, 192
   creation of, 27
   effect of oil discovery on, 55
   failure of sheep breeding experiment, 112
   meetings of Indian Council, 49-54
   rivalry with Navajo agency, 66, 120-21
   test site for Navajo voting rights, 188-89
   see also Northern Navajo agency
Scabies eradication program, 106-108
Scattergood, Henry J., 149
Schneider, F. L., 107
Scott, Hugh L., 106, 151-52

Sells, Cato (Commissioner of Indian
      Affairs)
   announces New Policy in Indian
      affairs, 132-35
   applies stock-raising homestead
      act to Navajos, 32
   attempts to allot public-domain
      Navajos, 122
   calls attention to Navajo need for
      schools, 172
   secures appropriation for land
      purchase by Navajos, 35
Seymour, Flora Warren, 175
Shirly, Jim, 159
Simington, A. W., 34, 122
Simms, Albert G., 124
Sinclair, Harry, 51
Smith, George Otis, 38
Smith, Marcus A., authors bill to
      forbid creation of executive-
      order reservations, 33-34
Soil Conservation Service, 197
Southern Navajo agency
   creation of, 27 (n. 17)
   extent of overgrazing on, 114
   public-domain Navajos vote against
      Wheeler-Howard Act, 169-70
   scabies eradicated on, 108
   see also Navajo agency
Southwest Trachoma Campaign,
      184-86
Spain, policy toward Navajos, 1-4
Stacher, Samuel F.
   and Navajo Tribal Council election,
      193
   criticizes bill forbidding creation of
      executive-order reservations, 34
   protests halt in allotment work, 122
   reports on land addition in Pueblo
      Bonito area, 116
Standard Oil Company (Indiana)
   purchases control of Midwest
      Refining Company, 50-51, 55
   challenges Harry Sinclair, 51
Stockmen
   affected by scabious Navajo sheep,
      107
   agree to consolidation of
      checkerboard, 116

Stockmen (Cont.)
   employ Taylor Grazing Act to control
      public domain in New Mexico,
      131
   oppose bill permitting Navajos to
      purchase land from oil royalties,
      121
   oppose Navajo expansion, 23
Stock reduction
   attitude of Navajo Tribal Council
      toward, 159-61
   Collier's efforts at, 158-63, 195-97
   effect of Depression on, 113-14
   failure of grazing fee experiment,
      112-13
   horse reduction program, 108-11
   impact of scientific sheep-breeding
      on, 111-12
   role in rejection of Wheeler-Howard
      Act, 169-70
   scabies eradication program, 106-108
   tied to boundary expansion plans,
      160-62
Stone, Harlan F., Attorney-General,
      74-75
Supreme Court
   asked to rule on Fall decision, 82
   in Joseph case (1871) rules that
      Pueblo Indians not wards of
      federal government, 58
   in Nice case (1916) rules citizenship
      and ward status of Indians
      compatible, 187
   in Sandoval case (1913) rules that
      Pueblos are wards

Taft, William H., restores Navajo
      withdrawal to public domain, 24
   withdraws public-domain from
      mining entry, 38
Taylor Grazing Act (1934), 131, 162
Theodore Roosevelt School, Navajo
      schoolchildren desert, 176
Thomas, Elmer, 145
Tocito Dome lease
   approved by San Juan Council, 54
   disapproved by Secretary Work, 65
   lease cancelled, 101
   leased at Santa Fe auction, 71

Trachoma
   and discovery of sulfanilamide, 185
   high incidence among Indians, 140
   prevalent among Navajo
      schoolchildren, 183
   Southwest Trachoma Campaign,
      184-86
   special school for Navajo children
      at Ft. Defiance, 186
Tuberculosis, high incidence among
   Indians, 140
Tusayan National Forest, 126

Western Navajo Reservation
   consolidation of checkerboard
      approved, 118-19
   creation of, 27
   embraces executive-order withdrawal
      of 1900, 22-23
   extent of overgrazing on, 114
   horse reduction on, 110
   scabies eradicated on, 108
Western States Oil and Land Company,
   50, 52-53
Wheeler, Burton K., 90, 145-47, 163-67
Wheeler-Howard Act (1934)
   acceptance by Indians, 167
   major provisions of, 163-66
   Navajo rejection of, 167-70
   Pueblo Indian influence on, 191
Wilbur, Ray Lyman (Secretary of
      Interior)
   urges transfer of Tusayan National
      Forest to Navajos, 126
   appointed Secretary of Interior, 149

Williams (E. T.) Oil Company, 50,
   52-53

Work, Hubert (Secretary of Interior)
   appointed Secretary of Interior, 64-65
   attempts to modify application of
      Fall decision, 76-78, 94-95
   briefly supports Fall decision, 94
   charged with fraud in Barnett case,
      138
   helps launch Southwest Trachoma
      Campaign, 184-85
   orders auction of Navajo oil leases
      on treaty reservation, 70-71
   organizes Committee of One
      Hundred, 65, 72
   pares Department of Interior
      expenditures, 143-44
   requests Attorney-General to rule on
      Fall decision, 72-73
   requests Brookings Institution to
      conduct investigation of Indian
      Bureau, 139
   sponsors bill consolidating
      checkerboard in Arizona, 118-19
   submits bill for consolidating
      checkerboard in New Mexico,
      116
   supports Lee's Ferry Bridge bill, 86

Works Progress Administration, 180,
   197

World War II, impact on Navajos,
   197-98